BEFORE FIDEL

BEFORE FIDEL

The Cuba I Remember

FRANCISCO JOSÉ MORENO

UNIVERSITY OF TEXAS PRESS

AUSTIN

Requests for permission to reproduce material from this work should be sent to:
    Permissions
    University of Texas Press
    P.O. Box 7819
    Austin, TX 78713-7819
    www.utexas.edu/utpress/about/bpermission.html

⊗ The paper used in this book meets the minimum requirements of ANSI/
NISO Z39.48-1992 (R1997) (Permanence of Paper).

Library of Congress Cataloging-in-Publication Data

Moreno, Francisco José.
    Before Fidel : the Cuba I remember / Francisco José Moreno. — 1st ed.
        p.   cm.
    ISBN-13: 978-0-292-71424-3 (cloth : alk. paper)
    ISBN-10: 0-292-71424-6 (cloth : alk. paper)
    ISBN-13: 978-0-292-71476-2 (pbk. : alk. paper)
    ISBN-10: 0-292-71476-9 (pbk. : alk. paper)
        1. Moreno, Francisco José.   2. Cuba—Politics and government—1933–1959.
3. College students—Cuba—Biography.   I. Title.
    F1787.5.M66
    [A3 2007]
    972.9106'3092—dc22
                                                            2006004517

To Jorge Tallet, friend
And to the memory of Kiko Baeza

There is a history in all men's lives,
Figuring the nature of the times deceas'd,
The which observ'd, a man may prophesy,
With a near aim, of the main chance of things
As yet not come to life, which in their seeds
And weak beginnings lie intreasured.

WILLIAM SHAKESPEARE, *HENRY IV*

CONTENTS

ACKNOWLEDGMENTS

It was while walking through the streets of San Francisco, discussing with Marvin Frankel our respective childhoods, his in the Bronx and mine in Havana, that the idea for this book originated.

As I began to put fingers to computer, I found progress difficult to make. Either nothing would come to mind or a torrent of memories would overwhelm my ability to write things down. I started the book and gave it up several times, and would use all sort of excuses to keep away from it.

Kerstin Eggers saw the first twenty or thirty pages I had managed to write in the first couple of months and became a firm advocate of the project. Without her persistent encouragement, constructive nudging and editorial counsel, I doubt I would have seen the task to completion.

Our son, Alejandro, undertook the thankless task of bringing some order to the untidy stream of consciousness that constituted the book's first draft. He has been an able and sensitive editor and only seldom could I object to his suggestions. I am very grateful for his assistance— and patience.

PROLOGUE

The plane was about to take off—a Super-Constellation on its daily run from Havana to New York. The four propellers whirling at half throttle, the doors closed, the stewardesses making sure the passengers were not walking up and down the aisle on takeoff, as Cubans were prone to do if left unattended, and shepherding them towards their assigned seats. It was early September 1959 on a sunny morning in the middle of the rainy season, like most mornings at that time of the year unless a storm was making its way from the Caribbean Sea into the Gulf of Mexico. It had taken me ten days, ten days to decide I didn't want to stay, ten days to turn down the two jobs I had been offered, a commission in the new Cuban army and a position at the labor union's national headquarters, and to forgo any others that might have come my way. I had returned to Cuba to take one of the two jobs offered, probably the one with the army. My exile was over, I thought. But here I was ten days later waiting for the plane to take off. Still, I sat there, questions and doubts in my mind, looking out the window and not seeing anything. We had struggled to overthrow a tyrannical government and had succeeded. We fought the good fight and won, and looking back I could see a path strewn with bodies of friends and acquaintances: Chúa, blown up; Porfirio, who made it through World War II in the Pacific without a scratch, torn apart by the Cuban secret police; Mario, tortured and shot and his wife crying and comforting their kids; Ñico, always in a hurry, his skinny long legs permanently in high gear—at least he died fighting; Fructuoso, and our never-ending discussions about Argentina and Peronismo, assassinated; also Carbó, who I liked but could never bring myself to take seriously; Machadito, who I always ran into, for some inexplicable reason, at the exact junction of Infanta and Concordia Streets, regardless of the time of day or day of the week, also murdered.*

The tortured and badly beaten were too many to remember and, ultimately, they had been lucky; they had survived. And then the new images: the excitement and optimism bubbling and overflowing like a freshly uncorked champagne bottle, a national *fiesta* which included even those who had never joined in, or even approved of, our fight against Batista's dictatorship. So as I sat in the plane waiting for it to get airborne, second-guessing myself with these remembrances and lingering doubts, I didn't notice the engines die and the door open; I just saw two uniformed armed men move down the aisle past me, stop three rows ahead, yank a middle-aged, heavy-set man out of his seat, and march him unceremoniously out of the plane. Doubts and remembrances evaporated, and I was left with the cold double realization that I didn't care if I ever saw the island of Cuba again, and that I had already been made into what I was always going to be.

*Chúa, whose full name was Francisco Cardona Orta, and Porfirio, who ran the Havana Law School coffee shop and whose last name I never knew, died in bomb blasts—either they were in the process of placing these devices or, more likely, the police so claimed after murdering them. Mario Fortuny, one of the leaders of the Triple A underground organization was tortured, shot and his body left in a car by his home. Ñico, Antonio López, was part of the small group of men that landed in eastern Cuba with Fidel Castro in December 1956, and one of the first to die fighting. Fructuoso Rodríguez, Julio César Carbó and José Machado participated in the attempt to kill Batista in March 1957 and were assassinated after a member of the Cuban Communist Party betrayed their hiding place to the Cuban police.

BEFORE FIDEL

FIRST BIRTH

CHAPTER ONE

I was born twice. Same country—two worlds. The first time I was delivered into a feudal family in a time that no longer was; the second, I was hurled into a revolution in a time that was never to be. I was brought into the first world in 1934 by a white doctor, into the second in 1952 by a black soldier. Eighteen years separated the two births, but in the tropics time moves on its own accord, unrestrained by the unimaginative inflexibility of numerical sequence, so the chronological progression is meaningless, if even discernible, and those years remain suspended in my memory, hazy silhouettes fixed against the cacophony of human frenzy, music and gunfire.

Cuba provided a vivid and dizzying introduction to life. Exuberant to stridency, aimlessly intense, hopelessly inchoate, pretentious and jejune, the island floated in a sea of noise, movement and ebullience as if engaged in a mad dash towards some imperceptible but irresistible destination. Speed of thought and action valued above clarity and accuracy in an unceasing feast of sound and color, presided over by a scorching sun, moderated only by the tenderness of the trade winds and scented by the perfumes of the tropical night.

My father had no noble title, but he certainly was a feudal lord. Luyanó was the largest industrial neighborhood in Havana, a sprawling continuum of working-class poverty sprinkled with lower-middle-class clean shirts and aspiring hopes. In the midst of all this our house stood out, an early-nineteenth-century structure that had been the country residence of the Count of Villanueva, a Spanish grandee, and our street properly was named after him. It was a large, solid, and spacious construction, converted into a school in the days of Fidel Castro, with windows covered by eighteen feet of wrought iron from floor to ceiling, and a main double

door entrance, also eighteen feet, in double mahogany. A garden protected the two sides of the house facing Villanueva and Rodríguez Streets,
itself surrounded by an aggressive six-foot black wrought-iron fence with
nasty sharp spikes on top and in the middle. One of my earliest childhood
memories is that of a little neighborhood boy hanging from one of those
spikes, screaming in pain as my father unhooked his hand.

Early memories are imprecise visions that emerge out of the foggy
recesses of the mind and present themselves in inexact sequence and in
response to changing circumstances. My first recollection is usually of
my mother, although sometimes it is my uncle Alfonso bending over my
crib. My father, grandmother, sisters, uncles and aunts all come in later
and in no clear order. I really don't remember the first time I became aware
of most of them; they surfaced as inhabitants of shadowy corners who
slowly, almost begrudgingly, took independent shape. Maybe there were
so many aunts and uncles that this was inevitable, or perhaps it was
I who was remiss to recognize and differentiate them, or that's how it
always is.

There was my grandmother, my father's mother, Doña Consuelo:
white hair, blue eyes, always either in the garden tending her flowers and
herbs or resting in her large rocking chair. She was the unquestioned
señora de la casa; she ran the house. She had had eighteen children, twelve
alive, eight of them living at home, and eleven who had supper together
every evening. It was much closer to a clan or a tribe than to a family,
and it took some time before I realized how out of the ordinary, even by
Cuban standards, we were—a throwback to some bygone era that clung
to time with unconcerned but unwavering tenacity.

My father was the eldest son and, therefore, the man in charge.
Things fell nicely into place because he also provided the house, which
came with his job. He ran the warehouse and shipping office of Victor
G. Mendoza y Cía, a large supplier of machinery and parts for sugar
mills. It was a double warehouse with an adjacent yard that served as a
baseball field for the neighborhood boys on weekends; the warehouse,
yard and living quarters occupying an entire square block—a fenced-in
and self-contained castle-fortress that insulated us, at least partially,
from our immediate surroundings.

We did not rule the neighborhood, but in our castle-fortress we were
above it—separate if not independent. It wasn't that we did not communicate with our neighbors, we did, but we didn't consider them neighbors,
just people who happened to live nearby. Women and old men would
come by and ask my grandmother for herbs for all sorts of ailments,
especially of the eye and stomach, and she would dispense her *jazmín,*

vicaria, albahaca and *yerba buena* with friendly aloofness; and boys would come by every afternoon to play *taco* or *quimbumbia,* or some other made-up game with my brother and me on Rodríguez Street, which was unpaved, or in the backyard after the warehouse and office had been closed for the day.

The black family that lived across Villanueva Street supplied us with a cook and three servants for years—the mother, Tomasa, replaced the first cook I remember, Adelaida, who had been with us for many years and who had left for reasons unknown to me, and who was much missed since Tomasa couldn't prepare a good meal to save her life. Tomasa's daughters, Chela, Manuela and Maíta, did the washing and the cleaning, especially on weekends, her husband, Papo, would run occasional errands, and their son, Papito, who had a head that seemed way out of proportion to his body, came over to play sometimes after school; and they were part of my life for years, but I never learned their last name, nor was I ever curious to know.

Despite our distance from the neighbors, we were very much part of the neighborhood and helped to give it its character as an aberrant urban relic of a world that was disappearing without ever actually having been.

My sisters were born before me but came after me in the social hierarchy of our family because I was the first son of the first son. My position was acknowledged by my assigned seat at the end of the long rectangular dinner table, directly opposite my father. My higher rank was accepted as a matter of course, although as far as I was concerned it didn't help me any in disputes with my sisters, or fights with my brother, or with anything else I could think of. Training as the eventual head of the family meant learning that responsibility was its own, and only, reward—if any young boy or emerging adolescent can call that a reward.

School fit in with everything else. I was scheduled to go to a private Catholic school outside the neighborhood and I knew this and must have been looking forward to it because when someone had the bright idea of sending me to a local school in preparation, I would have no part of it. The effort must have been halfhearted since the person who took me to the local school was Nené, who was never trusted with anything of weight. I was six at the time and my recollection of the event is quite clear. What I don't remember as well is the sequence of events concerning Nené, whether this was before or after his marriage to Rosaura, or before or after their divorce. Events in Cuba followed a pattern that although perhaps abstruse or recondite to others was in absolute harmony with the spirit of the place and the music of the day. To begin with, Nené was not a relative; he just pretended to be one. His mother, Nina, was my uncle Luis's mistress. Being his mistress, she was neither allowed to come into the house nor allowed to be in my grandmother's presence—that would have been a violation of a basic canon of propriety. Luis slept at her house every night after he had had supper at ours, and no one objected to the sleeping arrangement; obviously, it was not as important as the eating one. Nené would come to our house, never to a proper meal, of course, but to visit or have coffee or to go on errands for my aunts after he had stopped being a fireman. The reason he and his brother, Kike, and nephews, Yayo and Ando, pretended to be our relatives was as old as life: we were the local aristocrats, and they wanted some of our social prestige to rub off on them—and we had to find ways of correcting such a misunderstanding without being unnecessarily cruel, and the truth was that our objection to acknowledging any kinship with them had less to do with social pretentiousness than it did with intellectual embarrassment: Nené, Kike, Yayo and Ando were the dumbest bunch one could possibly imagine. Yayo would routinely spend entire afternoons trying to impress people by uncapping Coke bottles with his grotesquely large and malformed teeth. Ando, his brother, once got into an argument with me, on the day of my grandmother Consuelo's funeral, about the meaning of a popular saying that ran *Muerto el perro, se acabó la rabia,* When the dog dies, rabies ends. He insisted that the phrase meant that if a dog bit you and gave you rabies all you had to do was find that dog, kill it, and your rabies would be gone. The dispute between the two of us became so loud, and was so out of place at the funeral with the house full of people crying and eating and looking sad and trying to balance their coffee cups that Tarzan, my aunt Adela's husband, had to intervene and try to explain to Ando the error of his logic. Tarzan was no genius himself, a man whose specialty was inventing things that already existed, his most successful creation being the six-pronged ice pick, but even he had no trouble seeing where Ando's thinking had gone awry. Ando was subdued but not convinced and all throughout the funeral kept looking at me with a sarcastic sneer that proclaimed absolute confidence in the correctness of his interpretation. I remember wishing for a rabid dog to show up and bite him right then and there so he could try his logic.

In any event, Nené courted Rosaura, a local seamstress, in accordance with the mores and traditions of the time, and they went out properly chaperoned and waited for sex until marriage, and waited for marriage until they were in a position to afford it. Their courtship lasted twenty years, long but not unheard of in those days and latitudes, until Nené with much effort and through the influence of one of my uncles got a job as a fireman—civil service, livable wages, guaranteed vacations, eventual pension—and then they married. Six months into the marriage Nené showed up unexpectedly at home in the middle of the day and found Rosaura in bed with the local grocer. No one ever told me what ensued, but apparently Nené did everything wrong and ended up divorcing Rosaura with no legal case against her, which meant that he had to provide alimony and a share of his job's benefits. Outraged by finding himself in such a predicament, he did the only thing he could think of to preserve his honor and to spite Rosaura: he quit his job and never again sought proper employment, so there would be no benefits for her to share in. So the Nené who took me to the local school might have been waiting to marry Rosaura, or maybe he was already divorced. In any event, he took me to a neighborhood school a few blocks from home. Once there I looked around, said good morning to the teacher and told him I wasn't staying. I remember the man's bafflement and his asking Nené whether I was staying or not, and Nené shrugging his shoulders and not knowing what to say, and my grabbing his hand and leading him out of there and back home. It is amazing to me that I remember all this with absolute clarity but have no recollection of what happened when we got back to the house. Probably nothing.

My uncles were divided into two types: blue-eyed and brown-eyed. The blue-eyed—Luis, Enrique and Norberto—were all odd characters; the brown-eyed—Angel, Alfonso and Marcial—were normal, at least comparatively. The aunts could also be divided by eye color: Adela, Carmela and Pastora, blue; Consuelo and Charo, brown. The former were nurturing and the latter aloof, or perhaps only somewhat less nurturing. There was a blue-eyed uncle, Manuel, who was not an uncle although we called and thought of him as one. He was my grandmother Consuelo's cousin, and his eyes were an exact replica of hers. Manuel was my introduction to the blue-eyed weirdness that ran through the family. He lived a few blocks away with his mulatto mistress, Lola, and like Luis, had supper with us every evening before going to his woman for the night. Manuel also had a wife, whom apparently he had never gotten around to divorcing, and three grown children in a neighborhood at the other end of Havana. He was the only member of the family interested in books, strange books though, on chemistry and biology and surgery, and he kept a sort of lab in one of the back rooms facing the enclosed backyard. He also had some chickens in a coop near where the family chickens were kept, and he raised and trained fighting cocks. Manuel was a man of many idiosyncrasies, and I remember once coming back from school and going into the backyard and finding a chicken hobbling around on a wooden leg. In a last-ditch effort to save the animal's life through amputation, Manuel had designed and fit the chicken with the artificial limb, and the leg seemed to work, but the chicken died the following morning. Manuel's most outstanding idiosyncrasy, however, was one that took me some time to realize and which I never fully understood: he couldn't tell the truth. Well, not exactly. He could be truthful if he was talking on his own initiative, but if you asked him a question, any question, he would answer with a lie. It didn't matter what the question was, he just could not bring himself to answer truthfully, and when I detected this trait I asked one of my uncles, I think Alfonso, about it, and I immediately realized I had asked a stupid question. Was the sky blue? Of course Manuel was a liar. It was known, accepted and thought nothing of.

My father's family and my mother's family were worlds apart. Clannish, cohesive and rabidly supportive of one another in the face of the external world, the Morenos, my father's family, were an amalgam of individuals who differed markedly from one another and moved full steam ahead in their respective directions without doubt or vacillation, or ever paying the slightest attention to what other people thought. It was not that they would question or challenge the mores, values and opinions of others. It was more that what others thought was of no consequence; it was never discussed, taken into account or referred to—not even to question or dismiss; it just didn't exist.

My mother's family, the Sierras, were the opposite; they were concerned above everything else with propriety and appearance. There was a grandmother, an aunt, an uncle and their kids, five cousins in all, three male and two female, all of whom were much older than my siblings and me. My mother's mother, Gertrudis, who was referred to by us as Ayita and by everyone else as Doña Tula, was an unpleasant scrawny lady with a scalding stare, always sadly dressed in gray or black, who would occasionally lapse into Catalán, and who we would kiss perfunctorily in her wheelchair and escape from as fast as we could, something my brother and I could manage more easily than our sisters, who, being older and female, were subjected to a much higher dosage of her unhappy presence and sour character. Ayita lived with Aunt Cristina, my mother's sister— who, for no known reason, we children called Ana—and her family in the Loma de Chaple area, a quiet upper-middle-class neighborhood on a hill that always felt cooler than our own. Cristina's family was a pretentious bunch who, in Cuban jargon, *se tiraban los peos más altos que el culo,* farted above their asses. My brother and I dreaded the visits to their house, and although I can't speak for my sisters, I doubt they enjoyed them much either.

While my father's family didn't give a hoot about what anyone else thought about them, my mother's family was totally dependent on other people's opinions. Aunt Cristina, who was a handsome woman with a striking mane of shiny white hair, was always not only properly, but elegantly, dressed. Her husband was the star salesman of the same company my father worked for and had made quite a bit of money, but as he was both a womanizer and a gambler their financial footing was shakier than they pretended. Their eldest son had been sent to the United States to study, something not many Cubans could afford in those days, and since this cousin never learned much of anything anywhere the decision to send him abroad was probably more socially determined than educationally motivated. I clearly remember Aunt Cristina gloating over the fact that her son was "studying in the United States." The Sierras' pretentiousness was perplexing in its shallowness because they had at least one tidbit they could have boasted about had they been concerned with anything other than their affluence.

My mother's mother, Doña Tula, was a first cousin of Federico Capdevila, one of the most heroic Spanish figures in Cuban history. Capdevila had been an officer in the Spanish army back when Cuban opposition to Spanish rule was beginning to mount and had been appointed defense counsel for a group of eight Cuban medical students who were accused of desecrating the tomb of a known Spanish journalist and who were being railroaded through a military trial. The charges and the legal procedures responded more to the colonial government's desire to punish the Cubans and suppress further acts of defiance than to proper judicial practice or the search for justice. After a spirited defense and upon hearing the tribunal announce the draconian sentence of death for the eight young men, Capdevila, outraged, took out his sword, an official accouterment of every Spanish officer's formal uniform, and broke its blade over his knee in a symbolic gesture of disapproval and defiance. By doing this, he was deliberately and unabashedly declaring his contempt for the action of the military court and letting the judges know what he thought. His army career ended, for all practical purposes, right then and there—and he became the only Spanish soldier of his time depicted with respect and admiration in Cuban history books.

Justice and propriety were the two epicenters around which each family moved in complete contraposition to one another. In the Moreno household everything was discussed in terms of "right" and "wrong";

with the Sierras it was "proper" and "improper." Of course, determining what was right and wrong among the Morenos was always left to interminable and often heated discussions, although the family concerns seemed limited to cigars and politics with an abundance of knowledge about the first and an overabundance of opinions about the second. These discussions were limited not only in subject but also in time, space and participants. Debate did not begin until after dessert, when coffee was brought into the dining room and the women left the table and congregated in a small pantry by the kitchen's entrance. My brother and I were allowed to listen but knew better than to venture a comment or an opinion. Once, I did, and we were both told that *los niños hablan cuando las gallinas mean,* children talk when the chickens pee, and we immediately went to the coop behind the house and discovered, after long hours of observation, that chickens don't pee.

With the coffee came the cigars, all kinds of cigars, *brevas* and *cazadores* and *panetelas* and an array of others, and these were invariably followed by the critical appraisal of what everyone was smoking, an appraisal that went into painful detail about the quality of the leaf wrappings, the texture and coloration of the inner leaves, the virtues of Vuelta Abajo versus Vuelta Arriba (the two main tobacco-growing regions in Cuba), the aroma, the ashes, and so on and so on and so on. For a child forced to listen to at least part of the conversation before being allowed to leave the table, these cigar discussions were excruciatingly tedious, and my mind would fly in all directions, although I couldn't escape completely the ceaseless barrage of opinions and information which drove me to never put a cigar to my lips until many years after I had left Cuba.

Politics was something else. I didn't understand everything that was being said, but I found the conversation, references and arguments intriguing and appealing to my curiosity and imagination. The discussions were always couched in terms of war or its political variants: struggle, strife, confrontation, rebellion, insurrection, revolt, revolution. The whole history of Cuba since 1853, when the first armed attempt against Spanish rule took place, was viewed as a never-ending fight. First were the wars for independence, which lasted, with breaks in the military action but none in the overall effort, until 1898. Then the American occupation until 1902, after which a quasi-independence was granted under the colonial tutelage of the Platt Amendment, which gave the United States the right to intervene in Cuba whenever it pleased—and which the United States proceeded to do. From mutilated independence until 1933, when the American-imposed amendment was abrogated, Cuban nationalists struggled to turn their county into something other than a gringo protectorate, and these were years of corrupt and inept administrations, landings of Marines, racial massacres, endemic armed revolts, incipient labor militancy and chronic student unrest. Capping this era came the dictatorship of Gerardo Machado, a popularly elected veteran of the war against Spain who decided his constitutional term of office was too short and extended it arbitrarily in 1928, provoking widespread political unrest and providing a rallying point for all dissatisfied factions and individuals.

Most years drag themselves in and out of existence and disappear from memory without leaving behind anything but a perfunctory reference to a number; others slap a whole country in the face and make an indelible mark in its consciousness, becoming mandatory references for generations to come—1933 was such a year for Cuba. First, the dictator Machado was brought down by middle-class political activists with the tacit support of the United States, which was seriously concerned with the deterioration of the Cuban market for American products. Then, after a few weeks of confusion, emerged the man who was to reign over Cuba for the next two and a half decades: Fulgencio Batista, army sergeant, wannabe politician, and black. It wasn't that Batista was a full-blooded black man. Ethnically, he was a mixture of Indian and African probably with a little white here and there; but what caused him to be seen increasingly as black by white Cuba was not what he was but what he stood for. After coming to power in 1933, Batista could have been cast as either black or white, race in a Latin environment not possessing the absoluteness and permanency that it does in the Anglo world. A successful black, Indian or mestizo who accepts the ways of the whites, speaks and behaves as whites do, respects the same formalities and worships the same idols will, sooner or later, be viewed and classified as white. This of course doesn't mean that racial prejudice is absent, or any less cruel and arbitrary than in any other place; it simply means that in these societies it is possible for some individuals to move from the ranks of the discriminated into those of the discriminators. Batista, however, became blacker as time went by, and the foundation of the island's politics as I was growing up was the tug-of-war between the black sergeant-turned-general and the white Cuban middle class.

When Batista took over the army and the country through a coup d'état on September 4, 1933, he enlisted the support of the radical young nationalists who operated out of Havana University and let them run the government for slightly over four months while he solidified his control of the military by getting rid of the overwhelmingly white officer corps. For these four months the young radicals did what young radicals were supposed to do in a protectorate struggling to feel like an independent land: they nationalized American-owned public utilities; ran their government offices with a colorful and volatile mixture of passion, honesty and inefficiency; shouted anti-imperialist slogans right and left; and incurred the wrath of the new Roosevelt administration in Washington, which refused to recognize their government.

After four months Batista felt secure and made his move. He arrived at an understanding with the American ambassador, kicked the young radicals out of their official positions, replaced them with older pro-American politicians and got the new government recognized by Washington. He ruled the country from Camp Columbia, the army headquarters, and although his official position was commander in chief of the army, everyone understood he was *el amo del país,* the master of the country.

Batista's rise was a three-act play that began at the slow rhythm of an old and romantic *habanera* with distant sounds of African drums. The first act was the dismissal of the professional white officer corps, and this turned out to be low comedy. The officers, my mother's brother Fernando among them, never knew what hit them, and when they tried to react they were outmaneuvered and outwitted by the mostly mestizo sergeants, and were forced to show their ineptness for all to see as they were ridiculed into political oblivion. The second act was the dismissal of the radically nationalist student government, as the music slid into *danzón* with a stronger drumbeat and a more vibrant mixture of tunes and influences. The white army officers had gone without much pain or glory because they had been viewed as in cahoots with the fallen dictator, as part of the despised past political structure and as inept. But the removal of the student-controlled nationalist government was a different matter. Batista immediately became a Yankee lackey in the eyes of the idealistic nationalists and the incipient socialist and communist factions flourishing in Cuba, as in the rest of the world, in the train of the Russian Revolution. The end of 1934 and the beginning of 1935 saw the opposing camps clearly demarcated: Batista, the American embassy, American sugar interests and their Cuban associates on one side; the idealistic nationalists and the socialist and communist groups on the other; and the rest of the country, probably the majority, neither here nor there, just observing the action with the apprehensive detachment of those who are powerless and know their fate is in someone else's hands. The opposition to Batista grew in intensity, and by March 1935 it exploded in a general strike to the tempo of martial airs and the lyrics of revolutionary proclamations that mixed the rhetoric of the French Revolution with the aspirations of the Russian one. The strike gained momentum and appeared to be on its way to paralyzing the country and forcing the collapse of the government when the third act unfolded in the form of high drama, as the African drums moved loudly and forcefully into the foreground.

Batista broke the strike and squashed the threat to his rule by making a deal with the Communists—by buying them out. The Communists broke ranks with the rest of the forces supporting the strike—exactly as they had done two years earlier in a strike against Machado—and in return were given the right to organize labor unions and all the fringe benefits befitting the new dictator's allies. The deal, when coupled with the repressive measures taken against those who remained opposed to the government, destroyed the effectiveness of the opposition, consolidated Batista's grip and fixed for a long time to come the way Cubans looked upon the Communist Party since no dialectical legerdemain, or Marxist mumbo-jumbo, could disguise the fact that they had betrayed the strike.

The final scene was pure tragedy. The leader of the fight against Batista, initially a member of the nationalist government supported by Batista and the students, the man who had issued the decrees expropriating the American utility companies, the man who had come to symbolize idealistic nationalism and opposition to American interventionism, Antonio Guiteras, was captured and murdered—and with his murder all effective opposition came to an end. Two things about Guiteras come always to my mind: his full name was Antonio Guiteras Holmes, born in Philadelphia; and he went to his death from my aunt Cristina's home, where he had been hiding.

The counterpoint to politics was music. It is all but impossible to convey an accurate picture of Havana, even to think of it, without considering the sounds that encompassed and pervaded all aspects of city life. It would be like watching a movie without the sound track, where the mood and atmosphere become difficult to interpret, and scenes lose subtlety, complexity and often meaning. Sounds and music always frame the action, give it character, denote context, indicate direction and build expectation. Sometimes we are vividly aware of the background sound, sometimes we incorporate it unconsciously into the action—but it is always there. And so it was in Havana. There was noise and there was music and they were different; at times they ran on parallel tracks without touching, and at times they overlapped without integrating, and at other times they collaborated in peaceful harmony, and at still other times they fought and crashed violently into each other.

The street vendors would shout their *pregones,* their selling cries, announcing themselves and the virtues of their wares, and the radio would broadcast the music, or musics, since there were many of them in Havana, and the *pregones* sometimes became songs—"El manisero," the peanut vendor, the most famous but by no means the only one—and there were songs that had been, or were destined to be, *pregones* by appropriation, adaptation or transmutation. The lines were never clearly drawn, and there was a constant back and forth from street noise to music and back to street noise.

The city was a virtual battleground for rhythms and styles that seemed to share little in common; *boleros, guarachas, guajiras* and *danzones* were homegrown, but Cuban music did not monopolize the field and had to share it with music from Spain, Mexico, Argentina and the United States. From Spain came *pasodobles, zarzuelas* and flamenco; from Mexico, *corridos* and *boleros;* from Argentina, tangos; and from the United States, big bands, supreme among them, Artie Shaw.

Who listened to what was difficult to tell. Among my aunts and uncles there was a clear preference for Spanish and Cuban music. I liked all the music, American the least. My sisters had no use for anything that was not Cuban or American. Most of my friends liked Cuban music first and whatever else second, and I was surprised when I discovered that they did not share my enthusiasm for tango. What was conspicuously absent from the radio was Afro-Cuban music. It is true that most if not all twentieth-century Cuban music was heavily influenced by the rhythms, instruments and cadences that black slaves brought to the island, but still it was rare to hear the purer forms of Afro-Cuban music on the airwaves, even though the same music could be heard in the streets of all the popular neighborhoods in Havana and definitely in ours. Two or three months before carnival time the sound of *bongós,* bongo drums, would invade my house night after night, floating in from the black enclave on Acierto Street, right behind the warehouse, with a persistent and mesmerizing monotony that disguised for those not attuned to it, like me, its melody and meaning. Still, I was fascinated by the mixture of joy and sadness, temporal joy and ancestral sadness, the drums seemed to convey.

Havana danced frenetically and simultaneously to many tunes, and the incongruous behavior of its people kept pace with the melodies. There were those who thought of life in *bolero* form and indulged occasionally in mild melancholic romanticism; those who moved to the rhythm of tango, replete with tearful melodrama and emotional affectation; some who saw the world as a *corrido* and perceived existence as truculent challenge and boisterous violence; and some who viewed their surroundings as *zarzuela*, amusing and sardonic with sentiments and emotions always in a minor key; and still others who saw life as a wild animal to be fought, adjusting their vision to *pasodoble* time; and still more who faced life as *guaracha*, humorous and picaresque and not to be taken seriously; and the young who wanted to be part of the modern world and moved with the big bands; and a final group, perhaps the majority, who approached life as a combination of some or all of the above, exhibiting overlapping and contradictory tendencies that would have left an outsider convinced of their insanity but which to us, natives, made perfect sense.

Politics and music, fighting and dancing, these were the two beats that formed the harmonic texture of the island, and it would have been impossible to understand the country without taking into account these two forces and their interconnected rhythm. It also would have been impossible to fully comprehend Cuba without coming to terms with how and why this small piece of land, with a modest population of six million and no significant accomplishment to its credit, could have engendered in its inhabitants the high opinion they had of themselves. Maybe it was insularity, or maybe the twists of the country's history, or maybe some unpredictable genetic factor, or the Caribbean air, or the large amount of coffee we drank, or some undetectable cosmic variable that produced such high self-esteem, but whatever was responsible for it, there it was, front and center—and we all partook in it. This feeling of vainglorious satisfaction had its highest expression in middle-class Havana, but it was not limited to a social class or to a region; it ran through the whole island, and it was ingrained in the Cuban personality.

CHAPTER TWO

Calling me thin as a rail would have been an understatement. I looked more like a toothpick with an olive on top, and being underweight was my most salient trait as a child, at least in my family's eyes. I liked food, some of it anyhow, but I didn't eat much, to the consternation of a group of people for whom eating well, and by "well" they meant both quantity and quality, was not merely a matter of ingesting nutrients but an activity with metaphysical implications—and one of the very few points of agreement between the two sides of the family. Two of my father's sisters, Adela and Charo, and one of his brothers, Luis, were modestly plump, as was my mother's sister Cristina, and that was that. My father was thin, very, and my mother and the rest of the uncles and aunts seemed firmly anchored in some middle range that enjoyed total immunity to the amount of food they ate. And eat they did.

Lunch and dinner were both large meals, the major differences between them being that lunch was eaten quickly and not everyone was necessarily present, and the whole family would show up for dinner and linger at leisure over the dishes and lace food with conversation, and often conversation with food. Bread, rice and salad enjoyed entrenched permanency at both lunch and dinner; neither meal would be presentable without these staples. Soup, light or heavy depending on the time of the year, would come first, and if the soup was light, the beans would come as a side dish to be eaten with the rice, but they would be part of the soup if this was heavy; and the rice was always judged by how separate the grains were, with any degree of pastiness making it unacceptable; and the main course would usually be chicken, or pork, or beef, or occasionally fish, which did not have many followers. The food was consumed in this order, with the exception of the salad, which everyone seemed to eat at a different juncture and which consisted always of red and green tomatoes and almost always watercress; lettuce and other greens made their appearance in accordance with the seasons. Dessert was served immediately after the end of the meal, no lull here, and it would usually be fruit paste, often guava, and occasionally some fresh fruit in season, although the business of fresh fruits was tricky.

The number of tropical fruits available seemed to have no end, but only a few of them were acceptable at the dinner table. Mangoes, never. You could buy four or five of them for a penny and, with the exception of the most obscure varieties, they would go to the pig we fattened for Christmas dinner. *Mamey,* with its red pulp around a solid black pit, and *guanábana,* with its multitude of little seeds forcibly adhering to the stringy white pulp, were acceptable, along with pineapple, although pineapple more often came as part of a salad of my family's own concoction, mixed with avocado and with red wine as dressing. Fruits like *anón* and *chirimoya* were considered poor relations to *guanábana* and undeserving of our table, as undeserving as *caimito, mamoncillo, marañón,* papaya, *zapote, tamarindo,* fig, and the different types of banana, which were fine for breakfast but not for lunch or dinner. We ate all of these fruits, of course; we enjoyed the intense aroma they exuded and were puzzled by the paradoxes some of them presented, and sometimes were left wondering if there was a riddle to be solved in them, or a secret message to decipher. *Mamoncillo,* tiny and round, with a dark green cover halfway between skin and shell, and a delicious but meager amount of a delicate pale orange pulp, had to be eaten by the dozen or the score to satisfy even the weakest appetite, thus tiring your mouth before satiating your desire; and *tamarindo,* the veritable blending of heaven and hell in fruit form, a long light brown pod with three, four or even more individual dark brown seeds, each seed surrounded by a brown stringy pulp with a powerfully acerbic flavor that repelled your palate while it grabbed your taste buds with a delicious savor that wouldn't let your mouth get rid of the fruit, so it was not uncommon to eat *tamarindo* with tears in the eyes. It was only after dessert that the only lull in the meal would come, as the women got up from the table to bring coffee to the men, who then indulged their never-ceasing attempt to impart tobacco and political wisdom to one another while the women retreated to the kitchen pantry to make all the important decisions of the day.

I was so skinny that I was always at the receiving end of some well-intentioned and annoying effort to fatten me up, from liver steaks to brewer's yeast to malt drinks to horse blood potion, which I remember being dark red, to condensed milk and to whatever else anyone thought would put some fat in me. And I was told countless times by my mother that the reason I had died when I was three, when my tonsils were taken out, was because I was so thin, and therefore so weak, that my body couldn't handle the operation, and she would swear that my heart had actually stopped, and that I was brought back to life by the doctors, and that this was the reason they were so hesitant to perform the appendectomy on me that I badly needed. I never had any recollection of the dying episode, although I suppose if I had really died any memories would have been wiped away, but I always took that story with a grain of salt because, although my mother was not given to exaggeration, she was the only one who ever mentioned it and because, though I may have been as thin as a thread, I never felt weak but was rather full of energy and quite active, and in all certainty would have been diagnosed as hyperactive had medical knowledge moved at a faster pace. Whether I died or not at three, however, was ultimately unimportant, since physical death is a mundane occurrence and of all forms of death the least consequential. This the Morenos taught me well, in their never-explicit way, as they equally taught me that it was the death of the spirit, the failure to dream and have illusions, to look upon life as challenge and adventure, that was the only form of death that mattered.

The appendectomy I do remember—vividly. It was a pain in the lower right side of the abdomen that would come and go, and then would come and not go, and I remember driving to the doctor, who examined me and sent me home, and I remember the pain still there the next day, worse, and not being able to stand up straight, and going back to the doctor, who now made a decision with a very serious expression, and my mother was equally serious, and solicitous, which she seldom was. I remember being taken into another room in the hospital and having some awful big needle stuck in the middle of my back, and I have a vague, very vague, recollection of lying on an operating table, and then nothing, nothing until the next morning when I woke up and my mother was sitting on a chair next to my bed, and I realized the pain was gone, and I told her, and she burst into tears. Again it all had been the fault of my being so skinny and not having enough of whatever you needed to have enough of to get your appendix taken out without dying, or being close to dying; so back to fattening diets and fattening drinks that never seemed to have the slightest impact on my weight.

The problem with my weight, or lack of it, was aggravated by the fact that I was naturally a long-ball hitter. Being skinny and having a home-run swing was a dilemma I never managed to solve, although I tried many a solution—hitting the ball down instead of up, producing line drives instead of fly balls, placing the fly balls between outfielders, and even batting left-handed, which gave me a shorter swing but also a less effective one. It was a good lesson to learn, that hard as we try some problems defy our efforts and that we have to accept some shortcomings or compensate for them in some other way. And baseball, or what went for baseball on the streets of Havana, provided the training ground on which I became familiar with my strengths and weaknesses, and got to deal with challenges and adversity, mostly adversity, and learned to laugh, mostly at myself.

Americans used to believe that baseball had been invented by some fellow named Doubleday someplace in upstate New York, although it is difficult to imagine any game being invented in upstate New York. Now no one is sure any longer, and I believe some future research might well show that baseball was invented in Cuba by some Chicho Rodríguez who might, or might not, have been the same as Chacumbele, the semi-mythical Cuban who killed himself for mysterious reasons, making his name known throughout the island as synonymous with suicide, so when someone killed himself in Cuba people would say, "Le pasó lo que a Chacumbele," he went the Chacumbele way. And there were many Chacumbeles in Cuba, and no one was ever sure who the real Chacumbele was, or if there had ever been a real Chacumbele who had actually killed himself. All of which seems absurd and irrelevant but tallies with the uncertainties and unpredictability of Cuban baseball as played in the neighborhood, never a game with fixed rules but a blending of playing, struggling, arguing, laughing, fighting, inventing, making do and accommodating rules to circumstances; a flight into dreamland encased in a set of modifiable prescriptions that moved in response to the meagerness of the environment and the less than ideal conditions under which we played.

A formal game of baseball, eighteen boys, smooth field and a round ball, was a rarity for neighborhood kids, something reserved for special occasions, and I don't remember participating in any of those until I went to private school. In the neighborhood we adjusted the game to the number of boys available, and the ground was never smooth but full of pebbles, and stones and holes and undulations and hills, and the ball was never round. The few good balls with their covers intact would be saved for those very special days when we played a formal game against a neighboring team, so most of the time we had to make do with balls that had long lost their original cover and shape and had been wrapped in electric or hospital tape, and if you have ever done that to a baseball you know that regardless how hard you try, you always end up with a ball that is oblong rather than round, slightly pointed at the poles, and the more tape you put on it to secure its innards, the more oblong it gets, and as long as the ball stays in the air everything is as it should be, but when it hits the ground there is no telling what it will do, and with the holes and undulations and the pebbles and the stones, it was as much a game of chance as of skill. For pitchers the egglike ball was a blessing and they did marvels with it, because even if you had never pitched before, if you grabbed the ball tightly enough and threw it, it would curve, although you never knew in what direction; but for infielders it was an unpredictable bouncing and skipping nightmare to which our multiple cuts, lacerations and black-and-blues bore witness.

More often than baseball, we played *taco* and *quimbumbia,* both Cuban variations of stickball. *Taco* was the simpler of the two, for which you would saw off about two inches from the end of a broomstick and pitch this small piece, the *taco,* keeping the rest of the broomstick for a bat. The rules of the game would be adjusted to the rectangular shape of a city street, so you had to hit straight—fair territory was long and narrow, in front of the batter. One swing and miss meant striking out, and a foul would also get you out, and having the *taco* caught in the air before it hit the ground meant the whole side was retired, and lines would be drawn on the ground, or references to features agreed upon, as to what constituted a single, a double, a triple or a homer, and most of the time there would be no running of bases because only two or three boys would be playing on each side, but we kept count as if runners were on base, and the rules would accommodate the number of boys playing and the peculiarities of the street and the fancy of the players. Sometimes a cork would be substituted for the wooden *taco,* which helped the pitcher because the cork would sway and wiggle and waver and wag, and when hit it would not travel far, and to remedy that we sometimes drove a nail into the cork and secured it with tape, and that would help the batters a bit, but the tape would soon get ripped off, and the cork would eventually break, and when hit cork and nail flew in different directions with no one quite sure what was coming at him, so there was always disagreement between those wanting to pitch the cork and those who preferred hitting the wooden *taco.*

Quimbumbia was a more skillful game also requiring a broomstick or, more properly, two. A four- or five-inch piece would be cut off from one, its two ends whittled down as sharply as the whittler wished to make them, often piercing. The *quimbumbia,* the whittled-down-at-both-ends part of the stick, would then be placed on an even piece of ground or on top of a flat rock, and the game was played by tapping one end of the *quimbumbia* with the other broomstick so that it would fly straight up in the air, and once in the air it was to be hit the same way as the *taco*, and if you missed it or fouled it off you struck out. No pitcher was needed for *quimbumbia*, which was good since no one wanted to be too close to the batter, who having a full-length broomstick to hit with, was capable of a strong swing that could make the *quimbumbia* go fast and far, mostly fast and, because of its shape, in unforeseen directions. Unless you hit the *quimbumbia* smack in the middle, it would go up or down or right or left and on occasion back, and batters would often cut down on their swing, sacrificing power for accuracy, to make sure the *quimbumbia* was struck in the middle and would sail forward, but the really skillful batters were able to hit it accurately with a forceful full swing. The *quimbumbia*'s sharp ends made fielding it problematic, an endeavor fraught with peril. Even though you didn't actually have to catch the thing, just stop its forward momentum and push it back from the drawn lines marking hits, doubles, triples and homers, getting cut and bruised by the pointed ends was an inevitable part of the game. We never had any protection, not even makeshift gloves, and it is interesting to look back at the attitude of the adults around us, whose concern for the potential perils of the game was limited to passing remarks about the sharpness of the *quimbumbia*'s points or to general advice about protecting one's eyes, and contrast that attitude with our present pervasive preoccupation with the eradication of risk, which is well on its way to bringing about the safety belt for toilet training.

More than a game, *quimbumbia* was a form of warfare, or perhaps training for warfare, in which ability and daring could not be separated. The same could be said for baseball, both in the neighborhood and at school, although at school the violence was less openly admitted, camouflaged under euphemisms about dedication and commitment, but always the opposing team was *el equipo enemigo*, the enemy team. Perhaps this was the way it had to be because we were immersed in war, everything was war. Cuban history was war, Cuban politics was war, war was all around us; countries threatening war, countries preparing for war, countries waging wars, internal wars and external wars; communists at war with fascists, the Chinese at war with the Japanese, the Italians at war with the Abyssinians, the Spaniards at war with themselves, the Russians invading the Finns, the Germans attacking the Russians, the Japanese bombing the Americans; war in the newspapers, war on the radio, war in the movies— war everywhere.

The two men were by the iron gate that led into the garden, and as they
spoke they tried to slither through onto our side of the fence, but Adela's
body blocked their way. There was no question of pushing her aside or
slinking past her; she was there to stop them and that she did, and they
kept asking about Enrique, if he was in, when would he be coming home,
and she told them he was out and that she didn't know, although I could
see Enrique in the dining room sipping coffee and observing us. But
these men were policemen, Adela told me as soon as they left, implying
that policemen were not to be told the truth, that we were good and they
bad and dangerous, and that Enrique was on the side of good and had
to be protected, and that even if he weren't on the side of good he still
would have to be protected because he was one of us, and that was what
family was about. Years went by before I learned anything about Enrique's political activities and why the police had come looking for him
that day, and when I eventually did, it happened quite by chance.

I was twelve or thirteen and was waiting one day for the bus on Fábrica
Street when a black Cadillac with all the metal trimmings of the time
stopped in front of me, and a man in a cream-colored suit and slick black
hair got out and asked me if I was one of the Moreno boys. When I said
I was, he said he was Macho and began asking about my family, by
name, about my father and my uncles, and about my aunts, and I didn't
say much of anything while he was all words and effusion and friendliness, and after patting me on the head he got back into his *cola de pato*,
duck's tail, as the fin-spangled Cadillacs were known in Cuba, and after
telling me one more time to give his best to everyone in the family, tell
them that Macho was sending his regards and thought often of them and
other things along the same line, he got back into the car and left.

At dinner that evening I recounted the incident and was surprised
when the whole table broke out laughing without anyone bothering
to explain what was funny about it. Eventually my mother told me
that Macho, who was then mayor of Havana, and whose real name was
Antonio Fernández, had been one of three men plotting to assassinate
one of the top police henchmen of the Machado dictatorship. My uncle
Enrique had been another of the conspirators, along with a third whose
name I don't remember, even though I was told who he was and was to
meet his brother under perilous circumstances some years later when my
turn came for plots and conspiracies.

Macho got cold feet at the last minute and left Enrique and the third
confederate in the lurch, and since assassination plots and conspiracies were impossible to keep secret in Cuba, even if they never came to

fruition, word of it got around, most probably through Macho's boasting, since that would have given him the double benefit of appearing to be a tough and committed revolutionary without incurring any risk, and the version circulating was that Enrique and the other man had failed to go through with it. In the aftermath of the failed conspiracy, Macho, who knew exactly what was going on, had ample time to take himself out of circulation until things cooled down, while Enrique had a very close call and was saved only by the alertness of Adela and the rest of the family women who detected the police snooping around and were able, with the help of some of the men working for my father, to sneak him out through a back door into the adjacent warehouse and into a truck and out of the city. The third conspirator was not so lucky and was caught and badly beaten and had to wait in jail for several months until the regime fell, while Enrique spent those months hiding in a friend's house in the countryside.

This experience turned Enrique off politics for the rest of his life, but his name had already found a permanent berth in the police files, probably under the heading of terrorist or potential political assassin, and his subsequent abstention from active political participation meant that no police agency could identify him with any party or group, and this, rather than clear him, made him a permanent suspect in whatever plot, real or imagined, came to official attention.

The story picks up again several years later, my mother was not sure exactly when but knew it was after Machado had been deposed and Macho had become a known local political figure and city councilman for the Auténticos, the political party created by the no longer so young or so honest nationalists of the 1933 student-led government. The rest of the details she knew with great precision, the address, the last name of the people who lived in the second-floor apartment where the party was being given, and the occasion for the festivity, which, if my own memory serves me well, was the birthday of one of the young women of the family. Here I must take a moment to note that my mother was, among other things, the family historian, for both sides of the family; she saved pictures, kept dates and knew as much as there was to be known with the material at hand. The Morenos never spoke about family history; it had no place in their frame of reference, or at least not through any direct mention. It was my mother who knew about the Morenos' service in the Spanish army when my grandfather went to Cuba, and it was she who knew about the Moreno who was an officer in the Spanish navy in the nineteenth century and had sailed for the Orient in a warship, never to be heard from again—Moreno or warship. This last story I was indeed skeptical of throughout my entire time in Cuba, but it was confirmed many years later when I was working in Spain and having a romantic liaison with a Spanish woman with my same last name. As we began comparing notes about our families, we found that the same story about the disappearing Moreno existed in hers, and since her family had remained closely associated with the Spanish navy she knew of the disappearance in full detail, and I could not question her veracity and felt guilty about my lack of trust in my mother as raconteur of family history. So my mother's rendering of the Macho affair must have been correct, and it must have been correct also because when she told me about it some of my aunts were present and no one contradicted her, something my aunts wouldn't have been remiss to do.

Anyway, at some point in the party Enrique and Macho ran into each other, the first time they had met since the failed assassination attempt, and Macho, like the politician he was, smiled broadly and opened his arms to embrace Enrique in traditional Latin style. Enrique, according to witnesses, calmly, carefully and self-consciously, as he always did things, proceeded to take off his glasses, put them in their case, put the case into his pocket, and without uttering a word or changing expression punched Macho straight in the face and continued to punch and drag him down the stairs and onto the street until some of the men at the party, fearing for Macho's life, managed to pull Enrique off him. The family learned of the incident from people at the party who came running to the house to alert them, afraid that Macho's friends would come looking for Enrique and sure that, at the very least, the police would be called in and charges filed. But nothing happened—no one came after Enrique, the police were not called in, Enrique never mentioned the matter, and no one heard a word from Macho, who obviously had what it took to be a successful politician.

Not all of my uncles were like Enrique. Actually, I have never met anyone quite like him—a man suspended between fanaticism and sainthood, and disconcerting in the contradictory signals he sent out. He valued everything in direct proportion to its difficulty and would never spare himself, or think of sparing himself, a challenge. As a child I didn't like him much because he was aloof and detached and would look straight at me, staring, making me feel like I was being scrutinized and evaluated, and it was clear that he was not willing to make allowances for age or for circumstances or for anything. Once, only once, did he talk to me about baseball, although baseball was a frequent topic of conversation among the men of the family and all my uncles knew of my interest in it and that I played for the school team, but when Enrique mentioned baseball he was not interested in how well I was doing or in how much I was enjoying the game, he just wanted to know how hard I was trying.

Enrique had been an outstanding basketball player who had qualified for the Cuban national team as guard, but before this conversation I had not known that he had played baseball also, and after listening to my reasons for playing whatever position I was playing at the time, second base probably, he proceeded to tell me why he had played shortstop. His explanation was like a portrait of himself and his approach to life, and it took me a long time to understand what he was saying, or to make any sense of it. He had played shortstop, he said, because after analyzing the game he had concluded this was the most difficult position for him to play, the one he thought would place the biggest demand on his talents and ability, and he went on to admit that he had never been very good at it—but of course that hadn't been the point.

When it came to women the Moreno men fell into two groups: faithful and committed husbands, or the equivalent for those who had mistresses instead of wives, and happy-go-lucky bachelors. My father, Luis, Angel and Manuel were in the first category; Norberto, Alfonso and Marcial in the second. Enrique, as always, was in a category of his own. During my childhood, Enrique was the only bachelor uncle who did not have a series of girlfriends or passing amorous adventures but instead had only serious and apparently less than happy romances—although given his quest for perfection and the intensity of his personality, this was not difficult to imagine. At forty-one he finally found the woman of his dreams, Alicia, a woman his own age who came from a well-known political and literary Havana family, the Ichasos, and whom he had met during a vacation trip to Oriente province in eastern Cuba. Theirs was true love, and I was old enough to appreciate the change in Enrique's personality after they met, and it was only then that we grew close. I had already begun my pilgrimage through Havana's high schools when Enrique and Alicia started to invite me for lunch, first to an apartment downtown, later to a house in the Víbora district, one of my favorite parts of the city. I don't remember much of what we talked about, but what sticks with me is the warmth and peacefulness of those lunches and how welcomed I felt and how I was able to relax in their company. One of the few specifics I do remember is that Enrique was seriously considering going back to school to get a law degree. He had been reading books that had never interested him before, and I remember how Alicia had been able to bring out from within him a certain softness that complemented his basic stern personality, and how his intensity was losing some of its rigidity, and I began to understand him, or to think I understood him better, and saw how his inflexibility had been the manifestation of an idealism that was both naive and enviable, and that there was a certain purity in him that nothing could stain and which was both a curse and a blessing. Alicia and Enrique listened and showed interest in what I had to say, and we discussed history and politics and education without either agreeing or arguing, and, with the perverted sense of humor with which the gods rule the world, they were happy for three years, and then he died at only forty-four, and a few years later whatever was left of her went after him. I remember finding myself and my uncle Alfonso in the elevator at the funeral parlor with Enrique's corpse, and Alfonso crying and I wanting to cry but unable to because of Alfonso's tears, and I also remember the times I found myself in unfriendly police company or in a dark cell and thought of Enrique, and it was like getting a pat on the back, or a nod of encouragement when everybody else thought I was crazy or a fool or both, and although he wasn't there I knew he would have understood and approved—and I was grateful.

As a child, January 6 was the most important day of the year—and no saint's day or birthday or holiday ever came close. This was El Día de Reyes, or El Día de los Reyes Magos, the Epiphany—although if anyone had said epiphany to us we would have had no clue what that meant, despite years of Catholic school and prayer books and the first communion training and the daily masses, all mandatory, perfunctory exercises empty of meaning, interest, and above all devotion. We did not consider January 6 a religious holiday but a day of magic, true and glorious magic, when dreams came true and miracles occurred. When they did not, the hearts of many children were ripped apart, but for us and our friends and for most of the kids we knew, the miracles did happen and repeated themselves year after year. The day was a clear and unambiguous children's holiday, when school was canceled but adults had to work—which kept them out of our hair. It was a day when kids were expected to run around showing and trying their presents, which were not legion, as now, but few and selected, and because they were few, each one of them possessed a special meaning and was received with appreciation that often bordered on disbelief, even awe, and was never to be forgotten: the red bicycle, propped against the wall asking to be ridden; the scooter with the big black wheels and black hand grips; the first-baseman's mitt, looking at me from the table surrounded by four brand-new baseballs; the air shotgun, double barreled and black, waiting to be pumped and fired; the boxing gloves, hanging from their laces, shining and professional looking; the roller skates, steel wheels and leather straps halfway out of the cardboard box.

Christmas began on the evening of December 24, Nochebuena, and ended with the wonderment of January 6. On Nochebuena there would be an all-family dinner in the formal dining room, and the women would cook and adorn the house and decorate the table, extended to accommodate everybody coming for dinner, never less than twenty-five or thirty people, and the children would play and fight, and the men would smoke cigars and sit around waiting for my father to eventually call everyone to the table. The menu always included a salad with green and red tomatoes and lettuce and watercress and radishes, and dish would follow dish until the star of the evening, the roasted pig, made its triumphal entrance to everyone's delight, and the importance of the occasion was marked by the presence of wine, the only day of the year my father allowed alcohol to be served at home. Dinner was long and noisy, and we were allowed to eat whatever we wanted, and my favorite was always the *turrón*, nougat, which came in two varieties, one hard, *alicante*, and one soft, *jijona*, and I loved both and would eat as much as I could, and we went to bed with bursting stomachs.

When we woke up the next morning, the twenty-fifth, all the vestiges of the previous dinner were gone and a representation of Christ's birth had materialized on a long rectangular table, complete with manger and baby Jesus and Joseph and Mary and angels and archangels and shepherds and sheep and a donkey and a cow and always, for us, the three most important characters of Christmas, Melchor, Gaspar and Balthasar—the magi—and the display would occupy a good part of the living room. As the years passed, though, the representation of Christ's birth got smaller and smaller, and soon a Christmas tree appeared alongside it, and as the tree grew larger and larger, the image of a fat bearded fellow with a jocular expression, dressed in red and dripping snow, started to gain popularity, and as we mixed meters and yards, and inches and centimeters, and dollars and pesos in our daily routine, our Christmas festivities became a disordered juxtaposition of Spanish and American symbols. What did not change, however, was the length and precision of the season—exactly from Nochebuena to the Reyes Magos. And what didn't change either was the mysterious appearance of the Christmas decorations on December 25 and their equally mysterious disappearance on January 6, when they gave way to the bounty of the magi.

As children we took the whole process for granted and never concerned ourselves with how the transformations took place; we accepted process and transformation as the way things were.

One must give Batista credit for the double alliance he was able to forge with the Americans and the Communists. It is true that the Roosevelt administration was increasingly concerned with the German threat in Europe and that American antagonism to international communism had lost some of its earlier edge, but still Batista's ability to juggle his friendship with American interests and his alliance with local Communists must have required guile and cunning. From 1935, when his control was fully consolidated, to 1940 Batista ran the country as the power behind the throne, with the president and the rest of the government under his thumb. It was during these years that he let the local Communists organize labor unions and control them through the CNOC, Confederación Nacional Obrera, until 1939 and through the CTC, Confederación de Trabajadores de Cuba, afterwards, both national labor confederations, and in return the Communists gave him their support. In 1940 Batista got himself elected president and took direct and formal control of the government. He now had the open backing of the Cuban Communist Party, which had changed its name to the Partido Socialista Popular (PSP), a collaboration that became increasingly visible over the next four years and eventually resulted in some members of the PSP joining his cabinet and others occupying seats in both houses of the Cuban Congress.

It was during these years that I became an avowed anticommunist. For some unknown reason that must be embedded in the mysterious convolutions of Marxist-Leninist dialectics, the Communist minister of education, Juan Marinello, decided that private and public schools should have different days off. This meant that I didn't have school on Thursdays, when the neighborhood kids did, and had to go to school on Saturday, when they were off and the baseball games were played. I had never heard of Lenin, Stalin was just a guy with a big mustache in Russia, and the only Marx I knew was Groucho, whom I detested together with the rest of his brothers, who hard as they tried could not come close to the Three Stooges, or to Buster Keaton, or to the Argentine Luis Sandrini. But I knew that anyone or any group capable of depriving me of baseball through such an illogical, mean and abusive measure could not stand for anything good, and I became a lifelong enemy of the communist creed—I guess that's how political convictions take root.

My resentment of communism didn't necessarily trickle down to the personal level, however. My father's sister Pastora had married Miguel Pascual, one of the honchos of the Cuban Communist Party, and he was a hell of an uncle. He was one of the few adults who really enjoyed taking my brother and me to professional baseball games, and he did so regularly, far more often than any other man in the family. Occasionally he also took me to amateur boxing matches, since we were the only members of the family who enjoyed them and I thought of myself as a boxer, although a new weight category would have been needed for me at the subatomic level. Miguel had a brand-new car that he said wasn't his but the Party's, and two chauffeurs, Augusto and Perico, who took turns driving him around but who didn't work for him but for the Party, and during the summers, he had a house on Santa Fe beach, which was also not his but the Party's and where we would go for weeks at a time, and I truly liked Miguel, who lived up to the image of an uncle more faithfully than any of my blood uncles did, and who would also take me sometimes to the movies and who seemed always in a good mood and laughed a laugh that was more guffaw than laugh. But all my love for Miguel would not budge my antipathy for the evil force that had foisted school upon me on Saturdays.

The Maristas Brothers' school was in the Víbora district, not far from where Enrique and Alicia would eventually live, a pleasant upper-middle-class neighborhood with some big mansions and many spacious houses, slightly higher and breezier than the rest of Havana. It was an all-boys Catholic school, well known for its athletic programs in baseball and basketball, and I entered it when I was seven and managed to do slightly worse every single year until I left when I was twelve. I remember the routine well, probably because it never seemed to change: we wore khaki trousers, a blue short-sleeved shirt with the embroidered monogram of the school on the left side pocket, and a white tie, and the school bus would come in the morning around eight, then mass, classes until noon, bus back home for lunch, bus back to school, more classes—which could never compete successfully with the digestive requirements of a Cuban afternoon meal—and the bus back home at five. At the beginning I did quite well, but the need for more disciplined work collided with my hyperactivity, or with whatever prevented me from concentrating and paying attention, and the gap between my attention span and the need to concentrate grew steadily. Every year I would slide a few notches down in class standing and my parents, not really interested in academics, showed only mild concern, so my retrogression went unchecked and did not prompt a crisis—not until I was twelve.

As my attention to academics waned, my voyages slowly gained force and breadth. I began to mentally cruise the Caribbean with the Black and Red Corsairs and with Henry Morgan in search of Honorata de Wan Guld, and I would go to India with Sandokan, and roam around the world with Tamakún, and I would venture into the forests of Germany with the Grimms, and ride on the Russian steppes with Mikhail Strogoff delivering the tsar's messages, and I would roam the Cuban countryside at the time of Spanish domination with Manuel García near Havana or with Rustán in Oriente province; and Emilio Salgari and the radio and the movies and Cuban history books took my full attention. My mind would be too far away for me to hear what the Brothers were saying, especially in the afternoon, which was reserved for all the excruciatingly boring subjects like drawing and calligraphy, and when I eventually got to read *Don Quijote* there was nothing strange in his charging the windmills because that was what I had been dreaming about every afternoon at school for years. The only interesting school material—history, math, geography and reading—was jam-packed into the morning classes, and I would pay them as much attention as I was able to muster and had no trouble with those subjects, making do with what I learned in class since the homework I couldn't handle with any consistency, and I was not about to forgo *taco* or *quimbumbia* or any other game or reading tales of adventure.

Playing and daydreaming took most of my time. The school day would roll in and roll out with soporific monotony, like tropical rain pounding the pavement, each day inseparable from the preceding or following one, a state where all motion ceases and time moves slowly as if dragging itself through some dense sogginess, so I would look ahead to after-school games and to Saturday baseball and to adventure books to escape the weight of boredom. There was fighting, too, but you always had to be aware that fights at school and fights in the neighborhood were different matters. At school you fought out of passing rage or frustration, or to show off, and there was barely time to throw or receive a punch before all kinds of people would rush in to separate you from whoever you were fighting, so these were only scuffles in which one's chances of getting hurt were minimal. But fights in the neighborhood were open-ended propositions with no one especially interested in stopping them, in fact most people encouraged them to go on—the boys for fun or out of curiosity and the adults, including relatives, because they thought fights built character. But the encouragement did have its bounds: no weapons of any sort, just fists, and if the fight got too one-sided it was over with onlookers always more than willing to be enforcers if the bounds of fairness were transgressed, as if responding to some atavistic sense of justice. Within their prescribed limits, neighborhood fights had clear beginnings but uncertain ends: once you fought someone, especially if he got the best of you, you would want to fight him again the next time you saw him, whether out of pride, anger, to preserve your standing, or for whatever reason impels boys to fight. And bringing the conflict to resolution was a complicated affair, and a formula would have to be found, usually by common friends, to bring peace. The result was that school fights were far more frequent but less consequential than neighborhood ones, and I managed to keep my fights in the neighborhood to the necessary minimum to retain my standing. Whatever violence I had in me, and I certainly had some, found an outlet in baseball and boxing, and once the other boys knew you would fight if you had to, it was not especially difficult to avoid doing so. So that part of my life was under control, but school was not. My academic performance sank at a steady and predictable pace, and my grades collapsed accordingly, and when my fifth-grade teacher, Brother Ignacio, called me in front of the class and told me that the only thing I was good for was playing baseball, I took it as a compliment—and it was around that time that I began going to the Moon.

I don't recall exactly the first time I went, but it must have been during a school afternoon—the ideal time for sailing into space—and I did sail, I didn't blast off, not only because in those days one didn't blast off, but because the process was a slow one as if the wind would inadvertently fill my sails, and before I knew it, I was cruising through space in an imaginary pirate ship, and space was neither flat not curved but wavy like the sea. The Moon was just a vantage point, like the top of a very tall mountain, from which I could see things in a compact and comprehensive perspective without concerning myself with my surroundings. I was not much interested in the place itself; I would go to the Moon to watch Earth. It was a good spot to get an unobstructed, panoramic view of rivers and oceans and mountain chains and even of countries, which in most but not all cases I had no trouble recognizing, and it took many trips before I began to shift from the contemplation of vistas to the observation of people, who could also be seen with clarity if you just lay back, relaxed and opened your eyes.

CHAPTER THREE

By 1940 Cuba was a democracy—sort of. The Platt Amendment was long gone, a new constitution had been adopted and Batista was elected president by popular suffrage—but with the army counting the votes. For most of the next four years the contours of Cuban political life were molded by the reality and impact of World War II. Glenn Miller and the Dorseys joined the island's musical repertoire, while Batista's alliance with the Communists held and the radical nationalists mutated from irreconcilable enemies to loyal opposition. The violence and arbitrariness of the dictator's early years became milder forms of official high-handedness and profligacy—and, noteworthy for an accurate understanding of later developments in Cuban political life, both the Communists and the no-longer-so-young-or-radical nationalists fully partook in the system's corruption.

June 1, 1944, saw another election, this time an open and clean contest in which the army didn't count the votes, and Ramón Grau San Martín was elected president over Carlos Saladrigas, the candidate fronted by Batista and the Communists. Grau had been a professor at Havana University's medical school and had made common cause with the radical students in 1933, occupying the country's presidency for the four months of their nationalist government and being forced out with them. To oppose Batista's rule, Grau and his followers had organized the Partido Revolucionario Cubano, better known as the Auténtico Party, and this was the party that came to rule Cuba now. On the day power was transferred to Grau and the Auténticos, Batista went from the inaugural ceremony straight to the airport and into voluntary exile in the United States.

Batista had not been fully committed to his role as dictator. He didn't have to relinquish power in 1944 if he didn't want to. It would have been easy for him to rig the election while throwing some bones to the opposition, especially since the Roosevelt administration had its hands fully occupied in Europe and the Pacific and didn't need any trouble in its backyard. He had been a faithful ally, fulfilling Cuba's colonial obligation by declaring war on the Axis right after Pearl Harbor; no Cuban troops were ever sent into battle, but the Cuban economy was put at the service of the Allies and a number of Cuban merchant vessels were sunk in the bargain. In fact, Batista's decision to hold fair elections in 1944, and to abide by its results, was so unexpected that many of his supporters in the military felt betrayed. The Communists, in the meantime, had prospered amply under his protection, and the PSP elected three senators and ten congressmen in 1944.

The year 1944 left some clear memories in my mind: Grau was elected in June, in August we had the most violent hurricane I was to experience on the island, and in November my grandmother Consuelo died, her death marking the ascension of my mother to *señora de la casa* and signaling the beginning of the slow but inexorable dispersion of the Moreno clan. The first sign of the new order was the disappearance of the overhead grapevine that had covered part of the garden. I don't know who took it down or why, I just remember one day it wasn't there anymore, and I missed it. I missed its inedible sour tiny green grapes and the loss of its welcome shade, a dependable refuge from the burning sun; and it was this change in the garden, more than anything else, that marked for me the transition from my grandmother's to my mother's reign.

During the Grau years, Cuban public ferment shifted into high gear. The new government moved forcefully to rid the military of Batista's closest friends and take the labor movement away from the Communists; but otherwise there seemed to be no policy, no discipline, no order, and no goal, except maybe to turn public funds into private fortunes. The music that had been muted since 1935 now exploded in deafening stridency, like multiple bands playing in the same hall, at the same time and each its own tune—and all at full blast.

These were days of wild shootouts in public places between competing factions of the ruling Auténtico Party, of guns and anarchy in the schools, of blatant and open official corruption, and of rapid disenchantment with the new elected rulers. The weapons and the armed confrontations were always justified in political language by a number of armed factions that recruited primarily in the public high schools or the University, each managing to describe itself as "revolutionary" in one form or another, and all operating under the protection or indifference of the Grau administration. It seemed as if the country was in a state of near-insurrection, with incendiary rhetoric the norm among the young and angry cynicism among the elders, all accompanied by a notable crescendo in my family's after-dinner discussions, and as my father and uncles talked and lamented and argued, the frustration would condense in the air and swirl around the dining room with the smoke of their cigars. Those at the table who had hoped for better from the new government gave vent to their disappointment, while those who had been skeptical of the new government waved their prescience like a wand of wisdom and not as the creature of partisanship that it really was.

In Cuba, as in Latin society in general, politics was an acceptable excuse for violence. If you killed someone for the right reason—freedom, independence, justice, country—you brought pride and honor to yourself and your family. But the same action done for other reasons, especially if stained by money or material gain, brought dishonor and disgrace. If you robbed a bank and gave the loot to a political cause, you were a hero; if you robbed the same bank but kept the money for yourself, you were a criminal. So there was some logic to the overlapping and intermingling of corruption and idealism, to the disguising of crass pursuits in political vestments, and to the recruitment of the most vulnerable, adolescent boys, to supposedly idealistic causes.

All the fiery rhetoric, violence and chaos of Havana's political scene were equally present in the city's traffic. Street lights were placed only at the major intersections—everywhere else drivers were on their own. By tacit agreement, or by an unavoidable sense of self-preservation, the traffic on streets with bus or tram routes enjoyed the right-of-way. This practice, however, was only applicable at a small minority of intersections; the rest were left with neither lights nor established rights-of-way. As we understood it, all those approaching the intersection had an equal right to go first, so traffic flow was guided by noise and daring and recklessness, not by lights or signals. As you closed in on the lightless intersection, you would blow your horn: once, to announce that you were in the vicinity; twice, to signal that you were coming through. Under the best of circumstances, after you had honked once you would then listen for another horn, and if one was sounded, you would honk twice again to acknowledge that you had heard the second horn and to announce that since you honked first you were continuing ahead. There was an element of acoustic gauging of distances involved in the operation, too; even if you blew your horn first, another driver might try to estimate by the sound of your horn how far from the intersection you were, and if he thought he was closer, he would just go right ahead through the intersection blowing his horn twice rapidly and often increasing his speed just to be on the safe side. And even when everyone involved meant to be courteous, which was not often, it was in many instances difficult to tell who had blown the horn first, and the narrow, often contorted two-way streets did not make matters any easier. So personality, weather, family problems, work conditions, sexual frustration, acuteness of hearing, luck and a host of other factors rendered this arrangement noisy, irrational, unreliable and dangerous—and it fit us perfectly.

At the end of my first year of high school, I found a cause. Some of the Communist-introduced educational policies from the Batista years were still in place, and the one I ran smack into required that everyone attending private high school pass government-approved examinations in addition to those of their own schools. It meant that after you passed a subject, you would have to go through another test on the same subject but this time administered by one of the public high schools and at a time that was not necessarily synchronized with your school's exam schedule. It was a cumbersome system of establishing standards—originally intended in all probability to harass private schools—and it created bizarre situations in which a student would pass one exam and flunk the other, not an uncommon occurrence. Most people didn't seem to care about the absurdity of the arrangement, but I did, and I made it my personal crusade. If the Black Corsair could engage in a struggle against unfairness and injustice, what the hell, so could I—so I refused to accept bureaucratic arbitrariness. And since the Maristas school couldn't have cared less for what I thought about this or anything else, my wanderings through the high schools of Havana began.

First there was a public school—my first encounter with public education, with public-school students, with female teachers and classmates, and with the many subjects I considered esoteric and unnecessary, like art, music, drawing, and civics. I had a tin ear, I couldn't draw to save my life, I thought art was for sissies, and I considered civics a travesty, a way to provide jobs for unemployed teachers who would repeat pious nonsense after pious nonsense devoid of logical consistency or historical insight. At least this was how I justified disliking those classes—and my bad grades.

Since my day in the new school did not begin until the afternoon I would go by the closest Instituto, public high school, and watch boys only slightly older than I was with guns tucked under their shirts. I remember them doing their very best to show off their weapons while pretending to be hiding them, and I knew these boys were involved in politics, and associated in some way with the mysterious groups and individuals I had often heard of but never seen; groups that advocated all kind of reforms that must have been good because reforms were always good, especially when you had to fight for them. But I was too shy to talk to anyone so I just walked around a little and observed, and then ambled through the hilly streets of the Víbora neighborhood to my own school, and got there early enough so I could sit by the tall pine tree that presided over the vista of Havana and look out at the city stretched in front of me.

With public school also came girl trouble: Gladys. I didn't even really like Gladys that much—I was much more taken by Elisa, by her long black hair, her exquisite figure, and the fair skin that made her facial features stand out, and who was so beautiful that I did not dare approach her but simply admired from afar, as if she were some celestial creature that by fluke, or some mysterious design, had materialized among us. Not that I needed additional inhibitions; I had plenty of my own when it came to girls. I was an excellent representation of the Cuban idea of an *enamorado bobo*, literally a foolish lover, and in my case something close to an idiot.

And that I was an idiot with girls there was no doubt. I had barely noticed Gladys other than as a somewhat attractive but rather common-looking girl who sometimes I caught staring at me in class. And then one stormy afternoon, when the city lights had gone out and it felt like a hurricane had arrived out of nowhere, about a dozen of us left school and tried to make it home on foot. I had with me a raincoat and a hat which I had brought along that morning, either due to a remarkable stroke of foresight or, more likely, to parental imposition, and as Gladys had neither I gave her my coat while she used her books to cover her head. All of us kept on walking and laughing and getting drenched as the rain came at us horizontally and relentlessly, and at some point Gladys and I held hands, and at another point she turned around and kissed me, and I mean kissed me. It felt good, and I was glad, and I knew that Gladys was attractive and that it was good to have a girl like her kiss you; and late that night, long after I got home soaked and giddy and explained that I had given my raincoat to a friend and would get it back the next day, and was given the mandatory glass of warm milk with anise and cinnamon, the standard family remedy for a drenching as for anything else, I was still thinking of Gladys, and of Elisa, and of what you can and can't get, and nothing made much sense.

It turned out that Gladys had a boyfriend, or so he said when he approached me the following day at school and told me that Gladys had told him she now was my girlfriend; and he went on to make clear that the only thing for us to do was fight. My aunts had warned me repeatedly over the years that there was no limit to the trouble women can bring upon men, and I saw it now in this guy who was at least two years older than I was and considerably taller and wider. I had never been in such a predicament—all the fights and confrontations I had had in the past had been related to sports or games or things we boys did together and under circumstances I could control or at least predict—so my past experiences were of no help. I did not especially like the idea of fighting for a girl, particularly one who went around telling people she was my girl when I knew nothing of it, not even what being my girl meant. The other boy was earnest, and as I tried to answer him and put things in order in my own head, I realized there were things about him that I liked. He was clearly not from Havana and had some of the *guajiro*, the hick, in him, his looks and manners betraying a rural background that may have accounted for the way he had approached me, when we were alone, calmly and in low tones and with none of the antagonistic bellicosity and bravado common among boys, and men, in Havana. He talked without anger but with determination and a sense of grievance, as if he had been wronged or insulted, and I decided that the only thing to do was to hit him hard—with the truth.

I needed a solution without having to fight this guy bare-fisted, one on one, and without a cowardly retreat, so I began by acknowledging his right to redress given the information he had but assured him that I had no interest in Gladys and that we had just been innocently fooling around the day before. Without making any reference to her kiss, about which he probably knew nothing and which would have been a move in the wrong direction, I went on to tell him that this was not an attempt on my part to avoid fighting him but simply the truth, and that since his right to fight me had to be respected, I wanted to make something else clear that I thought had to be respected as well. I told him that I assumed he wanted to fight me, not just beat me up, which most certainly would have been the outcome of a regular fistfight given the differences in size between us, so we would have to find a more even and acceptable manner of settling the score. I then suggested the two options that had come to my mind: I told him that we could have a rock fight, not a new idea for me because in some of the many idle moments when I had allowed my imagination loose rein, I had thought of rock duels in which the distance between the fighters and the number and size of the rocks would have been agreed upon, and in which my agility and strong throwing arm would compensate for my light weight, and in which a bigger opponent would make an easier target. As I proposed this type of fight, and as I explained it to him, I grew fonder of the idea and confident in my ability to evade and throw hard and accurately.

My second option was swords—wooden swords. I expected the initial incredulity his expression now betrayed, but the idea was not devoid of merit, and I went on to explain it in detail, and as my explanation progressed my enthusiasm mounted. This was not surprising as my brother and I had been making wooden swords since I was seven or eight, and we had developed expertise in designing and constructing them and in fighting with them, against each other and every boy in the neighborhood who was willing, and I knew well-made wooden swords could be dependable weapons that could injure without threatening life, and my brother and I had sufficient scratches and punctures testifying to their capacity to hurt. Of course, these swords were not as good as real ones, but they would do, and as I elaborated on their virtues I also made a point that had bothered me in the past and that was quite pertinent now. The length of the swords should be inversely proportional to the lengths of the combatants' arms, so that ultimately the arm-sword combination would be of equal length on both sides. By calling attention to this point I was trying to remedy the glaring unfairness I had seen when the possession of a longer arm had intruded as an arbitrary advantage among those crossing blades, or sticks, and I was happy that justice and self-interest were moving here in the same direction—and I felt that with the utmost sincerity.

The more I spoke, the wider his eyes opened. I think he was trying to determine whether I was serious, making fun of him, or simply mad. Meanwhile my mind was working on a fallback position in case my suggestions were not accepted. I was determined that under no circumstances was I going to be beaten up—the very thought of it sending shivers down my spine—so I had to figure out what to do if he rejected my proposals and insisted on fighting then and there. I thought back to the wrestling scuffles and physical horsing around with my brother, and remembered how Roberto, who was younger and smaller, would sometimes grab my ankles and bring me down, making it impossible for me to use my hands or feet effectively. As long as he held on, the only solution was to fall on top of him and wrestle him on the ground, which eliminated the opportunity for either of us to punch or kick with much force. So as I espoused the virtues of rocks and wooden swords, I made up my mind that if the need arose I would grab his ankles and not let go, even if I had to cling to them with my teeth, and with that part of the problem solved I relaxed a little, although the aversion to being beaten up stayed—and was to remain with me permanently and serve me well in the political upheavals of years to come.

When I finally ran out of arguments I fell silent and looked at him, and was surprised that I couldn't tell the color of his eyes, and for the first time I realized he had freckles on only one side of his face, and I wondered how that was possible, and I waited for him to say something. I couldn't read his expression, which had not changed since I started talking, and I don't know how much time went by, maybe seconds, maybe minutes, before he stood up from the steps we had been sitting on, gave me a long look, and walked away, and I never heard from him again—or from Gladys.

My father was a most peculiar religious man. He went to mass every day, was very active in religious organizations, held the position of rector, equivalent to president or director, of one of them, said grace at every meal and would not touch dessert during Lent. But he would never discuss religious subjects at home, and as his children grew up, he made only mild efforts to keep them within the confines of formal Catholicism.

Once out of the Maristas school, I would not step inside a church again; as far as I was concerned, I had been to enough masses to last me a couple of lifetimes, and I had had increasing difficulty swallowing theological reasoning and taking seriously the pretentiousness and fatuousness of Christian ethics. Some of this sentiment was self-generated, but some, I am sure, was also prompted by the Morenos' irreverent disregard for all churches, sects, faiths and denominations—by the true ecumenical disdain in which they, with my father the only exception, held organized religion. My mother, although less vocal than most of my father's family, felt much the same and made it clear to her children that the only reason she went to mass on Sundays was to please her husband. I had lost my faith by the time I was twelve, if not earlier, although the truth is that I couldn't have lost what I never had, and I don't remember ever feeling any inner commitment to the cloudy reasoning that supported the religious tenets with which I was bombarded at school. What I do remember is that at some point, I must have been ten or eleven, one of the Brothers, I think Gil, was explaining to the class the mystery of the Trinity, and as he spoke he went on to assert, and to repeat with added emphasis and conviction, that a dogma was a truth that must be accepted even though we are not able to comprehend it, and as he said this a voice inside me shouted, "No Way!" I, who always liked to question and challenge and argue, sat back flabbergasted, trying to come to terms with the idea that a religion as powerful and well established as Catholicism could rest on such a flimsy foundation, and I would be damned if I was going to believe something I couldn't understand or that couldn't be explained. And beyond my gut reaction, there was an inescapable rational conclusion: if you don't understand what you believe, you don't know what you believe. Believing without knowing what you believed in put believing in a very unappealing light—and I felt liberated.

My lack of religiosity did not spring solely from this internal revelation, or from my family's influence; it was also spurred by the areligious and anticlerical environment provided by Cuban society at large. Middleclass Cuba did not have much interest in things religious and local Catholicism was primarily a provider of rituals and the acknowledged formal register of ceremonies; no middle-class Cuban would feel properly married without a church wedding, and even the most anticlerical individuals—anarchists, atheists and committed communists like my uncle Miguel—would go through them and have their children baptized. And for the most part women went to church, not to cleanse their souls but to ask for favors, and men, with rare exceptions like my father, would not go at all, unless very old and hedging their last-minute bets or young and to wait for the girls to come out after mass. And it didn't help my religiosity any that our parish's priest, Padre Gasolina, Father Gasoline, lived with a "niece" and some children in a house behind the church and was seldom sober when delivering his sermons, or that my father, although always properly polite to him, had given precise instructions never to admit the man into our house for he was not to be trusted with women.

If there was any real religiosity in Cuban life, it was among the poor blacks who still adhered to some of their traditional African, mostly Yoruba, rites and beliefs which they colorfully fused with Catholic symbols. Everything related to the African religion we called *ñáñigo,* and we used the term as adjective and noun to refer to beliefs, practices, people and priests. As far as we were concerned it was all superstition and nonsense, and there was little respect or interest among white Cubans for all this *ñáñigo* stuff, partly because it was black, which to us meant backwards and primitive, and partly because, since we didn't have much interest in our own Catholic religion, why would we care for some half-baked set of African beliefs? This attitude was best encapsulated by the joke I heard from one of my uncles about the Protestant minister who was trying to convert a Spanish atheist. The atheist, after listening carefully and politely to the minister for some time, finally said, "Listen Reverend, if I don't believe in the Holy Roman Catholic Church, which is the only true one, how can I believe in yours?"

Still my imagination was always captured and my curiosity engaged when I entered a black home and saw a little altar with figures of saints, usually Santa Bárbara or San Lázaro, facing the wall instead of the room, punished because they had failed to deliver on some particular request, turned around for a period of time directly proportional to the magnitude of their failure. And since it was only logical to reward as well as punish, the saints were presented with rum or sweets, or with whatever the members of the household could afford to offer, when they came through; and it seemed to me a more sensible way of relating to deities, if you had to relate to them at all, than on your knees in front of an instrument of torture. But these were only fleeting thoughts because I, and those around me, had little or no interest in otherworldly pursuits.

There were two Hermans the German. The first Germán el Alemán was a storyteller who occasionally appeared on the corner of Villanueva and Rodríguez Streets on summer afternoons when the drowsiness and the torpor caused by the suffocating heat weighed heavily on everyone and everything, and when life on the semideserted streets shifted into the gear of lethargy. Some of us boys would sit in a shady spot waiting for the air to cool down enough to play *taco* or *quimbumbia* or something else while giving the heavy Cuban lunch time to negotiate our intestinal tracts. We spoke of little or nothing at all, and it was then that Germán el Alemán would come by with a set of movie flyers, or perhaps he didn't come by but just appeared in our midst since we never knew where he came from or where he went after he left us.

In those days the local movie houses, the Ritz and the Ferroviario, distributed their flyers sometime in midmorning, announcing the movies to be shown that day. For five cents on weekdays we could take in two full-length movies, a cartoon or a short or both, and sometimes even an episode of an ongoing series where we delighted in recognizing that the last scene of the last episode never corresponded exactly with the first scene of the new one, so the train had not actually run over the beautiful girl, or the hero had not in fact been shot, and we took pride in thinking that we were too clever, too slick and alert, to have some gringo moviemaker get away with that, but we were as naive as children can be when they think they are anything but naive. Germán el Alemán would always arrive with a set of these flyers in hand and would begin his performance by reading them, very slowly, in their entirety.

Germán el Alemán was as Cuban as Cuban could be, so it must have been his pale blue eyes and dark blond hair that gave him his sobriquet, but it was the ease with which he would weave a story that mesmerized us. He would start in the same manner every time, taking one flyer first, then the other, and reading every single word written on them. He began with the name and address of the movie house, and the date, and then the extravagant adjectives like "magnificent" and "unbelievable" that were favored by the copywriters as introductions to the features' titles, and finally the names of the actors and actresses and the time of the shows, all the while ignoring the commercial inserts as if they didn't exist, not referring to them even for fun or criticism. And after reading what was being offered in each flyer, he would choose a movie, explaining his choice with a quick monologue in which he would answer his own questions as he went over titles and actors—but never actresses, who were background pieces—using the title as an indication of the film's content, and the leading actor to determine what type of movie it was, and always, to our tacit but strong approval, dismissing love stories or anything that did not promise some form of adventure, action or mystery. Once the choice was made, Germán el Alemán would stretch his legs, rest his back against the wall, run his fingers through his hair, and begin to project the movie on the screen of our imagination.

In a different society at a different time, Germán el Alemán would have been reciting Homer in the agora, or perhaps telling ancient stories by some watering hole in the desert as caravan riders sat by the fire sipping sweet mint tea, or he could have been in some Parisian bar or Italian coffeehouse during the twenties, entertaining both locals and émigrés with his tales of bizarre happenings, or today he could be in a Malibu beach house in shorts and a T-shirt writing scripts for a television show; but fate delivered him to us, and for a few summers he drove our minds to the realization that no movie could come close to what we could see when we closed our eyes and let our fancy roll.

Germán el Alemán would move from scene to scene, letting the title of the movie be the first idea upon which he would build his construct. I remember distinctly the day he chose *The Razor's Edge*. He began by describing a straight razor on a table and then the leather strap next to it, and the razor was the main character, the central figure, and when he gradually brought people into the story it was like they were under the power of the razor, and it took a while before they became characters on their own. When I eventually went to see the movie, it had nothing to do with Germán's tale, and I found the movie interesting but lacking when compared to the captivating narrative our storyteller had created for us. And I remember the long, thin frame of Germán el Alemán as he would appear from nowhere those summer afternoons to weave the yarn of his tales, and after a couple of summers he came no longer, and I was older and too preoccupied with other things to miss him then.

Germán el Alemán *dos* was German and no storyteller and came later. In the meantime, I was going to a new school, Colegio Trelles, a private lay school in the rich Vedado neighborhood, and I was back into the double examination mess, taking new subjects and trying to make up for the ones I had refused to take the official tests for. I liked my history, geography and literature classes but was bored by everything else and frustrated with math because for the first time I had trouble with the subject, now geometry, and couldn't stomach the lecturer, a pedantic medical student who taught by rote a discipline he didn't seem to be interested in. We argued constantly, and he disliked me almost as much as I disliked him, and I eventually just stopped attending his classes and instead used the time to wander through the nearby streets, and find places where I could go and sit and read, and explore in my mind the countries and regions I had learned about in adventure and history books. Although there were two or three pretty girls in my class, I didn't fancy any of them and either kept to myself or ran around with a group of boys who had adopted me because one day while waiting for the bus I showed them how to throw a knife. Two of them had been trying, without the faintest clue or success, so I asked one of them to lend me his knife and, after examining it and calibrating it in my hand, as much for effect as for preparation, I proceeded to land it right in the center of their target, a heart carved into the trunk of a tree. That was the grounds for their acceptance of me, although we never threw a knife again.

Truth be told, I had spent countless hours in my backyard learning how to throw knives and had become quite good at it. Throwing a knife well requires both accurate aim and precise control of the angle and force at which the blade lands, to make sure it not only hits but also penetrates the target. The difficult thing to master is the interaction between velocity and angle, which requires gauging how many times the knife is to whirl over itself, how many full rotations it will make before the blade's point strikes the mark and sticks there. I was drawn to throwing knives, I think, because my mother hated them. My brother Roberto and I had all kinds of toy weapons—pistols, revolvers, rifles, shotguns, machine guns and even a German toy cannon that one of my uncles had given me which took gunpowder and could actually fire—and never a question arose about any of them, but knives, my mother had determined, were something else, and we were never allowed to have one or play with one. Even when Eduardo, one of the men who worked for my father, gave me a rubber knife as a saint's day present, my mother impounded it immediately and I never saw it again. But by the time I began throwing knives, I knew how to procure and sneak them out to the backyard, and no one else in the house who saw me practicing by the *chirimoya* tree shared my mother's phobia, so no one bothered to stop me. I was then free to practice, and I quickly found out that throwing knives created a dilemma.

If I threw a knife hard enough to penetrate the tree trunk, a mistake with the angle of the blade meant that the knife would bounce back forcefully towards me, but if I weakened the force of the throw to reduce the speed of the ricochet, the blade would not penetrate deep enough to stay in the tree even if it hit the target at the proper angle. So safety and proficiency were at odds, and I had to find a way of reconciling them, or at least of determining which was more important and in what direction I should skew their balance. It turned out not to be a long-lasting problem as I soon found out I could substantially increase both by borrowing more and bigger knives from the kitchen. The bigger knives were perfect; longer blades could cover more ground with fewer rotations, and since all blades generally lose their angular velocity after two or three turnovers, with a bigger knife I could stand farther back from the tree. So with a better, larger knife, safety and precision became reconciled but not before I had a half a dozen cuts and bruises from ricocheting blows. I knew there was a lesson to be learned in this but didn't know exactly what it was and kept, for weeks on end, practicing my knife throwing every morning.

My school life and Cuban politics continued to deteriorate in unison. At Colegio Trelles I followed the opposite tack I had at the Maristas, taking the official standardized examinations in the subjects I thought I could pass while ignoring the tests given by my own school, and giving up entirely on geometry and anatomy, since one had left me behind and the other I absolutely abhorred and could only see as concerned with man as a bleeding and defecating machine. In 1948 the candidate of the governing Auténticos, Carlos Prío Socarrás, succeeded Ramón Grau San Martín as president of Cuba, and the cacophony got even louder, as if some form of extreme collective madness had descended upon the island. The few restraining mechanisms that had operated under Grau now ceased to function, and politics became a free-for-all in which official cupidity and concupiscence knew no bounds, and violence tagged along in a tropical orgy in which those in power lacked not only honesty but also taste, parading their ill-acquired gains with the boastful and aggressive ignorance of savages. And as the political debauchery reached an all-time crescendo, so did the anger and frustration of those unable or unwilling to participate in it, especially middle-class Cubans who saw the new president as another idealistic young man of the 1930s gone rotten, as the head of a band of marauders; and whatever hope Prío and his collaborators might have once inspired became transmuted into a demoralized, corrupt and inept political frenzy. As the decline of my high school career gained momentum, so did the degeneration of Cuban politics, and by identifying one with the other I found some solace in the sinking partnership.

It was right around then that Germán el Alemán *dos* appeared on the scene, resembling more a Panzer commander in a Hollywood movie than the business bureaucrat he was. He didn't speak much, but his grammar was impeccable, and his accent matched his receding blond hairline and Teutonic bearing. He had been a prisoner of war according to some, a veteran of the Russian front according to others, and people were interested in him, at least as much as Cubans were interested in foreigners, which wasn't a whole lot. In reality we were less interested in who he was than in what he appeared to be, or in what we imagined he could have been, and that must have been frustrating for him, or perhaps he welcomed it, since one never really knows what goes on in other people's heads. But to me this Herman the German brought music, classical music, and while maybe not the classical music that traditionally serves as introduction to the genre, since I assume Wagner seldom does, it was enough to do the trick and more. I ran into him one Saturday afternoon as he was carrying a pile of records towards his car. I asked him what they were, and he told me, and what he said meant nothing, but he went on to offer me some of them, and I found myself the proud proprietor of a tool of torture.

The records Herman had given me were excerpts rather than complete works, segments of *Rienzi, Tristan und Isolde* and *Tannhäuser,* and none in pristine condition. The only record player we had in the house produced horrendous screeching and scratching, which was not unexpected in those days when one had to worry about the needle, and the position and weight of the record player's arm, and about dust and the rotating base, and a multitude of other things that time and technology have mercifully rid us of. The machine's peculiarities added a touch of cruelty to the annoyance inflicted on my sisters and the few aunts and uncles still lingering around the house, all of whom were incapable of appreciating Wagner, and they would implore me to play something else, and would besiege me with questions, threats and snide remarks about how anyone could enjoy such music. But there was nothing they could do, because like everyone else, I was entitled to my time with the phonograph and I was determined to like this music because it was classical, not popular. That's what Wagner meant to me; it was a way of escaping from the little island burnt by the sun and under the siege of screaming maniacs engaged in a permanent binge of singing and dancing, and shouting, and robbing, and killing. And it was not only what they did but how they did it that irritated me—it was the roaring and aggressive vulgarity that I saw pervading everything, and that I equated with popular Cuban music and popular Cuban culture—as I could have equated it with anything else, I suppose.

Although I did not always enjoy the music of Herr Wagner, which could be grating even to me, I still got plenty of satisfaction from exasperating everybody else in the household, punishing the rest of the family for their ignorance and lack of taste. The more they complained, the longer and louder I would unleash the German on them, and eventually the complaining stopped and they just kept away from the high culture I was trying to foist on them for their own edification. Of all those I had wanted to punish, my sister Silvia was at the top of the list for what she had done to me with Gloria.

It had started on one of those carnival Sundays, when, after a Saturday night given to the street dancing of the blacks' *comparsas,* costumed groups, white Havana would go out in their *carrozas,* floats, open convertibles and trucks, with piles of glistening confetti and roll upon roll of colored streamers, and indulge in the remnants of whatever pagan rite was associated with the beginning of Lent. As we gathered in my house to board one of the trucks I noticed a thin and beautiful face with light hair and pale skin, and to my amazement she came over and stood next to me, and I forgot about the carnival and the other people and the onlookers, and could not believe that this older—she was fifteen, I thirteen—and beautiful girl could be as friendly to me as she was. I could not believe it because I was skinny to the point of appearing rachitic, and awkward with girls to the point of muteness, but after a few moments next to Gloria all that vanished that Sunday afternoon, and I went through the motions of the carnival as if I were in a different world where the only sounds were her voice and her laugh and everything else distant background noise. When we parted I was too shy and too afraid and too stupid to say anything to her but crafty enough to find out her address, which was in Marianao, a different municipality but part of greater Havana, near the school she and Silvia attended.

Two or three Sundays later, I walked the almost two hours to Gloria's house. I had not intended to walk the whole way there, but it was a beautiful sunny morning with a refreshing mild breeze that carried only a little moisture from the ocean, so I kept on walking instead of taking the bus or the tram, giving myself time to overcome shyness or to change my mind or who knows what, and I simply kept on walking until I arrived at her house around noon. I was lucky, she was on the porch talking to an older man, and I said *hola* and she was friendly and I stayed for about ten or fifteen minutes, and I said I was out on a walk with some friends and that they were not far and that I had to join them again. I'm sure I said it all mechanically and in one long sentence, like I was repeating something I had memorized for the occasion, which was exactly the case, and I knew that what I was saying was not believable, that it made little sense, but it didn't matter because I was talking to her and she was still friendly and smiled back and seemed glad to see me. That was enough, more than enough, and I felt good and I don't remember what else I said or if I said anything else, but I felt full of energy, invigorated, and I walked all the way back to my neighborhood in half the time.

Now there are certain deeds that reflect with the accuracy of a mirror the soul of those committing them, and what my sister Silvia did next cast hers in a dark light in my eyes. It was mean and unnecessary, and a transgression of all the canons of brotherly or sisterly love and, more important, of the family solidarity I had come to believe in and held in unquestionable esteem. I never understood her action or her motivation, never received an explanation for it, and it cemented my dislike for her. The very next day after I had visited Gloria, I came home from school in the late afternoon and Silvia passed me with anger in her voice and eyes, muttering something about telling Mother.

As Silvia led my mother into the kitchen I knew I was in trouble, although I could not figure out on what account. Since boys were not allowed in that part of the house—that was why Silvia had decided to talk to my mother there—I tried to get close enough to the kitchen window facing the backyard and the *chirimoya* tree to find out what was going on, and I heard bits and pieces of Silvia's indictment, and what I heard didn't make much sense: "she has a boyfriend," "she's older," "he's just a little boy," "he's interfering with our friendship." And there must have been more because I had trouble catching every word, and as they moved to the other side of the kitchen I could no longer make out their voices, and I was annoyed that I couldn't hear them and irate for having such a witch for a sister, and curious because what I had heard was beyond my comprehension and I couldn't square it with her anger. And her anger filled the whole kitchen and spilled over the backyard and it surrounded me and brought a bad taste to my mouth, and I was so disgusted by it that I stopped trying to listen and went around the garden and into the house through the front door, and it didn't take long for my mother to call me and lay down the law.

I was told to keep away from Gloria—and that was that, no explanation was offered and I didn't request one. I saw no purpose in challenging the maternal diktat and felt satisfied just holding Silvia responsible for it, and I was incensed, but at the same time I didn't feel like pushing the point, something I was more than willing to do on other matters and which usually took the form not of throwing down the gauntlet but simply of ignoring what I was told. I had found open challenges useless—no argument or reasoning could ever supersede family-mandated directives—if I felt strongly enough about an issue I would just go ahead and do as I wanted. This was an effective strategy because either I would never be found out or, by the time I was, circumstances would most likely have changed and the matter would have lost its immediacy.

My reaction to the Gloria admonition, however, fell into a different category, and while I felt no compulsion to abide by it, I felt no pressing desire to seek her out either. I was content with the idea that she had paid attention to me, or even, if I had gathered correctly from my sister's kitchen diatribe, liked me. This was pleasing and gratifying, but I had also heard Silvia mentioning Gloria's *novio,* boyfriend, and that put a damper on my enthusiasm as if the reference to another boy had taken something away from her. The whole question was far from clear in my mind, and even now looking back I am not sure what went on in my head, or if my head was involved at all, as I transformed Gloria from a girl I wanted to be near into an image to look at and admire from a distance, and it was as if following on the steps of El Quijote I had found myself a Dulcinea.

Maybe my attitude was the fault of my aunts, who had drilled into me from an early age the idea that there were two types of women, those you marry and those you fuck. Granted they never used the last term, since crudeness of language was not part of the family's repertoire of idiosyncrasies, but the message was clear nonetheless, and it came directly

48

from the women of the family who were in absolute charge of in-house education and who kept the men very much out of the picture. My mother also kept out of it, leaving my aunts fully in command, probably because she had nothing to add to the wisdom they imparted; if she hadn't approved of what I was being taught, she most certainly wouldn't have been quiet about it—even if it meant a confrontation with her husband's sisters. So perhaps it was this distinction between types of women that led me to have romantic thoughts of Gloria without feeling any urge to be with her, or maybe it was something more mundane like the difficulty of seeing someone who lived as far away as Marianao, or all the planning it would require to get around Silvia's watchful eye, but whatever the reason, I pushed Gloria onto a cozy back burner while I bounced from school to school with time only for baseball and nonacademic books, and for daydreaming and flying to the Moon.

I was leaving behind Grimm and Salgari with their fairy tales and adventures, and was beginning to discover *The Three Musketeers* and *The Count of Monte Cristo* and *Les Miserables*. I was captivated by the fantastic tales these books told, and even more by their descriptions of foreign, and thus mysterious and exciting, locations, all the while missing whatever subtle and not so subtle points there were to miss. I could read these stories and Zane Grey westerns and trashy detective books for hours at a time, while I couldn't read a schoolbook for more than ten or fifteen minutes. I knew I wanted to join the navy, but this was a problem because Cuba didn't have a navy, just a couple of old discarded ships the Americans had sold the country, more floating scrap metal than sailing machines. And while there was a Naval Academy, getting in was 90 percent political contacts and 10 percent qualification, and my family did have the contacts, but actually I was not so much interested in sailing as in traveling, getting away, discovering the world far from the blue and green hues of the Caribbean Sea, and away from the warm tropical air, and beyond the palm trees and the mosquitoes and the never-ending noise. I wanted to enter the country of D'Artagnan and see snow, and experience the worlds of Napoleon and Garibaldi and of the old Roman Empire, and I wanted to see the lands of the Red Baron and of the midnight sun, and walk into the Tower of London and stroll down Broadway and ride a horse in the Wild West; and I wanted to experience firsthand the land of tango and see the Spain that was so present in family conversations and yet so distant, and that's what joining the navy meant to me. So I held on to the illusion, knowing perfectly well there was no navy to join, but knowing equally well that the last thing you ever let go of are your dreams.

CHAPTER FOUR

The presidency of Carlos Prío Socarrás suffered all the ills of the previous Auténtico administration without retaining the few safeguards that had prevented the country from plunging into total chaos between 1944 and 1948. Now as the 1940s were approaching their end, Cuba seemed more like a large raft adrift at sea than a securely anchored piece of land, and there was no sense of political measure or proportion that anyone could discern. Street shootings increased in frequency and intensity, and official corruption reached heights never experienced before; the more outlandish and bizarre the act, the more likely it was to be committed. Politicians no longer bothered to go through the motions of disguising their actions, like the minister of the treasury who brought a truck around to pilfer the public vaults and who, without any bureaucratic circumvention or legal smoke screen, just took the cash home; or the mayor of Havana who carted away the City Hall furniture after running out of things to steal; or the ordinary policemen who supplemented their salaries by hitting on every merchant in the neighborhood for goods or cash or both. The president himself was believed to be on drugs because there was no rational explanation for his behavior and for his apparent total lack of control.

The few public figures who voiced outrage got nowhere in an atmosphere saturated with cynicism and apathy. Even the traditional guardians of public honor and idealism, university students, had fallen prey to thievery and assassination. The island resembled an asylum for the criminally insane where the inmates were free to go about as they pleased, while an orchestra played their trumpets and their *maracas* and their drums in a deafening raucousness of uncoordinated sounds that seemed to bother no one as it conjured an air of hysterical ebullience and glee.

But cynicism and apathy were largely masquerade, cover and escape valves for pent-up anger and frustration, ways to avoid facing up to the pitiable reality we all knew we were living.

Tango is pure melancholy expressed in language that aspires to poetry, and its lyrics and its music are perfectly matched for conveying a sense of unavoidable and irreversible sadness, and the Portuguese fado exudes irrepressible gloom in sound and melody, but traditional Cuban popular songs often manifest a sort of schizophrenic malady in which the sadness of the lyrics conflicts with the gaiety of rhythm and beat, and sometimes, after a lachrymose recitation of sorrows and calamities, the exuberance of the music pushes sadness aside, and the song ends with melody and lyrics in a mood totally different from its beginning; the original gloomy temper ignored, discarded, supplanted by a beat and rhythm that keep no connection with the initial unhappiness, as in "Lágrimas Negras" (Black Tears), which goes:

> Aunque tú me has echado en el abandono
> aunque tú has muerto todas mis ilusiones
> en vez de maldecirte con justo encono
> en mis sueños te colmo de bendiciones.
> Sufro la amarga pena de tu partida
> Siento el dolor profundo de tu traición
> y lloro sin que sepas que el llanto mío
> tiene lágrimas negras
> tiene lágrimas negras como mi vida

> (Although you have abandoned me
> although you have killed all my illusions
> instead of condemning you with just anger
> in my dreams I shower blessings upon you.
> I suffer the bitter sorrow of your departure
> I feel the deep pain of your betrayal
> I cry without you knowing that my cry
> has black tears
> black tears like my life)

and then, radically and suddenly shifting rhythmic, lyrical and emotional tempo:

Tú me dices que sí
y yo te digo también
contigo me voy mi santa
aunque me cueste morir

(You tell me, yes
and I also say yes
with you I go my sexy girl
even if it kills me)

Although in inverse order, the feeling Cubans expressed during the years of the Prío administration ran with parallel logical disjunction between careless cynicism and romantic idealism, and it was like being at a party where everyone was desperately trying to have a good time while they could because they all knew that it was going to end up in a brawl.

Relative to its number of inhabitants or square feet of territory, Cuba must have had the largest pantheon of heroes of any country in the world. Most famous was José Martí, a white, well-educated writer and poet who organized the 1895 revolt against Spain. He was its soul and inspiration and although not a fighting man, was killed in the first combat he ever saw, when he mounted his horse and charged the enemy against the advice of experienced soldiers. Then there was Antonio Maceo, black, with no formal education, a veteran of many a battle and skirmish, who died under mysterious circumstances with racist overtones not far from Havana; and José Maceo, his brother, also a general who died in the battlefield, too; and Calixto García who kept the fight against Spain going when almost everyone else was ready to give up; and myriad peasants and landowners and students and professors. And the heroes were not all Cuban born: Máximo Gómez was from the Dominican Republic, Orestes Ferrara from Italy, Narciso López from Venezuela, Frederick Funston from the United States, Carlos Roloffs from Poland.

One of the reasons there were so many Cuban national heroes was that it took Cuba so long to get rid of the Spaniards. All the other Spanish colonies in the Western Hemisphere had broken loose at the beginning of the nineteenth century when Napoleon removed the Spanish king from Madrid and put his own brother, Joseph, on the throne. This move sparked revolts in the colonies, uprisings that began with the reaffirmation of loyalty to the deposed king and of antipathy to the new French one, and ended in independence when the colonists, basking in their newly acquired preeminence and power, no longer saw a reason to accept anyone's authority but their own. But Cuba had been left out of this process and remained loyal to the mother country, and the absence of a pro-independence movement on the island during this period was so marked that after losing all their possessions in the Americas except for Cuba and Puerto Rico, the grateful Spaniards vested upon Cuba the title of *siempre fiel,* ever faithful, by which the island was to be referred in all official documents. La Isla de Cuba thus became La Siempre Fiel Isla de Cuba, and as always with this sort of thing, honors and wishful thinking were no match for reality—and reality for Cuba was the United States.

As sugar instituted its reign over the economy of the island in the first half of the nineteenth century, commerce with the United States grew in tandem, and as American interests in Cuba expanded, the gravitational pull began to shift inexorably away from Spain. When Presidents Polk and Pierce made offers to buy Cuba for 100 million dollars and 130 million dollars respectively, negotiations might have been successful had it not been for the opposition of the antislavery forces in the United States, which saw the danger of an additional pro-slavery state. The Cuban landed gentry were attracted to the possibility of joining the American Union and saw Texas as the example to follow. An "annexationist" faction grew among them that was responsible for organizing the first open and direct armed challenges to Spanish rule in the 1840s and 1850s. These Cuban players, however, turned out to be marginal actors in a much bigger drama, the confrontation between North and South that led to the American Civil War. The triumph of the North eliminated the possibility of Cuba becoming part of the United States and left independence as the only viable alternative for those rejecting the Spanish colonial yoke. Spain was a has-been power whose economic importance was being rapidly superseded by that of the United States, and from the nineteenth century on it becomes difficult to decipher political events in Cuba without reference to its powerful northern neighbor.

In the face of spreading antagonism to its rule, Spain poured soldiers into the island, and this worked for a while. The armed insurrection that had begun in 1868 petered out by 1871, an episode that Cuban historians, guided less by facts than national pride, refer to as the Ten Years War. But as is the rule with colonial conflicts, the end of hostilities was pause rather than resolution. Another brief armed struggle ensued in 1879, which because of its short duration came to be known as the Guerra Chiquita, the Little War, and in 1895 a major effort was mounted to oust the Spaniards, and this became the Cuban War of Independence.

And at the prompting of destiny, manifest or otherwise, and by the prodding of William Randolph Hearst and Joseph Pulitzer and their yellow press, and after the Joint Congressional Resolution of April 19, 1898, the Spanish-American War came and Cuba was given a new master. It was in the fight against Spain that the long roll of Cuban heroes started, to be generously supplemented later by those who fell fighting American suzerainty and homegrown despotism, and as Catholic worshipers choose saints to identify with and with whom they feel comfortable establishing a connection, I chose Ignacio Agramonte as my number one hero. He had been young, educated, white, and had turned down the opportunity to be a big shot in civilian clothes because he felt it his obligation to be among those bearing arms, and as a fighter he came to symbolize what I admired and what I increasingly saw lacking in the Cuba surrounding me: self-respect. It was said of Ignacio Agramonte that he originated *la carga del machete,* the ragtag Cuban army's version of the cavalry charge in which the machete of the rural worker took the place of the professional soldier's saber; and it was also said of him that he originated this charge when, in the middle of a confrontation with Spanish forces, he was told that his troops had run out of ammunition and was asked how they could continue to fight:

"¿Con qué peleamos, mi General?"
"¡Con la vergüenza!"

("What do we fight with, General?"
"With our self-respect!")

He then mounted his horse and rallied his men with the cry "¡Cubanos, al machete!" And without looking back, he charged the enemy and rode straight through the dry pages of history into the misty confines of legend and myth. So went the story of Ignacio Agramonte, and whether fact or fable it serves equally well the purpose of providing a measure by which to judge a man, or so I thought as a boy—and still do.

My brother Roberto and I fought a lot and played a lot together, and I felt it incumbent upon me to protect him because I was the elder. Sometimes this wasn't easy, especially since he would pick fights with bigger boys at school and then call upon me for rescue. At some point I made it clear I wasn't about to run to his defense every time he called, and this helped, but it didn't bring us any closer. Although in a certain way we were close, in other respects we were far, far apart. I saw him coming more and more under the influence of all that bothered and irritated me about Cuba; and like the rest of the family and the rest of the country, more and more absorbed by the boisterous vortex of emptiness that seemed to suck in everything. We seldom played baseball together because, being three years apart, we had different friends and ran around with different kids, but we would frequently, just the two of us, go and play catch and practice bagging grounders. Our games often ended in arguments and occasionally in a fight, and I always had to be careful to fend him off without really hurting him because, if enraged, he would kick and bite and hold on to my legs as if glued to them. Roberto was also our mother's favorite child, and the rest of us knew it but were not especially bothered by it, my sisters because as girls they were not on a competing plane with a brother, and I because being the eldest son I had all the attention I could handle, and in addition we were glad to indulge our mother a little since it was clear life had not indulged her much.

Life had not been easy for Felicidad Inés Manuela Clementina de la Sierra y Camps. She never completed grammar school because of poor eyesight and went through adolescence wearing very thick glasses, the thickest I ever saw, and as a young woman she had to live with her mother and sister Cristina at Cristina's home, where her sister reigned in an imperial manner. Cristina's husband would go on prolonged sales trips during which he worked and engaged in extramarital affairs with apparently equal zeal, and his adventures were so widely known they couldn't have failed to reach my aunt, who compensated for this humiliation with haughtiness and pretentiousness. My mother had no alternative but to graciously accept her condition of ward, so when my father appeared on the scene he must have looked to her like a knight in shining armor, or maybe like a rickety lifeboat, but, in any event, he was her chance to escape, to marry, to have children, to gain some independence and to have a life of her own.

She married my father and became Señora de Moreno, which literally means "wife of Moreno," or "woman of Moreno," depending on the interpretation one wants to give it, and which was the formal manner of addressing married women in white Cuba, but one that had no legal standing. The Spanish way of passing down family names is often confusing—and with good reason. To begin with, when a woman marries she retains her family name—she doesn't take on her husband's—and when children are born the children retain both family names, the father's followed by the mother's. My mother continued to be Sierra after marrying my father; he, of course, was still Moreno. I was, therefore, my given names followed by Moreno and Sierra, and the use of the two last names was mandatory for all legal purposes. That's the easy part. The confusion for outsiders, and sometimes even for insiders, arises in several forms. Most people in social or informal circumstances use only their first last name, so introducing myself to someone I would say, as I shook his hand, Francisco Moreno. But individuals with very common paternal family names like Pérez or García often use their two last names, so when they are introduced their names become Pérez-Something or García-Something, and some might even drop socially, but not legally, the first common-sounding last name and use only the second one. Others, if they count someone famous among their ancestors, or maybe out of sheer pretentiousness, or for whatever other reason might take their fancy, meld a double name, without the warning sign of a hyphen, into one. So a person introduced to you as Something Pérez Inclán could be referred to as Mr. Pérez, Mr. Inclán, Mr. Perezinclán, Mr. Pérez Inclán without a hyphen or Mr. Pérez-Inclán with a hyphen, and in the last instances his complete name would include another one, usually taken from the paternal grandmother. Now imagine this system passed down through generations, where both parents, or all four grandparents, may all have double last names, and you begin to get the idea.

Even after she married, life did not get much easier for my mother, installed, as she was, in the midst of an alien tribe. My grandmother Consuelo, the one with the beautiful blue eyes and the rose garden and the medicinal herbs, ruled the household with the loving despotism Latin women use to exercise power over their families; and my mother had to contend with a score of in-laws always around to monitor how she performed as wife to my father and as mother to his children. It was not until after my grandmother died, and aunts and uncles began to fade away, and the number of daily diners shrank to just her husband and her children and an occasional aunt or uncle, that she appeared to relax, and it was also then that she had her eye operation and could see better than ever before, and her thick, thick, glasses gave way to thin ones; and I don't know if it is true or just my imagination, but it was not until then that I saw her smile.

It was not until much later that I came to realize that my mother had a pretty face, and this realization was not prompted by filial sentimentality but by observing how much her features, once rid of ugly glasses and judging in-laws, resembled those of my sisters. I noticed, too, how much my brother's face resembled my father's, and it was surprising to see for the first time something that had always been in front of my eyes. But I did not ruminate on these observations, just took note of them and concentrated on escaping the confines of the island in any way I could, and that's how I discovered Johann Strauss, and moved on to Chopin, and to the other Strauss, Richard, and to Tchaikovsky, and to Rimsky-Korsakov. I knew nothing about music, but would be transported, by sounds that were to me the negation of things tropical, to faraway and enticing places where you didn't need a mosquito net on summer nights and where the flying cockroach, which should have been Cuba's national bird, was not to be found; and it was about this time that in a last-ditch effort on my parents' part to do something about my education, I was dispatched to an all-male, sleep-away, semimilitary, half-academic and half-vocational school on the outskirts of Havana.

The Instituto Técnico Industrial was definitely different; I was immediately struck by the popularity of the *danzón*, rural Cuba's version of the contredanse, among its students and taken a little aback by it, but I quickly found things easier than I had imagined. I actually liked being with boys from all over the island who lacked the smart-alecky attitude of Havana kids and were serious and well mannered. They had all been admitted into the school, as had I, through some connection that did not rule out merit but certainly outranked it when it came to getting anything from the government—this was a public school, and that is how things were with anything "public."

I started seeing how different these boys were when I attended baseball practice and saw that it was played differently by them, neither in the fluky and offhand style of my neighborhood nor in the self-conscious but whimsical way of the Maristas school where looking good was as important as being good, and which ended up sending a shortstop to the Yankees, Willy Miranda, who had a genius for making easy chances look difficult. But it was a learning experience to see how seriously these guys took their playing, how committed they were, how close to the ground the infielders kept their bodies, always ready to throw them in front of a grounder, and I noticed the marked intensity of pitcher and batter as they eyed one another, and I also realized how small I was, fifteen, and one hundred ten pounds of flesh and bone, mostly bone, next to seventeen and eighteen-year-olds who weighed twenty, thirty or forty pounds more than I did.

So without the fire in my belly to risk life and limb in pursuit of a spot on the school baseball team, which would have taken me at least a year to achieve, if ever, I turned to basketball, or more precisely, basketball turned to me. Mario, another freshman, had taken it upon himself to organize an intramural basketball league and was looking for recruits, so we formed three teams and began playing, and called ourselves teams A, B and C. For us, basketball was played quite differently than baseball. It was not a rough game, as was baseball, but a game of skill and concentration, and we dribbled, passed, shot and covered with as little physical contact as possible. There was a lot of attention paid to intercepting the ball, and to positioning, and there were fouls, but they were few and the result of miscalculation. Why we were so much more circumspect and rule-abiding when it came to basketball I don't know; perhaps it was that we didn't feel as secure in the rectangular wooden or cement court as we felt in the dirt or grass field, perhaps it was that basketball was still relatively new and foreign to us while baseball was part of the family, perhaps it was that playing cleanly was the most effective way of showing off, perhaps . . . well, whatever the reason, it was not limited to players but was shared by the spectators who saw contact in basketball as "dirty" and loudly disapproved of it, so the basketball I played that year was a skillful and pleasant game which I greatly enjoyed and which became integrated with the rest of my good feelings for that school.

My parents had sent me to the Instituto Técnico Industrial without a clear idea of what they wanted but with the hope that I would mature and mend my cavalier ways of dealing with school. I went like an exile from the metropolis who goes to a provincial town to purge his sins; I saw no alternative and looked upon it as a forced detour in a yet uncharted plan that would lead to an adventurous future, so I was surprised when I found that I did like the boys I met there and felt comfortable in the school's atmosphere. And a strange school it was, with a vocational purpose but an academic component that was very much to my taste, with teachers better versed in their subjects than the semi-illiterate Maristas Brothers and more enthusiastic in their dispensation of knowledge than the bureaucrat-educators of Havana public high schools or the part-time instructors of the city's private schools for whom teaching was one more activity among the several they juggled to make ends meet and who always appeared to be short in commitment and even shorter in inspiration. I found the routine at the new school very agreeable, with academic subjects in the morning and "shops" in the afternoon, and I got myself admitted to the only nonvocational program, chemistry. The chemistry teacher was Dr. Marrero, a very pleasant and relaxed man, on the heavy side and probably in his mid-fifties. Dr. Marrero allowed the few of us in his lab to come and go as we pleased, with no prescribed schedule, to conduct whatever experiments we were engaged in, and he would always wait until most of us were present—and there were not more than ten or twelve of us—to assign work or discuss results or explain what we were doing and why we were doing it. So I had plenty of opportunity to amble around the school in the afternoon and look into what other people were doing and chat, and I often would walk out to the nearby farm where the agriculture students were with their old tractor, some of them always working and others sitting on the grass enjoying the cool breeze that blew in most afternoons and sneaking a cigarette, and I would hang around there for a little while and then walk back to school as slowly as I had come out, and go to the lab and work on whatever I was working on and ask Dr. Marrero whatever I wanted to ask. And since he was an avid baseball fan who loved discussing the game and players, we would stay past class time listening to him expound on all the great players he had seen, and on the American teams that had visited the island in the twenties and thirties, and if someone had a question about chemistry he would answer it, and give it whatever time it needed, make sure it was understood, and then back he would go to discussing Martín Dihígo or Adolfo Luque or Alejandro Oms or Cocaína García or Lefty Grove, and unless I had basketball that day it would be dark by the time I left the lab and got back to the dormitory.

Many years later, in a future that was just one in a limitless number of possibilities, Pete Seeger took the "Guantanamera" song out of Cuba and into the United States and international renown. But the "Guantanamera" he took with him, with the unabashed credulity of a gringo radical, was a prim distant cousin of our "Guantanamera"; ours, the original, was a tune that would come on the radio every workday at three in the afternoon, when, to its melody, lyrics were added describing the crime of the day. Aside from the refrain, "Guantanamera, guajira guantanamera," there were no words to the music composed by Joseíto Fernández; the relation, in gory detail, of the most violent crime committed the day before was its only lyrics. And the most popular verse sung to the "Guantanamera" tune turned out to be the result of public imagination, and it came about because sometimes little countries jump ahead of their time, and we had our Lorena Bobbit decades before she became the avenging angel of feminine pride in the United States. But because of the cultural differences between the two countries, or maybe the different tenors of the times, the name of ours was of no interest and disappeared immediately from the public mind—but not the name of the mutilated man: Olegario. And because it was considered too racy a subject, it was not given the media treatment it was entitled to, and the mutilation never made it to the "Guantanamera" daily crime recital, although shootings and beatings and knifings and rapes were meat for its daily musical grind; but the people were not to be denied, and very soon, with anonymous authorship and no airtime, Olegario's plight became the most popular verse ever sung to the "Guantanamera" music:

> Pon tu pensamiento en mí
> Oh mi amigo Olegario
> Pon los huevos sobre el radio
> Y te crecerá el pipí

> (Place your thoughts on me
> Oh, my friend Olegario
> Put your balls on the radio
> And your weenie will grow back)

But perhaps my memory betrays me and it was Clavelito, Little Carnation, a popular country crooner turned psychic, to whom the verses were ascribed, but this is of marginal importance since Olegario's dismemberment was the kind of event that provided poetic inspiration for the daily airing of "Guantanamera."

It was the "Guantanamera" music that often filled the air as I lazily strolled about the school grounds, sticking my head here and there to see what was going on, and reassuring myself that I did not want, then or ever, to be doing whatever was being done in the "shops." How the radios came to be in there I never knew, although they must have been brought in by the teachers to alleviate the tedium of vocational afternoon teaching when the only sensible thing to do at that time of day was to catch whatever breeze might blow your way and wait for the midday meal to complete its intestinal sojourn and for the sun to be in marked retreat before undertaking any serious labor. And it became clear to me that we organized our activities out of sync with the flow of nature, and I thought about matters of this kind because I had nothing better to do at that time of day, and because there was something out of kilter between the lunch we ate and the climate we lived in, and because I missed the marching and parading we did after morning classes.

Extracurricular activities for those willing, or driven, to distinguish themselves ran on two clearly demarcated tracks: civilian and military. The civilian track consisted of running the student council, which required being elected to it, which in turn required making speeches and discussing school issues and organizing one's friends and everything else that accompanies electoral politics. This track had to exist, as politics was Cuba's third largest industry, after sugar and tobacco, and seen in that light it made sense for a vocational school to provide some training for it—although some of the most common and effective electoral techniques, like stuffing ballot boxes and resuscitating the dead, were left out, probably under the assumption that this would come through natural inclination and students would learn them on their own when the time came. I attended some of the meetings and participated in some of the discussions and was offered the opportunity to be a candidate for one of the class representative slots the following year, and I felt the lure to exercise power, never mind how restricted, but I also liked the military drills and the marching that went with the semimartial organization of the school, and whose didactic purpose must have been to complete the range of opportunities open to Cuban boys at the time: if you couldn't make a living at a profession or trade or in politics, there was always the army. The military and civic tracks were mutually exclusive and interested students had to choose one or the other, and to qualify as an officer in the student corps you had to show dedication and enthusiasm and everything that is supposed to go with military aptitude, but, above all, you needed the recommendation of the student-officers running the program, and this I could manage. So I had to choose between the civilian and the military tracks for the rest of my stay at the school, and this made me think long and hard, as long and hard as I was able to think about anything, and I decided on the military for reasons that were never completely clear in my own mind. But it turned out to be a moot decision since there was not going to be any rest-of-stay-at-school for me.

A few days after I came home for the summer, with my exams passed and the necessary backing to join the student officer corps, I received a letter from the school canceling the results of the final physics examination and demanding that the test be retaken at the beginning of the next school year. I was flabbergasted to learn that the reason given for the cancellation was that many students had copied their answers—from other students, the textbook, their notes or God-knows-what. I was outraged; physics had been my best subject and I had answered all the questions correctly and received a 100, the best possible grade. Hell, it had been a long time since I had done that well in any subject at any school, and if there had been any cheating it should have been caught then and there, and I felt insulted because I never would have cheated, not out of honesty but out of pride, and I wouldn't have helped anyone else cheat. I felt strongly that if I was willing to swallow my lumps, others should be able to swallow theirs. So my crusading zeal took over again and there was no way, out of principle, that I was going to retake that physics exam, and since there was no way back to school without taking the test over, school came to an end.

My decision to quit school was also prompted by a sense of adventure—by a longing for change and new experiences. At sixteen, I didn't have a concrete idea of the former or clear expectations about the latter, but desire for something new and different acted as an attractor, as a magnet, marking the path to be followed. There was no point in an open confrontation with my parents, so I didn't tell them about my intention to quit school but decided first to seek an alternative they could, even if reluctantly, accept. I started looking for a job and found one without much effort, and it was the type of job that, while not necessarily pleasing to my parents, would allay their misgivings, most of them anyhow. I went to one of my father's friends, Rogelio Valmaña, who was vice president of a large Cuban bank, and asked him for a position and he assumed, as I had intended him to, that I was there with my father's blessing, and he gave me a job. Cuba being Cuba, and the times being what they were, he also told me not to report to work until the summer was over so I could enjoy the rest of my vacation, and when I told my parents I had a job in a bank and wasn't going back to school they didn't put up much of a fight, in fact, seemed somewhat relieved, so I got ready to become an employee of the Banco Continental Cubano.

It was around then that I met Amarilis. I was at the first ice-skating rink Havana had ever seen, at least to my knowledge, and it was not even a legitimate rink at all but the frozen surface of a theater stage where some American ice show performed in the evening. It was open to the public during the day and I went—I had to go once I heard of it—and was fascinated by the coolness of the air inside the theater, and I rented a pair of skates and could barely stand up, let alone skate. As I struggled with the ice and the skates and my balance, an apparition materialized in front of me and offered to help; she was tall and thin and blond, and was wearing white pants and a pink sweater, and how the time passed afterwards I'm not sure. I know I skated, and skated and skated with her, and managed not to fall, and she was proud of her teaching. And I remember that when time came to go I did not want to leave, and she told me her name was Amarilis, and I didn't know what an *amarilis* was, or if there was such a thing as an *amarilis,* but if there was, it had to be something rare, and delicate, and beautiful. It was like my head was shrouded in a deep fog, and I didn't know what to do, but I did know I wanted to see her again, and asked for her telephone number, and she gave it. But when it came to girls I still didn't have a clue. This was partly because I had attended school almost exclusively with boys, partly because I had little or nothing to do with my sisters, partly because my home education concerning females didn't venture much beyond the marry/anything-goes distinction, and mostly because I was shy by nature and awkward by disposition, and couldn't think of anything to say to a girl, and because in a country of dancers and fast-talkers I couldn't do either. So I liked Amarilis and had her telephone number but was not sure what to do next.

In that summer of 1950, as I waited for my new future to begin, a lot of things came together. I was invited to join the Escuderos de Colón, the junior branch of the Knights of Columbus, which in Cuba was a very different organization from its counterpart in the States, more of an upper-middle-class social club than a religious organization, and it was in a big old mansion on Calle 12, in the Vedado district of Havana, far in physical and social distance from my neighborhood but not far from Amarilis. The Escuderos chapter was in the process of being constituted, so I would be one of the small group of its founders, and it turned out that there were only four of us so we could give ourselves whatever fancy titles the semisecret organization provided, and there was some mystery to the cloaked initiation ceremony and, more important, there was a big billiard table and a collection of foils, epées and sabers, and all this made it quite attractive, so I became a member.

One evening that same summer, my sister Marta and her boyfriend, Otto, took me to his club to see him play squash, and the game, as I soon learned, was not really squash but front-tennis, although everyone kept referring to it as squash, and it was played in a slightly reduced jai alai court with a tennis racket and a tennis ball, and as soon as I saw Otto and his friends playing I knew this was my game. I had no doubt that I could jump into the court at that very moment and make mincemeat of any of the four players; and it was no idle internal boast but a realization that came from some place deep inside me which admitted no doubt, and I knew then and there I had to do whatever it took to play the game, and two weeks later I was playing it.

It was also that summer that I went for the first time to a classical music concert. I met Mozart and Haydn at a Sunday matinee after someone in the family, my sister Marta probably, had given me the admission ticket someone else had given her, and I went out of curiosity and because it must have been before my front-tennis frenzy, when I would go and play or practice every day and had no time for anything else, and at the concert I couldn't judge how good the orchestra and the conductor were or anything else but was transfixed by the performance and dazed when it was over. I didn't know anything that beautiful existed, and could not help but contrast it with the raucousness surrounding my daily life. And fueled by the vehemence of youth and with the conviction of unquestioned ignorance, I thought something was very wrong with a society, a people, who placed Mambo over Mozart and didn't listen to Haydn but would enwrap themselves in *cha cha cha,* and I felt physically constrained and mentally deprived by the sweltering environs of a tropical island-prison. And this feeling exploded into full consciousness when later that same summer I saw *The Third Man,* and I had not seen nor will I ever see another movie which had the impact on me this one did one balmy evening at the Apolo movie house on the Calzada del 10 de Octubre. Neither the plot nor the charming wickedness of Harry Lime but the setting was what engraved itself into my mind with the force of a branding iron: the mysteriousness of war-torn Vienna, the shadows slithering through walls and pavements as the notes of the zither added lure to enigma, Calloway's dark, long leather coat, and the cabaret; these were sharp visual goads to my sense of confinement and to my desire for something different and adventurous. And I remember with perfect clarity walking out of the theater into the evening breeze with the absolute certainty that whatever the future had in store for me one thing I already knew: I would not, could not, live my life within the confines of a tropical island.

CHAPTER FIVE

On Sunday evenings Eduardo Chibás, the firebrand politician who had founded the Partido Ortodoxo (Orthodox Party) and had run as a protest presidential candidate in the 1948 elections, spoke on the radio, although it was actually shrieking and ranting and raving, condemning political corruption and government inefficiency and pointing out the many ills afflicting the country and ascribing them all to the negligence, malfeasance, cupidity and stupidity of Auténtico politicians and, specifically, to the Prío administration. I loved listening to his tirades because he would say in public what many said in private but no one else would broadcast or print, and because there was daring in his philippics and idealism in his jeremiads, and because he angered those who disagreed with him, and because in the middle of the profligacy, dissolution, turpitude and dishonesty that infected Cuban politics, he had managed to remain honest and forthright, and because his enemies called him *el loco,* the crazy one, because there was nothing else they could accuse him of, and because he had bolted the Auténtico organization and launched a new party that sought to return to the ideas and principles that had inspired the radical students and middle-class dissenters of the 1930s, and because he spoke with a lisp and couldn't pronounce the *erre,* the Spanish double *r.*

I went to work in September—at sixteen. I reported to the bank's branch on Zulueta Street, starting with a salary of fifty pesos a month for the initial six-month probationary period, which was the same as fifty American dollars since the Cuban peso was pegged to the dollar and both circulated freely throughout the island, and this initial salary was to be raised to ninety-five pesos when I became a permanent employee. This was indeed a good salary for a young, ignorant kid, way above the average wage brought by any similar job thanks to the muscle of the bank employees' labor union, which in militancy and proneness to violence was the closest thing to the American Teamsters organized Cuban labor had to offer.

The bank quickly taught me how the world really worked, how one went about changing it, what would happen when you tried to change it, and what would happen when you didn't. Six months into the job my position became permanent, which, given the legislation of the time and the power of the union, meant that the only way to get myself fired was by being caught stealing. After the same six months I was made union shop steward because no one else among the eight unionized employees in the office wanted the job, and I had no idea what that meant other than it was important, and that I would be in charge of union matters, leading my coworkers and speaking for them, and that made me feel grown up, and for the first time I was pulled in by the seductive appeal of power, and as a river follows its natural course, the rebel in me found another cause.

We like to pretend our actions and opinions come in the wake of some mental process or result from some form of understanding, but I am convinced they respond to forces and motivations of which we have only the vaguest awareness. We feel what we feel because that's the way we feel, and explanations follow in accordance with our individual preferences, schooling, creativity, and the nature of the time; and as I joined the union and became active in its work, I immediately felt driven to oppose its corrupt leadership. It was evident its leadership was corrupt because otherwise it couldn't be its leadership and enjoy the privileges and accoutrements of power in a society as base as ours and with a political system as knavish as the one we had. These people, I soon concluded in justifying my opinion, didn't match, or even come close to, what union leaders should be, not that I had any notion of what that was, but they were as good to do battle against as anyone else, and it was also obvious they were well entrenched in their positions and ready to defend themselves— but for me, just like for Don Quijote, the more difficult the struggle, the more glorious the charge.

The everlasting appeal of the self-appointed errant knight from La Mancha springs from his being both insane and quite sane at the same time. He embodies an approach to life that is both absurd and essentially correct, revealing the reality of unreality and the unreality of reality. It is an invitation to launch against windmills because they are there, and with a little effort they can be made to stand for whatever you want them to in the everlasting struggle between right and wrong, and in our permanent search for purpose. Its meaning is to be found in the implied admonition that we go through life being Sancho or Quixote, following stomach or imagination, crawling or flying. And this interpretation is romantic, and trite—and true.

With progress, television came and ice went, and I was more impressed by the disappearance of the latter than by the arrival of the former. The advent of television was a slow process with little initial intimation of the magnitude of the changes it carried in its train, while the vanishment of ice was a momentous event. It was not only that the rectangular and imperious monster of a white refrigerator had appeared in our midst out of the blue—my father must have meant it to be a surprise—and that the round and modest icebox, in the house since the world was created, a faithful and dependable provider of refreshing cold water at the easy turn of its always cold spigot, was never to be seen again; it was more, much more, than that because there had been not only a transmutation of substance but an alteration of location as well. The icebox had been in the seldom used formal dining room, in a little corner where it seemed to belong, while the refrigerator was in our daily dining room, demanding attention, imposing its ugly presence, inescapable as a topic of conversation as my mother and sisters, and the cook and the maids, and whoever else was around would feel compelled to sing its praises, and it is true that my sisters began to make desserts and ice cream and God knows what else, and it was also irrefutable that the thing had its merits, but, regardless, I missed the icebox. I missed its radiating coolness and the chunks of ice my brother and I would get from inside it when we came running in, drenched in sweat from whatever game we had been playing, and would not only drink the water but often press our bodies to the box to feel its invigorating chill. But the refrigerator emanated no coolness whatever, and to get water out of it was a slow and laborious process of reaching for bottles and pouring the water out without the opportunity to press our lips to a cold faucet, as we did with the icebox when no one was looking, and sometimes the bottles had not been filled, or the water was not cold enough; and I couldn't understand why the arrival of one had meant the dismissal of the other, since as far as I could see, they could have coexisted happily side by side.

The age of ice had had a fascinating side. Every day as my brother and I waited for the school bus, the ice truck would come by and stop right in front of us, on the corner of Villanueva and Rodríguez Streets, and steam would come through and around the heavy burlap curtain that covered its back, though it wasn't just steam but signals the ice was sending to the heat, warnings that it was ready to give battle—and what a battle it was. Despite the tightening grip of the tropical sun, the ice would stand its ground, and for every drop of its inner self that the heat wrestled away, the ice would send out a breath of coolness that was defiant of time and place and logic, and it would do this for hours on end, and by the time the ice had exhausted itself and only a few droplets of cool water stood as remnants of the struggle, the tired sun would be in retreat, and it was like a contest in permanent stalemate with ups and downs but without conclusion; the ice melted and the sun gave up, and the next day they would appear again to renew hostilities.

There would be two or three men and sometimes even four in the ice truck, working at the giant blocks with all kinds of sharp instruments, all of which had uncommon names because their blades were at strange angles to their handles, and each cut would be of a different size, although they didn't actually cut the ice but would make punctures and incisions and scratches right, left, center, above, below, and all of the sudden an almost perfectly square or rectangular block would appear as if it had always been there, previously buried in the main block and now liberated by the hand mattocks and adzes, or whatever their tools were called. I would look at the men at work and admire their dexterity and the speed at which they carved out the small blocks, and as they did this, chunks of ice would fly around and fall to the floor of the truck's bed, and the icemen would not even look as my brother and I collected them, and I would get one big enough to last me a while, and would put it in my mouth and rub it against my face or press it against my head to feel the drops of cold water meandering through my hair and running down my face and nape. But the advent of the refrigerator told us the ice age was coming to an end; that the ice truck, and the icemen, and the flying around of ice pieces, and the sculpturing of blocks to fit different size boxes were being erased for all time to come.

A *bayú* was a whorehouse. I didn't know then, nor do I know now, how Cubans came to use this term for a prostitution establishment; perhaps the word was adopted from the American "bayou," as the result of some local Freud trying to establish a link between the American term's connotations marshy, boggy and swampy and the merchandise offered at the place. Whatever the link, it seems lost in an unrecoverable past, and I would not rule out the possibility that the word, like so many of Cuba's street words, came from remnants of the Yoruba language spoken by many black Cubans, or perhaps even from the French, who at the turn of the century were prominent in Havana's prostitution business. But whatever the origin of the term, the *bayú* was a well-established institution and no adolescent boy would reach manhood without acquainting himself with the place and its wares. The degree of acquaintance, however, varied with the individual, and there were some men for whom the *bayú* was almost a way of life, their only form of communication with women out of the family, and who seemed never able to escape or break loose from it—even after marrying and having families. But for most men, the *bayú* was the provider of carefree sex, sex without the complications of marriage or the burdens of a relationship, and some even saw it as a kind of first aid station where they went only when they had to, and for as short a span as possible; however viewed, prostitution had its proper, if modest, place in a society in which mores, family vigilance over women and economic conditions restricted the opportunities for female sexual activity while fully accepting the need to satisfy the male sexual drive.

Havana's *barrio de putas,* red-light district, was centered on Crespo Street, somewhere between Old Havana and the main commercial part of the city, and was popularly referred to as "Crespo." It consisted of three or four blocks of brothels in which scantly clad women would stand by windows or doors trying to lure in prospective customers; and men, usually in small groups, would walk up and down the street, gauging what was offered and trying to make up their minds. It was never an easy decision, though, as each establishment differed little from the next. They all had a dark interior that masqueraded as a seductive penumbra but really served as camouflage for the less endowed and aging girls and were garishly furnished and decorated with religious pictures and icons; and some of the establishments served beverages and others did not, but there was always a *matrona,* an older lady in charge of directing traffic, keeping order and collecting fares; and all the *bayús* were populated by a handful of girls, mostly from the countryside, among whom beauty was the exception and grace or good manners totally out of reach; and contrary to the gayness and pleasure implied in the offer, or imagined by the purchaser, *bayús* exuded a palpable sense of joylessness.

The sadness could be seen in the faces and in the gestures and in the words, not of the women for which this was a place of work, but of the men; there was sadness in the lurking violence that could at any excuse or provocation jump to the fore and for which you always had to be on guard. It was as if the clients knew beforehand that whatever they were after they were not going to find, regardless of how much they spent or how long they stayed or how hard they pretended, and who were thus prone to vent their frustration at the slightest opportunity. This perception did not arise from any moral squeamishness about prostitution on my part; I wasn't really socially bothered by it beyond seeing it as the result of poverty and lack of education, and I didn't feel especially sorry for a whore, not any more than for an unemployed laborer—probably less since at least she was working. The sadness arose from the pitiful demeanor of the waiting clients, from the crudeness of the women, and from the ugliness of the places. It was not an intellectual sadness but the same sadness one senses when meeting a crippled person: an emotional and visceral current of discomfort which, after the mandatory rite of acquaintance, drove me away—to their higher-scale counterparts.

Love and sex in Cuba were seen as distinct—and virtually unrelated. Love was a feeling, sex an urge; the urge was disposed of with prostitutes and easy women, but the feeling was an amalgam of emotions that went from desire to devotion, and which required a different kind of girl. The distinction we made between love and sex, and the points of contact we found between them, however, cannot be easily rendered into English.

Cultures have different ways of shaping and organizing emotions, which are reflected in the words they use and in the nuances of their meanings. In English *to love* is a catchall verb that can signify a variety of emotions—those between men and women, parents and children, friends, or feelings for pets, for inanimate objects or even for activities, as in "loving your work" or "loving to golf." The Spanish verb *amar,* on the other hand, has no proper equivalent in English, and many of the meanings of "to love" come closer to *querer, tener cariño, estar enamorado* and *gustar* than they do to *amar.*

I adjusted quite well to the prevailing norm separating sex and love, and dealt with the urge as an urge and dreamed about Amarilis without doing much about it, probably because I was afraid to make a move, or maybe because I was distracted by front-tennis, and work, and union activities, and the increasing attraction of politics, and the discovery of the University. I was perfectly content to see her occasionally and dream of her a bit more often. It stayed like this for a few months, but then my life became more complicated, and the real Amarilis slowly but steadily faded away, receded into the background—without impairing or diminishing in any way my memory of ice skating while holding hands with a beautiful girl when I was sixteen and thought of myself as an ugly duckling.

After nine months in the Zulueta branch office I was transferred to the main office in La Habana Vieja, the colonial part of town with the old houses and narrow streets and cobblestones and the sea smell, and this was a very different world, with scores of people working there and the bank occupying a complete building. Although now based in the central office, my job was to fill in for vacationing employees throughout the many branches the bank had in Havana, a job no one else wanted because it meant changing locations and type of work every month, but it was its itinerant character and the novelty of each new assignment that made it appealing to me. At first I couldn't understand why others had not jumped at the opportunity to do a job that guaranteed a monthly change of locale and task, and it took me some time to realize that most people preferred to stay put and disliked, or were afraid of, the new and the different. At the bank there was a bureaucratic routine beyond which most employees were unwilling or incapable of going, and the power of our union bosses, and their corruption, rested on this as much as on their ambition and mendaciousness.

For the next few months I bounced from branch office to branch office, and found that each had been taken over by the character and manners of its surroundings. The dress and speech of the bank workers resembled in each case the peculiarities and habits of the neighborhood in which they worked, and the clients they served. In the branch by Havana's central food market the employees looked and spoke like butchers, fish mongers and pig farmers, and in the upper-middle-class Vedado area they dressed and spoke like the doctors and businessmen who were their clients. Food followed the same pattern, and lunch and snacks were consistent with the local environment; around the huge and cavernous central market there was *sopa china,* Chinese soup, which wasn't Chinese, and *arroz frito,* fried rice, which was Chinese and available at all times; and as one moved upwards in the social ladder of urban distinction, the choice of available food grew in thinness and elegance—by Cuban standards, that is—and sandwiches and *bocaditos* and *pasteles* would metamorphose from one neighborhood to the next.

I did like the moving around, but it did not calm my natural restlessness, which if anything was getting worse, and I remained active in union politics and one day I called the American embassy to find out if I could volunteer to fight in Korea and was told by a very polite official that no volunteers were being sought, and it was about the same time that I joined the youth section of the Partido Ortodoxo, the party founded by *el loco,* Eduardo Chibás.

By 1951 Cuban politics had reached a new peak of stridency, baseness and confusion, and Eduardo Chibás represented the only hope of bringing some order and decency and honesty to the island; the few respected public figures still left on the scene were flocking to his party in anticipation of the presidential election scheduled for June 1, 1952. But the epithet *loco* must have contained some truth, because Chibás opened his campaign by shooting himself in the stomach during his Sunday radio show. Well, not during the show exactly, because he had gone on for too long in the impassioned peroration he was delivering and had been taken off the air, only he didn't know it, and he went on to cap his harangue with what he thought would be a dramatic climax that would resonate through the island and clinch the presidency. It sounds absurd, and probably it was, but there was some logic behind his action, because in 1939, when he was a little-known member of the student groups that had fought Machado and Batista, he gained national prominence, and an eventual Senate seat, by shooting himself in the stomach and letting people believe that he had been the victim of an assassination attempt. So if a shot in the stomach had succeeded then, why not now?

Chibás probably thought the stratagem would work again, especially at a time when he was under fierce attack by the Auténtico politicians he was vociferously denouncing and trying to throw out of government—and he was right. Even though he was off the air when he shot himself "as the last call to the Cuban conscience," as he dramatically put it before pulling the trigger, there was enough theater and mawkishness to his action that the timing glitch turned out to be only a minor alteration in the script, and as is always the case in politics, reason didn't stand a chance in the face of melodrama. And he had shot himself in exactly the same spot as on the previous occasion, and the bullet followed now the same trajectory as then, and the public reaction was following the previous path, and he was recuperating as he had recuperated before—and then he died. It was as if one of the minor gods overseeing tropical affairs decided that "once was enough" and dispatched Chibás with some last-minute peritonitis.

I joined the Partido Ortodoxo right after Chibás's death, when the party was in state of shock, without a leader and floundering dangerously in the piranha-infested waters of Cuban politics. No one knew what was next; the elections were still forthcoming, the ruling Auténticos were a disgrace, and whatever other opposition existed was an even greater disgrace, because it was the party organized and financed by Batista after his return a couple of years earlier from his self-imposed exile in the United States, and it was clear that all he and his cronies were interested in was recapturing the privileges, sinecures and corrupt deals they had previously enjoyed. This party also represented all the high-handedness and arbitrariness associated with Batista's previous years in power, and its limited constituency was formed by crooked politicians and ignorant poor blacks, and such a party was no acceptable alternative. There were also, of course, the Communists who, with their Partido Socialista Popular, were more the representative of Soviet interests than a local force for reform, and whose past association with Batista and betrayals of popular causes hung heavy around their necks and which, therefore, constituted no viable alternative. In addition, it was also feared that some under-the-table understanding between the Communists and Batista was afoot, although this was probably more fantasy and paranoia than fact because with the Cold War in full swing, no Cuban politician who wanted to be president could afford to antagonize the United States.

Joining a political party was another forceful confrontation with reality, outer and inner, because my brief union stewardship at the bank's office in Zulueta Street had not been totally divorced from my dream life, from my search for dragons to slay. But with the Partido Ortodoxo came the realization that I did not want simply to join in to be just another rank-and-file member. I desired prominence. My involvement in union affairs could provide it, if I joined the party's labor section, but that was not the type of prominence I wanted. I did not view myself as a labor leader—there was something too limiting, too constraining, too narrow in that—so I joined the youth section, which was open-ended and, at least in theory, the training grounds for future party leaders. And joining the youth section of the Partido Ortodoxo meant joining its Havana chapter, and joining its Havana chapter meant meeting charisma.

Charisma is a hazy and mysterious quality that some individuals possess and which allows them to influence and control others, and although difficult to dissect or explain, there is no mistaking it for anything else when it confronts you, so without knowing exactly what it was, and incapable of describing it, I knew I had encountered charisma when I met Pepe Iglesias. Part of charisma's nature is that it can be packaged in any form, and Pepe Iglesias, whom we called Pepe Gatillo, Pepe the Trigger, behind his back on account of some shootout he was involved in during his high school years and in which some innocent bystander was the only casualty, was not at first sight impressive or prepossessing—medium height, medium build, brown eyes, brown hair, mild manners, bad teeth, very bad teeth. But when he spoke he emanated some kind of current that was sensed by those around him in the Havana chapter of the

Partido Ortodoxo's youth section, and when he spoke at larger meetings the charisma current was even stronger, and it was not what he said or even how he said it since most speakers said the same thing and spoke in the same oratorical barricade style. It was something else, something unique to him or to the way he appeared to others. Something ethereal but not tenuous, to the contrary, quite palpable; something you felt, felt strongly, yet couldn't describe. It went beyond agreeing with what the man was saying—that was taken for granted—it was more as if Pepe Iglesias were pointing the way, identifying the right course, issuing an unspoken invitation to follow him, and it was an invitation you wanted to accept.

The Havana youth chapter of the Partido Ortodoxo fascinated me. I had never before been among people my age who shared my interests and views and my concerns, who could speak eloquently about what was wrong with the country and how to put it right, who were interested in reading and would refer to Giovanni Papini, and Stefan Zweig, and Emil Ludwig and Curzio Malaparte when we met on Friday nights, and who could discuss how we were to set things right after the elections, when our party would be in power, and who explained how we were going to deal with unemployment, and bring about agrarian reform, and improve education, and instill public probity and a plethora of other things. We discussed and solved all problems and nothing could pale our enthusiasm or derail our naïveté and, believe it or not, we seldom discussed the actual upcoming elections—we were concerned with substance, not mechanics, and were certain the Partido Ortodoxo was going to win—and our meetings were presided over by Pepe Iglesias in an articulate, cogent and impassioned manner, and it was among these people that I wanted to secure my standing.

I had an idea of how to do this, but I needed the help of Juanito *el carnicero*, who was known as *el carnicero* because he worked in a *carnicería*, a butcher shop, delivering meat all over the neighborhood. He knew everybody, and everybody knew and liked him because he was a hardworking, pleasant and unpretentious guy about my age, or maybe a year or two older. He had been a fervent and vocal admirer of Eduardo Chibás and used his delivery assignments to spread the Ortodoxo gospel, and although he was not officially a member of the party, he was the face of the party in our neighborhood. I knew him and had discussed politics with him a couple of times, and sought him out and put it to him bluntly: we had to organize a local chapter of the Ortodoxo youth section which I would preside over and represent in the party's higher echelons, but he would have to do most of the organizing work. The reason it had to be this way was because he was in position to do the organizing, and I was in position to do the presiding and the representing. And he agreed, and we did it my way, and I felt good about having secured a firm base, but I also felt uncomfortable about building my position on Juanito's work, and although I could justify it in my mind, and nothing that I had told him was not true, there was an unsavory touch to my distribution of roles; I knew this was well in accordance with the nature of politics, but still, there was something in it that wasn't right.

The months after the death of Chibás brought an accentuation of the hysteria in Cuban political life as the governing Auténticos fell increasingly into disarray, and more and more respected nonpolitical figures came out in favor of the Partido Ortodoxo. The presidential candidate put forth by the Ortodoxos was a professor from Havana University who exuded boredom from every pore, but his very boredom was taken as a sign of talent and honesty, in one of those mental discontinuities in which wishful thinking prevails in absolute disregard of the laws of logic and common sense. Despite the Ortodoxos' growing public support, however, it wasn't clear that those in power would be willing to relinquish control just because they lost an election, especially since the likely winners were vocal and vehement, not only about enacting reforms, but also about punishing those who had abused governmental power for personal gain.

As 1951 unfolded, the rhetoric got more and more fierce, and the leaders of the Ortodoxo youth section issued truculent warnings and threats, as we advocated the creation of a special agency, with police and judicial powers, to investigate and punish all forms of past malfeasance by politicians and government officials; and it was amazing how sure and confident we were that what we were proposing was right and proper, and that it would get done, and that it would work miracles; and although we could hear the rumbling under our feet we did not realize the ground was shaking.

It was around this time, late summer of 1951, that I discovered my academic avocation. First I heard the frenzied clanging of the *tranvía*'s bell, as the streetcar rattled down the hill on San Lázaro Street in front of the bank's office in which I was working that month, then the screeching of the steel wheels braking on the steel rails, and soon after, the rising voices of a gathering crowd at the junction with Infanta Street, almost exactly across from me. As I went to the door to find out what was going on, I saw a group of young men leading the passengers off the streetcar, and proceeding to set it on fire to the cheers of the passersby and the former passengers. I crossed the street and asked a middle-aged man what was going on, and he told me that university students were protesting a proposed fare increase, and as the streetcar burned and the young men left, and as the firemen arrived and I went back to work, I knew I had to be a university student—and the next day at lunchtime I was at Havana University.

The situation didn't look promising since there seemed to be no way for me to enter the University without a high school diploma, and I was reluctantly trying to get used to the idea of night school to secure the damned piece of paper—because I had become determined to be a university student come hell or high water—when luck struck in the person of Wilson. I don't remember whether Wilson was his first or last name, probably his last, but he was a client of the bank and one of those countless people in Havana who seemed to make a living out of thin air, and whose collective endeavors went by the slang term *pugilato,* which is somehow connected to boxing but really defies explanation outside a third world context in which the willingness to work produces nothing unless coupled with some form of inventiveness that is able to get water out of a stone. Wilson's activities fell squarely in that category; he sold textbooks to Havana University students. Now this may sound like a proper and productive line of business, but you have to take into account that there were not that many students to buy the books; textbooks that sold in any quantity were tightly controlled by the professors teaching the courses or by their publishers, and what often passed for textbooks were mimeographed lecture notes, and these notes, as well as the regular textbooks, were frequently pirated by student groups and distributed free or at cost to whoever wanted them. But, regardless, Wilson was in business selling textbooks to students, and through his activities had become familiar with many of the rules and regulations governing Havana University, and he told me there was a backdoor to get in—and that he could provide all the books needed—at a reasonable price.

By the fall of 1951 I had taken and passed, with Wilson's books, the entrance examination to the Institute of Public Administration at Havana University. This meant that although I was not a full-fledged university student, I was "studying at the University," and at the beginning of the road to the School of Law. And that was exactly where I wanted to land since the choice of careers at Havana University was circumscribed by convention as much as by intellectual proclivity. Medicine, dentistry, engineering, architecture and the sciences drew the naturally predisposed in those directions who, with the exception of medicine, were not many; the School of Education was for those who were trying to obtain a teaching certificate, and its student body was 90 percent black and 100 percent poor; Business Administration, called Commerce in those days, was for accountants-to-be and smacked of tediousness absolute; and the School of Philosophy, which included Fine Arts, was considered the domain of girls, queers and weirdos. So that left two schools, Social Sciences and Law, which were closely intertwined in curriculum and space, and since the Institute of Public Administration was part of the Social Sciences one, I had to attend this school first in order to get to Law. It was my good luck that the most expeditious way available to me for entering Havana University led directly to what was the political heart of the institution.

My interest in becoming a university student was not as arbitrary as it might seem, especially to someone unfamiliar with Cuban history and with the role the University and its students had played from the days of the Spanish control of the island. Havana University, the country's sole institution of higher education, had been a hub of pro-independence activism under Spain, and the fulcrum of every protest movement since the inauguration of the republic. Its students and professors had often openly opposed abuse and oppression, and had been frequently jailed and occasionally murdered. The University had also contributed a large share of the venal and inept politicians who had run the country since independence; the institution, in fact, was the training ground and feeder for national politics.

In 1951 Havana University was a sad shadow of its idealistic self as student leaders were closer to gangsters than to their patriotic predecessors, but the negatives were overshadowed in my mind by the burning of the streetcar and by my readings of Cuban history, and I saw Havana University for what it had sometimes been, and for what it could be a symbol of. Once I visited the place for the first time, perched on a hilltop and stroked by the soft sea breeze, and once I walked on its center square, the Plaza Cadenas, abrim with nostalgia and replete with revolutionary ghosts, I was hooked.

There were two kinds of students at Havana University—official and free. The official ones registered formally at the beginning of the academic year and were expected to attend classes and take whatever tests and examinations were required by the instructors. The free ones were allowed to register for a single final exam right before these examinations were administered at the beginning and at the end of the academic year, in

September and June, and did not have to attend classes or comply with any other course requirement. The free route was probably created because Havana University was the only university in the country and there were many students not able to attend classes in Havana, and thus forced to study at home, on their own or with local help. This free option allowed the opportunity for these students to descend upon the island's Mecca of learning to secure the seal of approval needed to turn their labors into professional credentials. But whatever its origin and institutional purpose, the free option was a blessing for me as I worked in the bank, plotted union insurgency, dreamed of reforming the country under Ortodoxo rule, read history, remained firm in my determination, sooner or later, to seek nontropical horizons, and thought about girls without doing much about them. So in September 1951 I enrolled as a free student and took my first set of exams.

Fidel Castro was the first to arrive at, and the last to leave, the first public meeting my neighborhood youth section organized—with Juanito *el carnicero* doing all the legwork and I in charge of inviting the speakers, all of them Ortodoxo candidates running for seats in the House of Representatives for the province of Havana. The electoral system was one of proportional representation in which each party would be allocated seats in proportion to the total number of votes received by all its candidates combined, and then the seats won by each party would be assigned to its individual candidates in descending order from top vote-getter down until each party filled all its seats. Our objective was then to maximize the number of people voting for Ortodoxo candidates regardless of the specific individual they chose to vote for, and to this end I extended invitations to about ten of those running for office in Havana province. Most ignored the invitation since, after all, this was our first meeting and there was no guarantee how many people we could produce for them to address, and also because the nature of the contest, although province-wide, led candidates to concentrate on areas in which they were known or in which they thought, for whatever reason, they could maximize their own individual votes. So we ended up with only three candidates but were lucky enough to get the two Castros—Orlando and Fidel.

Orlando Castro was the candidate we in the youth section favored because we knew him. He was from the city of Havana and had helped to found the Partido Ortodoxo when, together with Chibás, he had bolted the Auténtico. I don't remember inviting Fidel Castro, who then, very late in 1951, was one of the least known and least favored of the Ortodoxo candidates running for the House of Representatives in Havana province. His reputation was that of a "university politician," a euphemism for the political gangsters who were involved in armed fights between groups with such truculent names as the Unión Insurreccional Revolucionaria (Revolutionary Insurrectionist Union), Movimiento Socialista Revolucionario (Revolutionary Socialist Movement), and Acción Revolucionaria Guiteras (Guiteras Revolutionary Action), all of which were somehow tied to Havana University, and all of which mixed idealistic pronouncements with plunder and murder. I must point out, however, that the ferocity of these groups' names did not result solely from their members' proclivity to the feral and the blusterous, that it was in harmony with the manners of the Spanish language, for in Spanish "revolution" and "revolutionary" have traditionally been associated with terms like "idealism," "commitment," "patriotism," "self-sacrifice," all with strong positive connotations, and this linguistic bent was thus in accord with our political culture and predisposition. But be that as it may, I don't remember inviting Fidel, although I suppose anyone in our section could have invited him, but when he showed up I was glad to have him since almost no other candidate had accepted our invitation, and his past associations had nothing to do with my original reluctance to invite him—I simply didn't like the guy.

The meeting was held in a *solar* in Municipio Street, a *solar* being the next to the last stop in the downward scale of urban living quarters available to the poor, a kind of tropical tenement house only one short stop away from indigence, which in Havana took the form of makeshift dwellings made up of cardboard and other cast-off materials and restricted to specific sections of the city. But as *solares* went, this one was not too bad, or at least it didn't look too bad at night. The space was dominated by a rectangular patio, with a two-story structure to its right, each floor containing a long line of single rooms. Each room would have been inhabited probably by an entire family, and all the families in the building would share the two bathrooms—one upstairs, one downstairs. The evening was cool, and at night the place felt quiet and peaceful, and the talk was all about politics, and with the few refreshments and cigars we had brought for the occasion the conversation veered away from what must have been the daily concerns and preoccupations of the people living there, and before I had a chance to become acquainted with them, or to thank properly the old black lady who had made the place available and ask her what kind of cigar she was smoking, there was Fidel Castro already talking and smoking a cigar with her. ¡Mierda!

I had never before known anyone quite like the people I met through the Ortodoxo youth section. There was Pepe Iglesias and his charisma, of course, but ultimately he was just one of many and not even the most interesting of the bunch. These new acquaintances came in all shapes, styles and races, but there was one among them who was truly legendary. In many ways he was the opposite of Iglesias, without charisma and without ambition, but almost inadvertently emanating an intense glow that drew you in and made you want to be not his follower but his friend. His name was Kiko Baeza, and in an environment in which we rarely knew one another's full names, we all knew that his was Francisco Orlando Baeza Pérez. He was older than most of us, about seven years older than I was, and usually dressed in a dark suit with a sober necktie in total disregard of the tropical heat and of the white or bright colors favored by everyone else. And as complement to his almost lugubrious attire he wore thick eyeglasses set in a heavy black frame over a pox-scarred face, and he spoke slowly, in a deep voice, and enunciated clearly, something the immense majority of Cubans seemed incapable of, and you could not but be impressed and truly taken in when you got to know him.

His grave, almost somber exterior was countered by a lighthearted personality and an avid and vivid imagination, all encased in a thought-ful predisposition, and Kiko Baeza, who had never finished high school, made a living writing doctoral dissertations for Havana University stu-dents who were too busy, or too lazy, or too stupid to write one them-selves. There was no subject in the humanities or the social sciences he would not tackle, and he wrote with such flare that some of his clients had trouble living up to his work when they were called in to defend their theses in front of their professors—which Kiko surely would have willingly done for them had circumstances allowed it.

I witnessed a couple of conversations in which those commissioning work from him requested moderation, asked Kiko to make his work good but not too good, and Kiko would agree with a soft, tenuous smile which in my naïveté I took at first as a grimace but which eventually I realized was a true smile, a bit sardonic, but an honest smile nevertheless, be-cause Kiko Baeza thought the whole thing was a joke—the University, the professors, the intellectual pretentiousness, the jargon, the abstruse and obtuse subjects. I tried to discuss the ethics of what he did with him but soon realized we had no common ground on which to base such a discussion since I looked up to formal education, and thought there was something in it worthwhile and worth protecting. But my vision, I must admit, was founded on nothing but ignorance and idealization and wishful thinking, and I had no idea of the theory, the facts, the history, the philosophy, the logic, the goals or the structure of higher education. I simply figured that if it was there, and if it was looked up to by so many, it must perform some beneficial function—a notion also prompted by my desire to defend the institution to which I now felt drawn. Kiko's thoughts on the matter, however, came from a deep-seated and immovable conviction that formal education in the humanities and the social sciences, at least that afforded by our only university, was simply a standardized way to issue licenses for jobs and an intellectual travesty, a big, sad joke not totally unrelated to criminal fraud.

A creature of tropical underdevelopment with a truly bohemian personality and a powerful inner flare, Kiko Baeza would take twenty or thirty books on some subject into his room and bury himself there for several weeks, coming out only for meals because a meal he would miss under no circumstances. He would eventually emerge triumphantly with a heavy ream of handwritten pages, which under no conditions would he consent to type himself, that constituted the warrant to a doctoral degree for some teacher who wanted a raise, or for a minor bureaucrat wanting a promotion, or for some frustrated housewife in search of recognition or as an alternative to cheating on her husband, or for anyone seeking a doctoral degree to satisfy need or longing or vanity or whatever else the Caribbean heat had put into his or her head.

Kiko would work in mysterious isolation and when he resurfaced among us we knew the job was done—but not completed, because the most delicate part of it still lay ahead—collecting payment. It was often the case that those commissioning work from him were reluctant payers, and Kiko would recite for our entertainment the excuses and explanations and evasions he had heard, and repeat and mimic their pleas and expressions, and deconstruct the reasons they had given him for evading or delaying payment, and Kiko would expand on how these people would restate their promise to pay him eventually but wanted the work turned over to them immediately, assuring him that the sooner they had their theses, the sooner they would have their doctorates, and the sooner they had their doctorates, the sooner they would be able to pay him. Kiko would recount these experiences with true amusement, never rancor, and he always ended up turning the work over to those who had commissioned it, payment or no payment, and so it went that

Kiko did not always get paid, or paid in full, when completing a work, or that sometimes, unexpectedly, he would get paid for work done months or years before. But whether he got paid in full or in part, on time or later, money always had the same effect on him.

Money was for Kiko Baeza something to use, to spend, to dispose of as soon as possible in pursuit of some immediate gratification, and above all, something to share, totally and generously. No sooner did money come into his possession than Kiko would inform all his friends and invite them to restaurants or nightclubs, and in a couple of days he would be as broke as he had been before and quite comfortable about it, or at least never showing signs that the lack of money had any ill effect on his attitude, habits or appearance, and we, his friends, would go back to providing him with whatever help our own means allowed. But we never gave him cash—unless he asked for a loan, which he would always religiously and punctually repay—because his sense of dignity wouldn't allow handouts, and because his several sisters supplied him with enough help to cover all his basic needs and daily expenses, so we would treat him to what he appreciated above everything else, a meal.

A meal was to Kiko Baeza what a mystical vision had been to Saint Theresa of Avila, a combination of spiritual and carnal ecstasies, a pleasure that superseded all others in blissfulness and amounted much more to a true communion with the divine than anything the hucksters and hawkers of religion could possibly offer. Kiko would not only take pleasure in eating the food, something he always did slowly and circumspectly, but also would find joy and satisfaction in examining the menu, evaluating the alternatives, making a selection and placing the order, and he would take pleasure in having the silverware properly arranged, and in being served, and he would try to determine how the food had been prepared, and would watch how it was presented and brought to the table, and ultimately how it tasted. The whole process was a marvel for me to observe since I had never been interested in food and saw eating as a necessity that only occasionally brought enjoyment, but what I noticed above all else, as I watched Kiko enshrine and sanctify the ordinary act of filling one's stomach, was how he was able to relish in whatever was to his taste without being disturbed by what didn't meet his standards and expectations, how he took the good and remained untroubled by the bad, at most making a passing comment how this or that could have been a bit better, but always concentrating on what he found agreeable and pleasing—a sybaritic, laid-back, latter-day Californian, misplaced by the gods in a torrid and underdeveloped Caribbean island.

There was something else that set Kiko apart from the rest of us. Our antipathy to the local Communist Party, ingrained in our psyches by its betrayals and former alliance with Batista, and by the indecipherable jargon, secrecy and holier-than-thou pretentiousness of its members, did not stop us from leaning towards socialist views, albeit in a generic and far from specific fashion, and pertaining mostly to the role of government in redressing social wrongs. And this "socialism," or perhaps more accurately "social concern," went unquestioned and unchallenged among us, and I had taken it for granted without giving it much thought until I heard Kiko question it while putting forward the proposition that perhaps our view was misguided, and that a straight capitalist solution would be the better remedy to our country's ills. Upon listening to him, I realized how many things I was taking on faith, faith founded on ignorance, and how little inclined most of us were to inquire into our opinions or to scrutinize our beliefs.

Kiko Baeza was not the only peculiar individual hovering around the youth section of the Partido Ortodoxo—Kiko himself wasn't even a member of the party but an old friend of Pepe Iglesias from high school who gravitated around Pepe's circle of political friends without being one of his followers. There were others whose singularities, if perhaps less engaging than Kiko's, were difficult to ignore, especially for someone who knew as little about the society surrounding him as I did and who had limited acquaintance with the world beyond my tribal family, my schools and my steady, and by local standards well-paying job. It was at the Partido Ortodoxo that I first met on equal footing the rest of Havana, those who had never known three square meals a day, those who wore ragged clothes because they had no others, those who were ignorant but did not allow their ignorance to interfere with their ambition. And as I grew more familiar with these people the ordered picture I had created in my mind of how things worked in life, in political life anyhow, did not tally with reality. At the beginning I did not question my ideas but saw these individuals as the oddities of a system in disrepair, and it took me some time to realize that in our midst oddity was the rule and order the exception, but this realization was slow in coming and, fortunately, did not prevent me from enjoying their eccentric, erratic, whimsical and often preposterous behavior.

Chúa wanted to be a *concejal,* a god-damned city councilman! At first I thought he was kidding, but no, he was serious. It was late one evening and we were having some *mediasnoches,* the gentler version of the traditional Cuban sandwich, when he asked if I would support him when

the time came to get the nomination and run for that office, and I asked
him in return why he wanted to do that, to be a councilman, for in my
own innocent and romanticized version of politics, wanting to be a
councilman was like aspiring to being a trash collector or a street ped-
dler or, at best, a clerk in a third-rate store. I listened to Chúa telling me
that was what he really wanted, and I couldn't make sense of it but told
him he could count on my support, not knowing what that really meant,
and we parted company and I walked home marveling that someone had
actually told me his ambition in life was to be a city councilman. As time
went by, and as I found out how good a baseball player Chúa was, a
hard-hitting third baseman who played for the strong amateur team
Fortuna and who had caught the eye of the professional teams' scouts,
that night's conversation took the form of an incomprehensible mystery
shrouded in the thickness of tropical mist, and it was not that I couldn't
conceive of people running for office or wanting to be politicians, but
what amazed me was someone aiming so low, someone who could have
aimed far higher since Chúa was second in command to Pepe Iglesias in
the Havana youth section, which itself was the most important chapter
of the organization, and was personable and likable, with none of the
showiness or hard edges or peculiar personal traits of most wannabe
politicians—and on top of that he was one hell of a good baseball player.

There was also Paquito, short, dark, fat and fixated with "Cara al
Sol," the anthem of Franco's Spanish Falange, which he would sing
every time we were alone in a low conspiratorial voice on the assumption that I was familiar with its lyrics, which I was, and on the assumption that I shared his admiration for Franco and Spanish fascism, which
I didn't; and there was the other Paquito, tall, fair, thin, the owner of a
brand-new car whose trunk was always filled with the lingerie he sold
for a living, who had been to school in the States, came from an expensive neighborhood, dressed well and had no intellectual interest, real or
pretended, of any kind, who stuck out like a sore thumb in our ragtag
camp, and who never gave an inkling of his reasons for being with us,
even though he talked a lot and always seemed to be in a state of excitement, or as we would colloquially say, *acelerado,* speeded up. And
there was Secundino Macías, short, black, skinny to transparency, in a
permanent state of undernourishment, who was talkative when he had
eaten that day and laconic when he had not, and we often found excuses
to buy him something to eat and came to believe that our first patriotic
duty, once our party had won the elections, would be to find him a job,
and this turned into conviction when walking with him one evening down
Neptuno Street we realized he was wearing only one shoe and retracing

our steps found the other a block and a half away—he had lost it and had not noticed. And there was Fermín whose oratorical skills were a commingling of highly charged emotional rhetoric, voodoo incantations, stage gesturing and irreverent humor, and whose speeches mixed political punch with a quasi-religious eeriness that transfixed his audience when, in the middle of a political peroration, he would turn around, back to his audience, and pursue the same topic but now talking to some invisible beings and with a totally different intonation in his voice, and after a few moments of that he would turn again towards his audience and resume his original tone and continue his discourse as if nothing had happened. And there was Parrita, whose name was Parra but couldn't get anyone to use it, and whose given name I forgot or never knew or perhaps it was Daniel since that rings a bell, and he inhabited a parallel universe always out of place with what was going on around him, moving in a different direction from everyone else.

Once I played a dirty trick on Parrita at one of our weekly meetings, when the two of us were sitting next to each other in a corner of the room and a little apart from everyone else. Without forewarning I felt a storm gathering in my stomach and gas passed through me with explosive impetus, and as the sound of the blast resonated throughout the room I stood up looking down at him, and with as much disgust in my inflection as I could muster said, "Parrita, you are a pig!" and sat down. And he went red, and green, and purple, and green again and couldn't bring himself to utter a single word, although I could see that he was trying to, and he stood up, but words still refused to come out of his mouth, and the whole room laughed looking in our direction as he sat back in absolute dejection, unable to make a sound and realizing that there was nothing he could possibly say. Even worse, when the meeting was over I tried to tell everyone that it had been me and not Parrita, but they all thought I was just trying to protect him. I apologized to Parrita for my crudeness and explained to him that it had been a harmless joke—maybe not in the best of taste but harmless nevertheless—and that I was sorry to have embarrassed him, and I thought the matter had been put to rest and went out of my way, at least for a time, to be friendly and courteous to him. And I most likely would never have thought of the incident again, but months later, maybe even a year, I found myself at a party talking to Omar's sister, quite a dish, seductively thin with bright green friendly eyes. After talking to her for a long while, I sat down next to Parrita, who was also at the party, and no sooner had my rear hit the seat than he lowered his head and bit my right upper thigh a few inches above the knee. It was like being struck by lightning from a clear blue sky as his teeth tore through my pants and into my flesh, and I yelled in pain and surprise, unable to believe what was happening. And as quickly as he had bitten my leg, he let go of it, stood up and left the room and the house, and people came over and asked what had happened, looking at my torn trousers red with blood, and I said I didn't know, which was true—and Omar's sister didn't speak to me again.

There was Pepín, too, coarse and boisterous, always making fun of everyone and everything and especially of Kiko's crush on Julio's sister, Aracely, and believed to be *muy simpático* by most. Although one must be careful when using this adjective because *simpático* has little to do with the equivalents usually ascribed to it in English: pleasant, nice, likable, appealing, congenial, and even less with anything related to sympathy. It is a term that most non-native speakers of Spanish have great difficulty mastering and which often makes them sound silly. The difficulty in its usage arises from the fact that the term lives halfway between objectivity and subjectivity. When you say "Pedro es simpático," you are trying to formulate an objective appraisal, but when you say "Pedro me cae simpático," I find Pedro *simpático,* you are explicitly admitting the subjectivity of your judgment. You could complicate things more if you were to say "Pedro no es simpático, pero está simpático hoy." All of which amounts to the fact that when you label someone *simpático* in Spanish, people quite often are not sure what you mean and tend to reserve judgment on your assessment, so more often than not, ascribing to someone the quality *simpático* says more about the one emitting the judgment than about the one judged.

Most people who knew Pepín thought him *simpático,* showing, I suppose, that the sum of subjective *opiniones* can pass for objectivity. Then there was Julio with the five sisters and who never spoke out about anything, perhaps because he was the lone male in a household full of females; and there was Orestes, always in need of a scrub, with nails whose natural color must have been black because they never showed any other, who was continuously and invariably involved, according to his own telling, in some conspiracy with members of the political mafia that controlled organized violence under the Prío administration. And there were others who came and gained our attention for a moment and were gone the next: Angel, another of the many Castros in the Partido Ortodoxo, who aspired to national prominence and would talk about nothing but what we should do to those in power when our term came; Omar, who already had national prominence and wanted us to help him keep it; *el cojo* Gaicés, whose legendary virility was the theme of a song popular at the time; and there were also, who could forget them, the three Pino Guerra sisters, two brunettes and one blond—and there was no man around party headquarters who did not have a crush on one, two or the three of them—and they were superficially dissimilar but inwardly united by some powerful sexual attribute which rendered them equally alluring despite their different ages, looks and personalities.

We rushed into 1952 with *bongós* and *timbales* and *maracas* ablaze, in an apoplexy of excitement heralding the forthcoming elections of June 1, holding high the symbolic broom of the Partido Ortodoxo, with which we were going to sweep away the past. We were convinced of the unavoidable overhaul of political life that was to follow our equally unavoidable triumph, never thinking for a moment that the election could be lost, or that any force could thwart our mission or bend our resolution; and in the deafening din of the tropical music enfolding us, no one could hear the faint beat of the muffled drum, or the distant airs of the approaching funeral march.

SECOND BIRTH

CHAPTER SIX

The second birth is very different from the first.

The first time you are born you are not conscious that you are being born, and awareness arrives gradually, in stages, giving your senses time to adjust and time for things to fall into place. The second time your awareness is instantaneous and overwhelming, and all your senses and nerves and systems of perception and manners of discerning burst out at full gallop. You are fascinated and surprised, and you try to grasp what's going on around you and come to terms with the marvel of the occasion. You realize that nothing is what it was, and that it is not you who is different but the world around, which has acquired new colors and hues and shades, that old correspondences no longer hold, and that you are in limbo—suspended between admiration and disbelief—taking things in without comprehending them, but not caring too much about this failure because you know this is not a time to understand but a time to behold.

It was March 10, 1952.

The day before, a Sunday, Kiko and I had been watching an evening news and commentary program on television, and had seen Jorge Mañach, university professor and senatorial candidate for the Partido Ortodoxo, dismiss with incontestable academic certainty a question concerning rumors that Batista was preparing a military coup. I hadn't even heard the rumor, and the idea of a military takeover had never entered my mind; perhaps I thought we were beyond such roguery or, more probably, ignorance and inexperience had prevented me from contemplating such a possibility. Either way, I was willing to accept without question the reassuring wisdom emanating from such a learned and distinguished source. It could not have been otherwise, because to be a professor in an underdeveloped land is to be one of God's spokesmen, and Mañach was so positive in his exposition and so confident in his conviction that such a turn of events was no longer possible in Cuba, and so certain that Batista, the man who had willingly accepted electoral defeat in 1944, was above such a dastardly deed, that it would have been impossible for any sensible person listening to the professor to have questioned his judgment. And after hearing him, Kiko and I went to have something to eat and didn't even discuss the issue, so preposterous we thought the possibility of a military coup. When we finished dinner I took the bus home and went to bed—and the world I had known ended.

I don't remember who woke me, or if anybody did, but as soon as I opened my eyes I sensed that things were not normal, that something quite out of the ordinary was in the air. It was still dark outside, only a few minutes past five, but all the lights in the house were on and everyone else was awake. I thought it odd that no one was preparing or serving breakfast, the *café con leche* and buttered fresh-baked bread that was our daily introduction to life, but then I realized the bread man, the *panadero*, would not yet have come by with his rolls and baguettes. Still, the absence of coffee when everybody was up and about was an indication of extraordinary circumstances. My mother was glued to the telephone, and the radio was on but only the sound of static came in as my sisters moved the dial back and forth. I don't remember asking anyone in particular what was going on, but the question would have been redundant, and it was my father who, with a serious expression and in a whispering tone, told me, "Dicen que Batista está en Columbia," they say that Batista is in Camp Columbia, which, translated into political language, meant that he had staged, or was in the process of staging, a military coup.

The agitation inside the house contrasted with the stillness outside. Everything was quiet—no street vendors, no buses, no traffic down Villanueva Street, no pedestrians. The air was cool, as it usually was this time of day, and the sun was just beginning to rise over a strident and clamorous city which today was eerily silent. Eventually the *café con leche* appeared but not the bread, and still no one my mother talked to knew what was going on, why there was no traffic, no radio, no newspaper vendors loudly hawking their merchandise. Finally, well after six, the first sign of life came in the form of an almost empty bus rolling slowly down Villanueva.

I had to know what was going on. I don't remember anyone trying to dissuade me from leaving the house, but it wouldn't have mattered if they had because I was determined to find out what was happening. I had no clear idea where to start, but as I left it occurred to me that the most logical plan was to go to a location that would have to show signs of unfolding events. I opted for the presidential palace, the seat of the government—or at least where the president had his office—and my decision was easy because both bus routes passing by my house went right by the palace. I boarded the first bus that came by, after waiting quite a while for it, and there were only three or four other passengers in it, which was rare, very rare, for that time of the day.

In the early morning the city was usually moving into full swing and buses would be congenitally congested—so much so that some of the male passengers, never the women, would hang precariously from the boarding steps with their bodies protruding inches, if not feet, from the vehicle, twisting, squirming, contorting and wriggling to avoid hitting pedestrians, telephones poles or any other impediment street or traffic placed in their way. And the buses would be filled with the noise of new arrivals asking those already on board to make room for them, and the *conductor,* who was not the driver but the fare collector, would be calling on people to pay up and requesting the money to be passed on to him since he himself was bound to be pinned down by the surging crowd, and some passengers would be asking for their change back or claiming they could not reach their pockets with their two hands engaged in supporting themselves on their shaky perches, and others would be talking to friends who always seemed to be several seats removed, or cracking jokes for the general benefit, or simply shouting something to someone. But this morning the bus was almost empty and the few passengers in it completely silent.

It was different, oddly different; the endemic public garrulousness was absent, the streets were deserted, the bus driver and the *conductor* were subdued, and almost in a whisper one of the passengers commented that the traffic lights were not working, and another, equally quietly, pointed out that there were no policemen on the streets, which was another major abnormality because, with its overpopulation of policemen, there were always some on the city streets, mostly sipping free coffee while trying to appear busy—but not today. The streets of La Habana Vieja, the colonial part of town, seemed even emptier and quieter, and I was now the only passenger, and the driver and fare collector talked in an inaudible hush while constantly moving their heads around in search of movement and information. I asked them if they had already gone by the presidential palace in a previous run that day and both shook their heads, no, and I asked them if they knew what was going on there, and if the bus would be allowed to follow its normal route and go past it, and the driver shrugged his shoulders while the *conductor* did not acknowledge my question. So we three kept silent and within a few minutes we approached the building and saw sandbags in front, and a machine gun mounted behind them, and lots of sailors, all very unusual since normally there were only a couple of policemen guarding this entrance with no sandbags or machine gun and definitely no sailors, and as the bus rolled by we saw the sailors were fully armed and behind them, in the building's courtyard, more uniformed men, also fully armed, and all wearing stern expressions. Those by the entrance glared at us as our bus went by, but no apparent attempt was being made to divert traffic, and there was no doubt now in my mind that something big was under way. I got off the bus and, after another long wait, climbed on another, this one headed towards the University and the bank office on San Lázaro.

I went to the bank to see if anyone was there who could tell me what was happening. It must have been around eight o'clock by then, and I wanted to find out as much as I could before going to the University, where I was sure there would be people who knew. The branch manager was already in the building, a big, rotund and affable man who opened the door as soon as he saw me and began immediately to pour out a torrent of rumor, gossip and hearsay that made little sense and contained no solid information. But he was determined to let imagination fill the gaps, and he told me that Batista was trying to take over the government and had taken control of the Camp Columbia garrison, and that there were units loyal to the government in the interior of the country marching at that very moment on Havana, and that these units were coming in three separate armed columns and would be in the city within hours and, of course, the bank would remain closed, and after listening to him for a few minutes it was pretty clear he didn't have the foggiest idea what the situation actually was. It was the assistant manager, a very fat lady named Mercedes who lived next door to the office and was listening to a small radio she had placed on the center of her desk, who had what little reliable information was beginning to surface. She confirmed that Batista had in fact taken over the army headquarters—the only thing that appeared certain at the moment. I told them of my intention to climb up the hill and go to the University, and they both tried to dissuade me, thinking the police or the army would already be there or would be preparing to attack the place in case of any resistance and that, under any circumstances, it would be a very unsafe place to be.

Before walking up to the University, I went to have something to eat at the coffee shop across the street from the bank and saw that more people were out now and that there was more traffic, and in the coffee shop I found that people were more talkative than earlier, although still communicating in quiet voices rather than in the normally clamorous Cuban manner. No one seemed to have specific information about the situation, but there was general agreement that indeed Batista had succeeded in taking over the military. My head was spinning and I had difficulty coming to grips with the notion that a military takeover had actually taken place. I couldn't entertain the thought that a coup, especially one led by that bastard Batista, could be a fait accompli, a done deal, and I was certain that if an attempt had been made, and it was becoming quite apparent that one had, opposition to it was bound to emerge. After all, we had a government, and the Auténticos in power would not allow Batista to kick them ignominiously out; and we also had a widely popular Partido Ortodoxo, and the Ortodoxos would never permit the democratic process to be subverted and wouldn't let someone come and rob them of the electoral victory that was coming their way. I was sure that whatever the initial success of Batista in the barracks, his attempt would be checked.

I walked up the San Lázaro Street hill to the University. By now it must have been close to nine in the morning, but the air was still cool and I could feel the ocean breeze on my face as I climbed the long set of steps. As I reached the top and headed for the Plaza Cadenas, the University's center square, I saw students milling around in groups. The largest one was in front of the Law School, which wasn't surprising, and by the time I got there someone had just finished addressing the students. I asked what was up and one of them told me that arms were being sent to the University, that some of the student leaders had gone to collect them and were expected to return within the hour. At first everyone in the place seemed to have more information than I did; I was told that there had been no resistance to Batista in Havana, that the military and police forces had offered no opposition to his coup, and that no one knew where the president and his cabinet were, although it was assumed they were preparing some counteraction, perhaps with the support of military garrisons in the provinces. Some people even mentioned the names of the officers who commanded these garrisons, throwing the names into their explanations and interpretations to give them an air of authenticity; but these were clearly no more than guesses, or wishful thinking, and after listening for a while to what everyone was saying and what the groups were discussing, I concluded that, aside from the fact that Batista had taken over Camp Columbia and that there was no fighting going on in Havana, nobody knew a thing here either.

A group of students that originally had been standing in front of the School of Education had now moved towards the Science building, diagonally across from where I was, and I walked over there in time to hear a young man, a student leader I assumed, asking for anyone who knew anything about arms to identify themselves, as they would be needed to show others the basics of firing a gun. Four or five young men raised their hands and moved towards him, and that was all he said and then he left in the company of those who has raised their hands. Eventually the two large congregations, the one by the Law School and the one by the Science building, divided up into smaller groups in or around the Plaza. There must have been three or four hundred students there all together, and I don't remember seeing a single girl or a single professor, just the male students and the *bedeles*—the uniformed concierges who took care of the buildings, who were old and mostly black, who had held their jobs for generations, and who were institutional features of the schools. Also missing was the University police force, which supposedly kept order since the national police was, by law, not permitted on campus.

As I went from group to group I could sense the anticipation and anxiety over the expected arrival of arms, but no one had any idea when they would arrive, or from where, or how and under whose direction they were to be used. The groups kept growing and shrinking and moving from spot to spot around the Plaza, but the first hour went by with no arms, no leaders, and no news, and when the second hour was over it was the same. By noon I realized that there were only about one-third of us left, and by half past twelve only about two dozen, and by one o'clock, with the place almost deserted, I left and walked down the steps and down the San Lázaro Street hill back to the bank's office. I still had no idea what had actually happened, or not happened, and the traffic was still lighter than normal, and the bank was still closed to the public, although a couple of the regular customers were inside talking to Mercedes, who opened the door as soon as she saw me, and who wanted to know what the students were up to—which was, to my chagrin, nothing.

I called home and my family didn't have anything to add to the little that was already public knowledge: Batista had taken over the military, claimed to be in control of the country, and no one was trying to stop him. No government reaction, no calls to resistance, no fighting—nothing. I kept trying the telephone and finally reached some Ortodoxo friends who told me that Pepe Iglesias had called an emergency meeting for three o'clock that afternoon, and they gave me the address, which turned out to be near Malecón Boulevard and not more than a ten-minute walk from where I was. The news of the meeting lifted my spirits; I was now certain something concrete and effective must be brewing. It couldn't be otherwise with Pepe Gatillo in it, and it made sense for the Ortodoxos to lead the resistance, since we had the most to lose if Batista got away with a military putsch less than three months before an election we were sure to win. The Auténticos in the government were on their way out anyway, and they knew it, which could explain their reluctance to take an open and strong stance against Batista and his soldiers, so if the Ortodoxos didn't do it no one would. The idea that Batista could trample over rules and laws and institutions and take over without encountering determined, if not fierce, resistance was something I couldn't accept, or even imagine.

At three o'clock in the afternoon I met the real Pepe Iglesias, the man behind the charisma, behind "the trigger" sobriquet, behind the presiding chair of the Ortodoxo youth organization. Pepe didn't have much to say and, contrary to my expectation, was calm and collected, didn't foresee any counteraction to the military takeover by the government, didn't have a course of action to recommend, showed no inclination to lead in any direction, and went on to explain with unerring logic that we had nothing to fight Batista with, and that even if we could get our hands on some weapons, we wouldn't know how to operate them or what to do with them. What he said made sense, which was the worst part of it, because I had not gone to this meeting looking for sense but for hope, and I had expected him to show the way, some way, but he had nothing to offer and he didn't seem especially interested in offering anything. And I went from puzzlement to outrage as time kept going by and nothing was done to turn things around, and I simply couldn't believe, did not want to believe, that a bunch of miserable soldiers could kick everybody in the ass and that everybody would just take it.

Over the next couple of days the complete demise of the elected government became evident in all its pitiful detail. The president had fled the country, his ministers and his military high command had vanished, evaporated, some following the fleeing president, others seeking sanctuary in foreign embassies—a picture in the newspapers showed the deposed minister of interior in the Mexican embassy with a rosary in his hands praying to a picture of the Mexican liberal and anticlerical hero Benito Juárez—and others simply abandoning their offices and going home. Not a shot had been fired, not a single act of resistance had taken place. Batista was now president—by the grace of his balls.

Pathetic. What had taken place was not simply the overthrow of the Auténtico government, but the demolition of the entire political system because with the ruling party had also gone the Ortodoxo opposition, equally unable to offer any resistance, unwilling to stand up to the soldiers despite the blistering rhetoric that had been its hallmark, and despite its trumpeted commitment to democracy. The Auténticos had been obliterated; the Ortodoxos, castrated.

I was angry, and yet there was something else—excitement. I felt excited as I rode through the almost empty streets of the city the morning of the coup, and the excitement accompanied me to Havana University and to the meeting with the Ortodoxos, and it did not abandon me when I had to admit late that day that nothing of what I had wished for, and expected, had happened or was about to happen. Excitement, because, from the moment I woke up that morning of March 10, 1952, the world was a different place: the monotony and tedium of daily life, the intrusive boorishness of Havana, the incandescent relentlessness of the tropical sun, the oppressive horizons of the predictable drudgery that ruled the present and conformed the future, had all taken sudden flight and a new landscape had emerged, as if Sandokan had encountered a resplendent city in the thick of the dark jungle, as if the Black Corsair had all of a sudden seen the unexpected glow of a safe harbor from the prow of his battered brigantine. To hell with Sancho Panza, the windmills had become real.

The angels of destruction and creation descended over the Cuban political scene with the swiftness and force of a celestial hurricane—what had been could no longer be, and what we thought was going to be receded into a foggy background, and as the barracks-rabble, old cronies, and reprobate politicians grabbed public offices and sinecures with equal contempt for both form and substance of public decorum, the dynamics of the new situation pushed the country into a rapid and thorough political transformation. The Auténtico and Ortodoxo parties were dead. When President Prío fled the country on March 10, in the cravenly and undignified manner in which he did, he took with him whatever resolution and will to political life there might have been left among the Auténticos; theirs was a natural death, as the once young and idealistic men and women who had originally created that party now worried themselves solely with the preservation of their ill-obtained riches, and, no longer in touch with the idealism of their youth, showed neither traces of civic responsibility nor signs of personal courage or self-respect. The Ortodoxos had more honest individuals in their midst, but ultimately they were equally reluctant to confront Batista, to actively oppose his coup, so with the implacable logic that changing political circumstances produce, they were also quickly consigned to oblivion. The country's two major political parties became overnight the discarded peels of rotten bananas. But the same whirling wind that had blown them away brought in now a new cast of characters—those willing to take a stand and fight.

The first to appear onstage was Aureliano—Aureliano Sánchez Arango, a law professor and student leader of the 1930s who had been President Prío's minister of both education and foreign affairs. He was the only member of the government who had retained a reputation for personal honesty, although also reputed to be haughty and authoritarian, and he captured public attention as the sole member of the deposed regime unwilling to bend to Batista's will. He eluded the soldiers sent to apprehend him the day of the coup and went underground instead of acquiescing to the new order, seeking refuge in a foreign embassy, or escaping the island. And even though no one knew exactly what he was up to, and many of us harbored doubts and misapprehensions about a man who, even if personally honest and not a professional politician, had been part of the previous administration, Aureliano became a rallying point for those opposing Batista and willing to do something about it.

I kept attending the meetings of the Ortodoxo youth section, but they had become wakes for dead dreams. The party leaders had been shown for what they were: politicians thirsting for power and its perks and devoid of the principles, the moral fiber, the civil courage and the personal guts required to take a stand against a dictatorship that had been imposed on the country by a group of renegade soldiers and political crooks. The leaders of the Ortodoxo youth section proved to be no different from their elders, and no call to action ever came from them, not even from Pepe Gatillo. For a while I kept attending these meetings, not knowing what else to do, but I needed to find new bearings, to navigate the new circumstances in pursuit of the ideals that had been simultaneously negated and brought to the fore by Batista's seizure of power. It was sad to see the group and the party I had belonged to in this new light, and to see individuals with whom I had shared political ideas, dreams and hopes scatter aimlessly in different directions. Some of the former regulars stopped coming around immediately, while the rest could not agree on any kind of activity to oppose the government, and there were even some, to my amazement and disgust, not interested at all in opposing the new regime but calculating when and how new electoral opportunities would emerge and how they could take advantage of them.

The public reaction, or more properly the lack of it, to the political changes was impossible for me to understand—unfathomable. I just couldn't comprehend how people could remain unperturbed by such a turn of events, by such an affront, because as far as I was concerned, Batista had insulted and humiliated the whole country. His transgression was not a political or legal abstraction but something concrete and palpable: the imposition of his will on the rest of us. When rhetoric and double-talk were put aside, what was left of the new situation was the stark fact that this guy and his cronies were telling the country that they were going to lord over it and that we had to take it—like it or not. And the sorry reality was that most people, including elected officials, party leaders, public figures and civic personalities, seemed willing to take it, or at least unwilling to challenge it, which was essentially the same. I was only eighteen, totally inexperienced, grossly uneducated, without any clear idea as to what to do, but I was sure, damned sure, of one thing: I wasn't going to take it.

Angry at the passivity of the country in the face of Batista's action, I searched for ways of venting my displeasure and showing my low esteem for those so willing to accept the new state of affairs. So I decided to strike a personal blow of defiance that would demonstrate what I really thought of the society I lived in; I took Ivonne, a beautiful brunette whore whose trade she unmistakably proclaimed in dress and countenance, to one of the most popular meeting places of the Havana middle class, the America Theater.

I know it might be hard for people today, given the differences in circumstances, fashions and mores, to realize how the pretentious middle class of an underdeveloped country could be so committed to their ideas of propriety and manners, and how attendance to a place that showed a movie and a floor show could have had any social status. But they were, and it did, especially on Saturday evenings, when attendance at the movie theater would be circumscribed to well-groomed patrons from the upper-class neighborhoods of Havana, with women fully attired and the men in suits or freshly pressed linen *guayaberas*.

The *guayabera* itself was one of the few concessions middle-class Cuba made to the Caribbean climate. Of uncertain origin, probably from the Philippines via the Manila Galleon and Mexico, the pleated and multi-pocketed airy shirt ranged in Cuba from the countryside to the towns and from the humble *guajiro* to the wealthiest and most prominent men;

and as it became urbanized and universal the *guayabera* branched out into types and styles that, while retaining common generic lines, proclaimed the social distinctions between those wearing the different variations. Those worn by the poorest were generally short-sleeved with a soft collar, made from cheap cotton in pale colors or shining white; the higher-class version was long-sleeved, starch-stiff in the collar, pure linen, and impeccably off-white. This version of the shirt gained acceptance as a substitute for a suit in semiformal occasions, and it was into a multitude of genteel *guayaberas* and gaudily but expensive dresses that I paraded the whore who looked like a whore. Heads turned and whispers could be seen as well as heard, and I felt I was getting the reaction I had sought and made a point of showing Ivonne off as much as possible. I hoped my point would be driven home by the fact that it was as clear that I was one of them as it was that she wasn't, with my own linen *guayabera* and her whorish clothes leaving no room for doubt. I wanted to state my lack of respect for them; tell them that they were no different from the whore on my arm. They had shown total lack of dignity and courage, doing nothing to challenge a handful of mutinous soldiers and professional scoundrels, and I was trying to show exactly what I thought of them, and it was a silly gesture, a ridiculous gesture—and the next week I was behind bars.

It was a cage more than a proper cell: cement walls on two sides and iron bars from floor to ceiling on the other two; an almost perfect square, with the walls painted green, a darker green than the rest of the police station's lobby. Earlier that evening, four of us, Pepe, Antonio, Fermín and I, had been minding our own business after leaving the Ortodoxo party headquarters, walking slowly down El Prado Boulevard towards the sea, and we had just stopped at an ice-cream vendor when the police cars came and the policemen ordered us inside. We did what they said, not knowing what was going on, and they put me in the same car as Pepe Gatillo, and I looked at him for guidance, but he just shrugged his shoulders in a gesture of unconcern. The policemen's faces were grave but not menacing, and the order to get into the cell and not to talk to one another dry but not brusque; these were the days when there had not yet been any violence between the new government and its opponents, and it was like the two sides were shadow boxing, sizing up the antagonist and taking his measurement for future reference. Eventually, several hours after our arrest, the police captain in charge of the station came in and was briefed by the desk sergeant, who told him some kids, us, had been distributing antigovernment leaflets and had been seen entering the

Partido Ortodoxo headquarters. The sergeant read to him what must have been a sample of the leaflets; the captain heard it and didn't react to it in any visible way. When the sergeant was finished, the captain disappeared into the interior of the station without looking at us, came back a few minutes later sipping a cup of coffee, sat down behind a desk next to the sergeant and signaled someone to bring us to him. He looked at us with some curiosity and in a civil tone asked what we knew about the distribution of the antigovernment material, questioning us one at a time and getting the same answer every time: nothing—which was the truth. He then leaned forward and subjected us to some words of wisdom about young people being used by conniving and dastardly politicians, and how we should be aware of them and keep our own interests in mind. Finally, pleased with his words, and probably following standing instructions, he let us go. It was too late in the evening to find an open café, so we went our separate ways, but not before agreeing to a man that the only people stupid enough to go around distributing antigovernment literature and then marching back to party headquarters were those yokels Fidel Castro kept bringing around.

Fidel was the only Ortodoxo politician who appeared energized by the new situation, and he kept holding meetings in one of the back rooms of the Prado 109 house with groups of young men from the countryside. Their rural origins were clear from their speech, clothing and demeanor, and Fidel must have sought these country boys out of desperation because we kids from Havana were not only disinclined to follow him but were, in fact, highly suspicious of him. Here was Fidel Castro, who as a student had been associated with the gangster-like groups operating from Havana University, who had been accused of involvement in at least one assassination, whose father-in-law was one of Batista's ministers, and whose wife's brother, Rafael, was a vitriolic pro-Batista propagandist and secret police officer, openly advocating armed action against the government. He had made no open and public break with his pro-Batista relatives and had no political following of his own, and so the paranoid among us thought he was a police spy or agent provocateur while the rest thought him somewhat unhinged, or in Havana slang, *algo tostado*—somewhat mentally toasted—and in either case unreliable and untrustworthy.

Pepe and I left the police station and walked together for a few blocks, and then I continued on my own, on foot all the way home. It was a long walk, but I felt like staying out in the coolness of the predawn air, thinking about the evening's events because I had not thought at all while in the cell. I had instead concentrated on the officers' comings and goings, trying to figure out their routine and what they were up to, and I had looked at the walls and at the desks and at the chairs and at the place's only decoration, a big ugly picture of Sergeant Batista in the uniform of a banana republic general, with a smirk for a smile; and I had looked at Antonio and Fermín and had seen them looking as uncomfortable as I felt, and I had watched Pepe, Pepe Iglesias, Pepe Gatillo, our charismatic leader, who seemed completely unperturbed by our predicament, and I was amazed to realize how much a person can show of himself without saying anything, without making any effort to communicate. Pepe's message could not be misinterpreted: he didn't give a shit. Not just about the police and whether we were going to be incarcerated and formally charged or simply let go as we eventually were—that was just a minor part of it. His lack of interest ran deeper; now that his seemingly assured electoral future had been derailed, he didn't seem to care much about what was going on politically, and it was clear to me right then that there was no fighting spirit in him, only ambition thwarted and plans disrupted, and that he was now trying to determine how best to reorient his life. I began to realize that his goal had not been very different from Chúa's interest in being a municipal councilman; he had just set his sights higher.

The changing circumstances were quickly revealing people's true character, transforming them from what they had pretended to be to what they were. Pepe Iglesias's transformation was the first one I saw, and I saw it at close range, and it made me think, and I kept on thinking about it while I walked the streets of a Havana that was dark, cool and very quiet in the very early hours of the morning. The city seemed empty, or suddenly inhabited by a breed of people different from its normally exuberant and excitable population. I trailed for a while behind an old black man in a shapeless Panama hat too small for his head and who moved with body oscillations as if slithering rather than walking. It took me a long time to catch up to him, though he wasn't going fast, and it took me even longer to pass him as he quickened his pace when he felt me closing in, but his movements didn't betray any change in rhythm so maybe it was I who was slowing down as I approached him, and when I drew near him I saw a big unlit cigar in his mouth, but the tilt of his hat and the angle of the shade created by the street lights prevented me from seeing the face around the cigar, just blackness from the collar of the shirt to the brim of the Panama, with the protruding silhouette of the cigar the only marker of what should have been a face, and all of a sudden he was no longer there; either he had stopped or I had fallen asleep while walking or I had been moving faster than I thought—or he had never been there.

I went back to thinking about Pepe, someone I had admired as a firm, clear-minded, eloquent and purposeful individual, one who had seemed able and willing to set the path, but now where that person had been there was nothing, like the dark space under the old black man's Panama hat. I kept on walking through the night and the empty streets, and saw no one else for a long time, then a policeman reclining against a lamppost, and as I went by him I couldn't tell if he was sleep or awake, if was real or if I was imagining him as I might have been imagining the old black man with the cigar and no face, and I expected the policeman to say something as I walked by him, but he didn't, and I kept on walking, enjoying the cool air and feeling happy and sad; happy to have been in jail, even if briefly, and to have found the experience tolerable, and to have gained from it a sense of self-importance; sad that Pepe would not be with us, for although I wasn't sure who we were, or what we were going to do, I knew Pepe the Trigger wouldn't be there.

CHAPTER SEVEN

Aureliano! The most wanted man in Cuba, his picture on the front page of the newspapers and his powerful-sounding name, with almost as many syllables as letters, flying the flag of revolution and symbolizing the promise of retribution—the talk of the town. Where was he? What was he up to? When would he march on the government? He seemed to be the only one challenging Batista, and his name was beginning to take on mythical dimension. Everyone seemed to have known him—when he was a leftist student leader, when he was in jail, when he was a professor at Havana University, when he was a minister in Prío's government. A multiplicity of qualities were attributed to him without any accompanying evidence, and references to him were made in low voices and with serious expressions; a legend was emerging—a legend-on-credit, based on deeds to come, but a legend nevertheless—and this was just what was needed to keep the anti-Batista spirits up. The police were looking for Aureliano, the press speculated daily about his whereabouts, the street was full of rumors on what he was planning—and I was on my way to meet him.

The meeting had been arranged by Raúl Roa, dean of the School of Social Sciences at Havana University and an old revolutionary firebrand from the 1930s, to whom I was directed by a former teacher of mine and political activist of the Roa generation, Asunción Díaz Cuervo, after I had gone to her for advice and assistance in getting in touch with Aureliano's people. It appeared as if Aureliano was the only one willing to confront the government, the only one engaging in action proper to the circumstances. The Auténtico and Ortodoxo parties had lost total relevancy by failing to respond adequately to Batista's challenge, although their scrawny institutional skeletons remained marionettes in the hands of a few bankrupt puppeteers; the Communists, as ever, were engaged in interminable and incomprehensible dialectical double-talk and, given their past conduct in Cuba, could not be trusted anyway; the students at Havana University had begun to agitate, to stage public protests and rallies attacking Batista for overturning the legitimately elected government of the country, for violating the constitution and for instituting military rule, and I participated in their protests and attended their rallies, but these were more efforts to show what Batista was and what he represented than actions to get rid of him. Of course, there was always Fidel Castro, but he offered little basis for trust and lacked any visible means with which to challenge the government, and there was also Rafael García Bárcena, a poet, high school teacher and visionary whose ideas on how to get rid of Batista hung somewhere between the ridiculous and the demented; he instructed his followers, mostly high school boys and a few starry-eyed university students, to secure domestic weaponry—kitchen knives, axes, straight razors, BB guns, slingshots, old revolvers and whatever else they had access to—and would then post them on assigned street corners and pass review of his "troops" from the window of a public bus. Bárcena was either totally ignorant of the first law of revolutionary dynamics—ideas and money get arms, arms get power—or just chose to blatantly ignore the middle bit. This left Aureliano as the only game in town, the only one in Cuba who seemed willing and prepared to face up to and overthrow the tyrant.

Roa had been expecting me, and I was led into the dean's office right away by a *bedel,* one of several Armenteros brothers who worked in that capacity at the University, who knew me as a student and who had treated me before with dismissive friendliness but who now, on my way to see his dean, showed unusual amiability. Roa was waiting for me and he couldn't have been friendlier—not what I had expected from a dean. He was not very tall, but he was wiry and spoke fast, very fast, moving incessantly and without giving me a chance to say anything. But I didn't have anything to say, because I was mesmerized by his talking and by his gesticulating and his being Robespierre and Danton and Saint-Just and Lenin and Trotsky and Zapata and every revolutionary I had ever heard of rolled into one. I was in a political rapture, I felt like even his glasses were projecting fervor and idealism, and it took him only a few minutes to explain the evils of the military government and the need to overthrow it, to enumerate all the problems Cuba had ever had or would ever encounter and to solve them all, to exalt the virtues of Aureliano and to prescribe the ousting of Batista as the first step to regenerate the country.

And it was all music to my ears, political manna from above, as if he had been reading my thoughts and putting my ideas and dreams into words, opening the doors to a heaven where armed angels with beatific expressions and luminous bandoliers readied themselves for the charge of the just. By the time I left Roa's office I had joined the Triple A, Aureliano's underground opposition organization, and was about to have a clandestine meeting with the government's most wanted man. And at that point I was beyond excitement. I was in a revolutionary bliss that defied words and that elevated me to the top of the world from where I could look down upon the rest of creation.*

But before I got to meet Aureliano, I was thrown back into labor politics. Almost by miracle, I had become the head union steward for all the employees of the Banco Continental Cubano. I had been in the middle of one of my monthly assignments away from the main office when news went out that Manolo Rodríguez, the previous steward, had been fired from the bank along with his second in command, Aramís Labrada. It was never clear why the two were fired, and rumors circulated that they had been caught in some scheme to rob the bank, but all anyone knew for certain was that they had both been fired and carted off to jail, that some legal procedures had been initiated against them and the union needed a head in the Banco Continental Cubano. I quickly found out that an election would be called immediately to replace the departed pair, so I telephoned one of the very few people I knew at the central office, Antonio Mauris, who had worked in the Zulueta Street branch when I was the union representative there, and asked him to put forward

---

*Before I left his office that day, I asked Roa the meaning of the Triple A's name. He replied that he had been the one to suggest it and that it didn't have any meaning. That in a conversation with Aureliano immediately after Batista's coup, when they discussed the need to create an underground organization, they searched for a name that would not be divisive or bring up undesirable connotations, and soon concluded that such a sanitized and implication-free name did not seem to exist in the Cuban political lexicon. It was then Roa said, that he suggested using the triple A. He had seen a car with the sticker of the American Automobile Association on his way to the meeting and that was how the idea occurred to him. Whatever the veracity of Roa's explanation, the adoption of the three A's was reminiscent of the very effective ABC underground organization that opposed Machado in the 1930s. I never heard anything to counter or dispute Roa's story, which, given his very close personal ties to Aureliano at the time, and his own imaginative bent, seemed credible. The enemies of the Triple A, in a pejorative twist to belittle the organization, claimed the three A's stood for Asociación de Amigos de Aureliano, Association of Aureliano's Friends.

my name as candidate for the steward job. Antonio asked me who I wanted to be my running mate, the deputy-steward candidate, and I told him to find someone he thought was honest and well liked, and he found Feliciano Hernández.

The election was held the following week and I won. I won for two reasons. One was that no one wanted the job—that is, no one of substance, or who had been around for a while, was interested in the position. The second reason must be divided into two parts: first, almost no one among those voting knew me, they just knew whatever the couple of individuals who actually knew me had told them, and second, and far more important, they hated the guy who ran against me. His name was Guerra—his first name might have been Jorge, but I'm not sure and nobody ever called him anything other than Guerra, and he was tall, loud, aggressive, ignorant, inarticulate and a militant practitioner of *santería*, which was anathema to the white bank employees. Many of those who voted for me did so as a political statement; although they knew little about me personally, they were aware I opposed both the Batista government and the leadership of our union, which itself had become supportive of the dictatorship. Politics was beginning to spill over all areas of life dominated by the country's white middle class, and bank employees were white to a man and very definitely middle class.

I won with a solid majority of the eighty or ninety people who had troubled to go to union headquarters to vote. Guerra had a small but very combative group of supporters who had gone around putting pressure on people to vote for their man, and, if unchecked, they would have succeeded. But parliamentary techniques have their own way of determining events and we were able to get around their tactics of intimidation by calling for a secret ballot. The Guerra people had assumed the vote would be public, a showing of hands, as was customary, and that they would be able to see how individuals voted. A secret ballot would undermine their bullying tactics and they knew this but were caught unprepared and by the time they realized we were requesting one it was too late. I, for my part, had only minor interest in union issues and saw the whole thing as a big personal and political adventure—as a chance to open up a front against the government.

Finally I got the call to meet Aureliano, so there I was, union leader and university student and still thin as a rail and as innocent as my eighteen years dictated, waiting in front of the Apolo movie house in the short-sleeved dark blue shirt I told the man on the telephone I would be wearing. I didn't wait long. A dark sedan pulled up next to me, and without any doubt, knowing this was it, I opened the passenger door and got in. The driver didn't utter a word but kept driving up the Calzada del 10 de Octubre towards the Víbora district. Once in that neighborhood, he drove and drove, up and down all kind of streets, turning right and left, and left, and right, and I began to feel sorry for the man, as it was obvious he was trying to disorient me, but the more he drove around, and the more turns he took, the more I knew where I was—this was the neighborhood where I had gone to school and I knew it like the palm of my hand. At one point I tried to make conversation, but the driver kept his lips shut tight, probably concentrating on the zigging and the zagging, as the streets were dark and the signs hard to read. I felt like offering assistance but thought he might take offense, and as I was enjoying the game I kept quiet until he finally stopped in front of a two-story house and said his first word: "aquí."

My heart leapt—I was going to meet the elusive Aureliano.

The house was typical of the neighborhood; different from the others yet the same. The details of all these houses varied, as did the colors of the outside walls and the shape of the gardens and the type of fences and gates separating them from the sidewalk, but there was a something—a pattern, a regularity—unifying all the differences, making them look alike. I'm not sure what it was, maybe their height, all two-story, maybe their width, maybe their gardens and little fences, maybe their age.

We got out of the car, the driver knocked at the door and a middle-aged woman opened it. He entered first and then signaled me to follow, an impolite way of proceeding but one dictated, I assumed, by some law of underground protocol, and as we entered the woman pointed to a sofa in the living room. She didn't say anything to me, didn't offer the mandatory cup of coffee, but told the man something in a very low voice that I couldn't make out. As I sat on the sofa and waited I took a look around. As one entered the house there was a narrow stairway immediately to the right, leading to the upper floor, to the left was the small living room in which I now sat, and straight in front of the door was a short rectangular hallway that led, probably, to the dining room and kitchen. The house had looked much bigger from the outside; once inside, it felt quite small.

There were so many things running through my mind that I couldn't align them in any useful order, so I just focused on a dark speck on the far wall as it moved slowly and hesitantly, first up, and then down, and then to the left, towards the window, but never to the right, towards the inside of the house. The moving spot reminded me of myself, of my jumping mind moving in different directions prodded by excitement, curiosity, pride, fear—all mixed in some emotional soup that rendered it a total blank when I should have been thinking of what I wanted to discuss with Aureliano, of the things I wanted to say, of all that I wanted to find out. As I focused my eyes on the moving spot I realized that it was an animate being, a bug on night patrol, and then the woman came into the room and, still without saying a word, sent me upstairs.

As I climbed up the steps, a man who looked only a few years older than me, but not many, was coming down, and as I got to the top I could hear the woman telling him to go and sit on the sofa where I had been waiting. When I got to the top of the stairs I looked around and saw a clean-shaven, medium-height, middle-aged man at the doorway of one of the rooms. His right hand was moving towards me. I shook it and entered a rather small bedroom furnished only with a bed and two chairs. He introduced himself, Aureliano, and offered me one of the chairs, taking the other for himself and sitting directly in front of me. As we faced each other the bed was to my right and as much as I didn't want to stare, I had trouble taking my eyes off the submachine gun and the pistol lying on it.

I didn't hear his first words. I mean, I heard the sound of his voice but not what he was saying; my mind glued to the weapons on the bed— very black on a light bedspread, seductively and mysteriously offering some undefined promise. Maybe they were for me, I allowed myself to dream, although I didn't have any idea what I would do with them beyond admiring them and enjoying their possession and feeling important. Aureliano kept on talking, so I gathered my will and forced the weapons out of my line of vision and out of my mind and tried to concentrate on listening, and I must have had such a dazed or foolish expression on my face that he looked at me, stopped talking, smiled and started all over again.

He spoke and I listened, and he spoke very differently from Roa, slowly and without much body movement, and his words matched the calmness of his style. He knew about me, about my Ortodoxo affiliation, about my union activities, about my attending the University, and said he needed my help to fight Batista, and this made me feel good, very good, and I thought of the weapons on the bed again; but he went on to explain his plan, a plan that seemed rational and sensible and which implied a nonarmed role for me. His strategy was to recruit people in the military, and to stage a countercoup with them and others individuals with military experience, and he wanted me to help organize support for this action among political activists and the general public. As if foreseeing an objection to such an "auxiliary" role, he went on to affirm categorically that under no circumstances would he allow young people with no military training to put their lives in unnecessary peril—and added, either to drive the point further home or as the true reason behind his position, that lacking training and experience, young people, regardless of their enthusiasm and commitment, would be a hindrance rather than a help in the action he was planning.

I understood what he was saying and couldn't deny the sense it made, but I still needed to ask some questions, prodded probably by my reluctance to let the weapons on the bed go. "Is the young fellow you were talking to before I came up going to be working with me?" I asked. Aureliano moved back in his chair, passed his right hand over his black hair and replied with a tenuous smile of satisfaction visible only on his upper lip, "Oh, no, él es un militar." "Oh, no, he's a military man." I was very impressed by his answer, probably the way he wanted me to be. If he was meeting with a military man his plan was certainly moving ahead, and this meant that there were people in the armed forces not under the thumb of Batista. I felt exhilarated by the news, and the questions I had promised myself I would ask Aureliano came out of my mouth all rolled into one: "¿Se está avanzando?" "Is progress being made?" "Sí," he replied, "estamos avanzando con rapidez." "Yes, we are moving fast ahead."

There was nothing else to say. I was not about to forgo the chance to contribute to Batista's overthrow, so I shook Aureliano's hand, told him what a pleasure it had been meeting him, wished him good luck, assured him I would get to work on my assignment right away, and asked to whom I should report and coordinate my work with, to which he replied, "Raúl Roa." And I was in a cloud as I walked down the stairs towards the man who had driven me there and the woman who had opened the door when we arrived, and through my inner cloud I saw that the young man who had passed me on my way up the stairs, and whom Aureliano had identified as a military man, was still there, sitting on the living room sofa, and I thought it strange.

It was now the driver's turn to go up to Aureliano. I was left waiting downstairs with the woman and the young military man who was sitting on the sofa with his body tilted forward and his eyes on me, and then on the floor, and then on me again, and I tried not to stare back. The woman was standing up by the door, not blocking it physically but as a psychological barrier in front of it, since one would have to brush against her to get out of the house. No words exchanged. The three of us lost in our respective selves—total silence. No outside noise filtering into the house from the quiet neighborhood either. It was an uncanny and almost oppressive moment whose nature I could not understand or justify but could not fail to sense. But the moment was brief and the driver quickly returned downstairs and motioned me to follow him to the car. The young man also got up from the sofa, but the woman told him gently, "Un par de minutos más." "A couple of minutes more."

A change had taken place. The driver didn't say anything, but his driving told me—and the expression on his face, too. No more misleading turns up and down different streets, no more distracting rights and lefts; we went now in a direct line from Santa Catalina to the Calzada del 10 de Octubre to the spot where he had picked me up. His previous solemn and mysterious countenance had given way to a still serious but much friendlier face, one of polite, if slightly condescending, camaraderie which told me I had been anointed.

The house was dark when I got home, so it must have been past eleven o'clock, maybe even past twelve. I had walked through the empty streets of my neighborhood after leaving the car, and as I walked I practiced being followed and trying to lose my tail, so I would turn around all of a sudden, retrace my steps, go through open spaces where I could get a clear view of anyone behind me as I pivoted right or left. But my heart was not in the exercise, and no one was after me anyhow; it was just an excuse for extending the walk because I was enjoying the freshness and coolness of the night air, and I walked fast to let speed increase the impact of the breeze, and it was like sailing I thought, although I had never sailed, but I had been in boats and in a kayak I borrowed sometimes to paddle into the waves searching for the combination of air and salty sea water that would crash against my body and envelop my vision in a translucent sparkling mist that spoke of freedom and adventure.

I took the big rocking chair and moved it to the end of the porch close to the jasmine so I could immerse my senses in its perfume. I should have been thinking about the commitment I had made earlier that evening, of ways to help Aureliano, of the best manner to organize support for the Triple A, of how to identify potential recruits, of planning actions to challenge the government. I should have been thinking of all those things, but I was not. As I sat there breathing the heavily perfumed night air, lazily rocking to and fro in the big chair, I thought of the Black and Red Corsairs and of beautiful Honorata de Wan Guld, and I thought of Sandokan, and of Ignacio Agramonte and Tony Guiteras, and of my uncle Enrique, and for some inexplicable reason I couldn't get out of my mind some verses of García Lorca I had read a few days before:

La luna vino a la fragua
con su polisón de nardos.
El niño la mira, mira.
El niño la está mirando.
En el aire conmovido
mueve la luna sus brazos
y enseña, lúbrica y pura,
sus senos de duro estaño.[†]

The jasmine. It must have been the jasmine that carried the words of Lorca into my brain. What else but jasmine could be so indelibly impressed in the lines and stanzas of the Gypsy verses? But perhaps it was just my age, that one time in life, when there is a short break between the two systems of control that govern our existence. When no longer children, yet not quite adults, we escape the tyranny of the family without having yet succumbed to the tyranny of social rules and conventions, and for the first and probably only time, we are free. And we find freedom difficult, because freedom always is, and find it also glorious, because it also always is; and it is during this brief respite that our imagination, prodded by conviction, disdaining distinctions between the real and the ideal—because it sees these distinctions coming less from the wisdom of maturity than from the cowardice of egoism—finds its unshackled self.

Earlier that evening I was eighteen, but I had grown older as the car sailed through the dark streets of the Víbora district in search of the

---

[†]Some poetry does not suffer translation well. This is the case with Federico García Lorca's *Gypsy Poems,* an interplay of imagery and sound. The rhythm and musicality of the words are not subject to translation, and it is the rhythm and musicality, not the words themselves, that convey the emotion and meaning of the poem. As an illustration of what I mean, here is the literal translation of the poem:

The moon came to the furnace
in her bustle of nards.
The boy looks at her, looks at her,
the boy is looking at her.
In the excited air
the moon moves her arms
and shows, lewd and pure
her breasts of hard tin.

mysterious house, and of the man inside it who flew the flag of justice and waved the sword of vengeance. Now, as I dozed in the big rocking chair, enfolded by the overpowering scent, with the spark of imagined deeds in my eyes and the lines of Lorca in my brain, I had moved back in time and was thirteen or twelve, and there was absolutely nothing unreasonable or surprising about the traversing of ages—it was in comfortable accordance with the balmy undulations of tropical time.

CHAPTER EIGHT

My fellow employees at the bank were rapidly becoming a nuisance. They expected me to solve their petty individual problems: change vacation time, secure a transfer to a more convenient location, argue for a raise or promotion—all problems I had no interest in, and which I would delegate to my second in command, Feliciano. Feliciano, "the happy one," was one of those rare beings whose names are literal descriptions of their dispositions. He was permanently in good humor, always smiling and willing to listen, forever prepared to forgo office work for a "union" coffee break, and more than happy to liberate me from the petty duties I found boring and a waste of time. In the permanently tumultuous and accelerated processes of my brain I had other goals; I wanted to overthrow the union leadership and turn the Bank Employees Workers Union into an antigovernment force, make it into an effective tool in the fight against Batista's tyranny. So I could, with the good conscience that self-righteousness grants, use the union job in pursuit of my own goals, for purposes of high politics; and I felt neither remorse nor discomfort over my lack of interest in the day-to-day welfare of my coworkers.

After being elected union steward I was transferred to the bank's transit department, where work was done in two shifts, one beginning at 7:00 A.M. and the other at 1:00 P.M., allowing me some free time during the day. The department was known as the "hole," and it was a large and windowless rectangular room slightly below ground level at the very end of the bank's office space. The room held some ugly big black contrivances for sorting checks, which for some reason were called *tamboras*, bass drums, and four large tables with neon lights and adding machines all over them, and those who worked there seemed to have little in common, in appearance and demeanor, with anyone else in the bank.

They dressed informally, which in those days meant a sport shirt rather than coat and tie, often unshaven, always in a rush, clamorous and garrulous, and went about their work emitting a collective hum, like a hyperactive swarm of bees. They were, needless to say, looked upon distrustfully and disdainfully by nearly everyone else in the bank.

The hole was where the bank placed those who didn't fit anywhere else. Because of the Cuban labor laws of the time, it was practically impossible to fire anyone unless they were caught with their hands in the till—although in reality these laws applied only to workers who had a strong union protecting them, who were almost exclusively white-collar and from Havana. We, bank employees, were the best example of this labor elite, and when our bank was faced with incompetent or troublesome workers, unable to get rid of them, a place had to be found where they would do the least damage. So into the hole they went. By the time I got there, the hole was a blend of reformatory for the maladapted, parking lot for dunderheads and refuge for the unconventional—and by far the best place in the bank to work.

I liked the hole. I liked its people, its informality and its hours. The length of your workday did not depend on the clock but on how fast and accurately you processed the thousands of checks coming from and going to other banks. To work efficiently, you had to become part of the machine, to maintain yourself in a kind of suspended animation and never, ever, fully read the numbers on the checks. You couldn't actually translate the figures into amounts in your head and then trust your brain to remember those amounts as you found their equivalent in the keys of the machines; that would have been far too slow and inaccurate. The trick was to go from eyes to fingers without letting your mind get in the way—look and punch, never think. And I was good at it from the very beginning, second only to Sergio Medina, a soft-spoken skinny kid who knew a lot more than I did about classical music and whose uncle was the host of a radio classical music program. Soon, however, I caught up to and then surpassed Sergio—in the processing of checks, that is, never in knowledge of classical music.

My ability to work fast, faster than anyone else, quickly got me accepted in the hole. This counted much more than being the union boss or anything else, because each shift worked as a team and no one could leave until all the checks had been properly tabulated and balanced.

"What's he doing here?" I asked myself as I stepped off the bus and saw Paquito, not the short admirer of Franco but the tall lingerie salesman from the Ortodoxo youth group, sitting on an empty wooden box right across from my house. He didn't give me a chance to say a word. "Turn around and don't look at your house," he said as he put his right arm around my shoulders, directing me away and towards Municipio Street. "What's going on . . . ?" I began, but Paquito put his left index finger over his mouth telling me to shut up, and he brought his face close to mine and whispered, "The police are after you."

I had no idea what he was talking about and didn't try to guess but just walked in silence with him until we got to his car, which was parked a few blocks away. When I saw the car I thought of the underwear that was surely in the trunk and wondered what ladies' garments he was carrying this time, and I would have asked him, but his expression was so grave that I decided my curiosity could wait. And it was not until we were in the car and it was moving away from my neighborhood that Paquito, without saying a word, handed me a copy of the afternoon newspaper he had been carrying.

I couldn't believe it. The lead column on the front page was a description of how the police had almost captured Aureliano the night before, how they had just missed him by a few minutes but had arrested the couple who owned the house in the Víbora district in which Aureliano, according to the paper, had been hiding. There were pictures of both the man and the woman, but I had never seen either of them. Way down the article, however, there was a description of the last person to visit Aureliano at this house, a young man, the article said, the police were now trying to identify and apprehend. The description was very detailed, sex, approximate age, height and weight, hair and eye color and even clothing, and it took a moment for my mind to process the information, an instant of cerebral blankness followed by a strange physiological reaction, as if a hard lump was descending down my esophagus at the same time my balls were moving up my throat.

I was silent as I let the information sink in, while Paquito waited for me to say something. He finally parked the car and looked at me, waiting for me to speak, but I wasn't sure what to say, where to begin. I knew Paquito from the Partido Ortodoxo, but he had, as far as I knew, no connection with the Triple A, so why was he waiting for me by my house, alerting me, and how did he know the person described in the paper was me? As if reading my mind, and enjoying my puzzlement, he went on to tell me that Raúl Roa had called him and had simply asked him to find me and tell me I should go into hiding. Roa hadn't explained anything, and the only reason he had called Paquito was because he was a friend of Paquito's family and knew Paquito to be an Ortodoxo and assumed, correctly, that he knew me. It was only when he bought the afternoon newspaper, as he waited for me across the street from my house, that Paquito realized the reason for the warning he was delivering.

Emotions hate solitude; they never visit us one at a time but appear in combinations and arrangements that have no regard for the canons of common logic and respond to a sequence of their own making. I was afraid and confused, and exhilarated and proud, and glad that the police, the police of the dictator, were after me. ¡*Carajo*! But I had no idea what to do because I didn't know what was going on, and Paquito was no help because he knew even less. At least I knew that the man who had driven me to the meeting with Aureliano and the woman in the house when we got there were not the man and woman in the newspaper. But who were these people? What had happened to the man and woman I met? What about the young guy, the one who was supposed to be a military man?

I left Paquito. He felt good about having helped me, and probably also about having obliged Roa. For my part, I had to figure out how I should be feeling, so I walked for a little while, bought two evening newspapers and found an almost empty Chinese restaurant where I could sit down, read, and figure out what to do next.

I had some pork fried rice—I always had pork fried rice at Chinese restaurants—and I looked through the newspapers and found nothing new. In fact, the early afternoon paper Paquito had showed me had more information about the incident than either of the evening ones. These two just reported the near miss; the arrest of the couple and some general references to Aureliano having held meetings in their house up until nearly the very moment the police arrived—nothing more, nothing about me. I was relieved that my description was not deemed important enough to be included, which was definitely a good sign since these two newspapers were mouthpieces of the Batista government and would print only, and exactly, what the police wanted them to. But something about my absence in the later papers bothered me. It meant that identifying and finding me was not of much interest to anyone; in other words, that I wasn't all that important.

I called my house and spoke to my mother. No, no one had been looking for me; no visitors, no phone calls. I told her I had eaten out and was going to a union meeting. I walked some more and thought through the situation, and the more I thought about it, the more I became convinced that the police had not gotten to the man who took me to the house or to the woman I met there. I assumed the police could have found who these two were through the couple they had arrested, but knowing who they were and finding them were two different things, and the fact that they were not mentioned in the newspapers, that there were no references to them at all, meant that either the owners of the house had not given their names to the police or that the police had made the arrested couple talk but were not letting out what they knew. But if I, the least important spoke in the wheel, had been alerted to the developing situation, they surely must have been too and were most likely in hiding by now. This meant that the only people who knew who I was were safe, and since there was nothing in the evening papers to question that, I didn't think there was much need for me to worry, but just to make sure, I telephoned Roa.

Ada, Roa's wife, answered the phone, and I made a point of asking for Dean Roa in a very formal manner, saying I was a student trying to get some information, without mentioning my name. "Paquito told me that you suggested I change courses," I told him, or something like that, when he came on the line, and there was a brief pause before he replied, "Yes, that was before I spoke to your professor. I thought it would be a good idea, but after talking to him I think you are doing fine." "How's he?" I asked, assuming we were reading one another. "Oh, he's fine," Roa said. "And his wife?" I added, taking a shot in the dark, hoping Roa knew about the woman who had been in the house but was not in the newspaper. "She's fine, too," he said, and added, "I think they're going on vacation someplace." We spoke for a few more moments about school matters and what courses I should be taking the following year, and before hanging up he asked me to stop by his office within the next few days.

I felt reassured. If I had understood Roa, both the man who had taken me to see Aureliano and the woman who was at the house were safe. The couple in the paper, the owners of the house who were in police custody, had never seen me, and although the military guy with us in the house had been identified by the evening newspapers as an undercover government agent, it was safe to assume he didn't have a clue about who I was. If he had known about me, I reasoned, no detailed description of what I looked like and what I was wearing would have been released to the press, since it could only alert me. No, I thought, if he had known who I was the police would gone for me and, I sadly reflected, they would have had little difficulty finding me. Armed with such assumptions I decided to go home, but first I called once more, and ambled for a while in the neighborhood, and as I went to bed that night I took comfort in the fact that my bedroom was at the rear of the house, and that if the police were to show up at the front I would have several avenues of escape available through the back—and although this assurance rested on imagination more than on fact or experience, it let me sleep easier.

The next morning offered a rude awakening. There on the front page of the paper was a picture of the owner of the house, the man on the front page of the previous day's papers, but now he was dead. Actually there were two pictures of him: one, a close-up of his face, which seemed to have only the vaguest resemblance to the face in the previous day's pictures, and the other of his body lying face down in a courtyard next to the wall of a building. According to the report, he had fallen out a window of the Buró de Investigaciones, the secret police headquarters, as he was being questioned. The identification of the building made the photograph even more disturbing; I could easily picture the place, and its surroundings, and its atmosphere. *Esto se está poniendo feo, muy feo,* this is getting ugly, very ugly, I told myself as I read and reread the article, and kept looking at the dead face. Defenestrated! I had never taken that word seriously—a whole verb devoted to the act of pushing someone out a window had always seemed ridiculous to me. I remember reading about some Czech politician who had been killed that way, which was how I learned the word existed, and I had kept it in my mind as a kind of Eastern European peculiarity, a gloomy Slavic way of disposing of people with a blatantly implausible excuse. Fall out of a window during interrogation—who the hell could believe that?

I wasn't in the mood for breakfast. I left the house in a hurry mumbling some excuse to my mother and began to walk in the general direction of the bank but without any idea as to what I should do, if anything. I didn't want to think of the dead man, but I forced myself to, and I stopped along the way and sat in front of a cup of *café con leche,* staring at it more than drinking it, while I tried to put my mind in order, which, given my hyperactive nature and the news of the day, was not easy, but I kept on trying, beginning at the end. Why was this guy killed? I asked myself and was surprised that the answer was not difficult to guess.

He was killed because he didn't talk. If he had talked, had cooperated, why kill him then? Sure, there could've been an accident, but being pushed out of a window, fucking defenestrated, no chance of that being an accident. Maybe a cover-up for an accident? No, not that either. The police didn't need any cover-up, they could do whatever they wanted, kill, torture, imprison; there was no one to question, challenge, stop or punish them. That was the bottom line and everybody knew it, and that was what we were trying to get rid of. So he didn't talk, which meant either he knew something but wouldn't tell or he didn't know what his questioners wanted to learn—a miserable situation to be in.

Those were the only two possibilities I could think of: the man couldn't talk because he didn't know, or he wouldn't talk because conviction had prevailed over fear. I opted for the first because it seemed the more reasonable of the two, not because I was passing judgment on the human condition; and because the face I had seen in the newspaper was soft and round with a flaccid contour, and lacking the strong lines I would have identified with a heroic stance. Absurd, I now realize, but what do you expect from an eighteen-year-old? So I concluded that the poor man didn't know much and that his ignorance had done him in with the police interrogators—not a very patient bunch, I was sure. So he didn't know what the police wanted to know. And what was it that police would have wanted to know?

The police would have wanted to know where Aureliano was, and who were those with him that night. My conversation with Roa led me to believe Aureliano was safe, which meant the dead man knew nothing about his whereabouts after Aureliano had left the house. And the fact that the man who took me there and the woman who was in the house were now in hiding, according to Roa, meant that the dead man knew who they were, and had probably told the police. If they had been unknown to the owner, there would have been no reason for them to hide. I concluded that the unfortunate man had just lent his house for the evening to trusted friends, the man who drove me and the woman there when we arrived, but had not been privy to anything else. Maybe he knew Aureliano would use his house that evening, but nothing else. I felt reassured, drank my *café con leche,* and went to work.

The year 1952 was coming to an end and I had my hands full with politics and the University and front-tennis, at which I was getting very good, and with the bank; and then more than my hands could handle since, without knowing exactly how I got there, I was making love to the sexiest woman I had ever met. Her name was Blanca, and she was tall and shapely with the kind of green eyes that some Cuban mulattoes had and which brought an exotic element to the mix. We just began talking one afternoon in the Plaza Cadenas, casually and about nothing, and within a couple of days we were in bed. And the only reason it took even that long was my own ignorance about finding the proper accommodations for such a purpose.

Havana was full of *posadas,* houses of assignation, catering simultaneously to pretended morality and economic reality. Some were on busy streets and others in secluded areas, some obvious and cheap, others difficult to identify and expensive; enough of them to satisfy a wide range of variation in sensibility, taste and pocket. So before you brought a woman to a *posada* you had to figure out both whether she would be offended by the suggestion and, provided she wasn't, which one you should take her to. And these were not light matters, since I had never done anything like that before and had no knowledge, practical or otherwise, of how to go about it.

If I was going to err, it was going to be on the side of good taste and seclusion, largely because I realized that there might well be a connection between my decision on this matter and Blanca's willingness; but this did not make things any less complicated, since the truth was that I didn't know how to put the proposition into words, words that would fit my idea of a polite way of asking a woman to get in the sack. When she asked where we were going I couldn't get a clear answer out, and when I couldn't find the damned place she said we were walking in circles, and I kept making vague reference to "this address" without using the word *posada,* and when I finally found the metal gate that led to it and we went in, the actual building was completely hidden behind a row of black bushes, and it was so dark all around us that I lost my footing and went down on the wet grass. Since I fell without a sound, Blanca thought I had just disappeared and began calling my name in a low voice until I was up again next to her, with *guayabera* and trousers soiled and wet to the touch. It still took an eternity to find the door and ring the bell, and the sound it made was so subdued, almost inaudible, that I was seriously considering giving the whole thing up when the door finally opened.

There was no one behind the open door, the way it was supposed to be, because a *posada,* a fancy one anyhow, had to assure the absolute privacy demanded by the mores and pretenses of the Cuban psyche. Sex was widely practiced but narrowly acknowledged, males were expected to engage in it before marriage, the more the better, across all race and class lines, but females were not, especially if they were middle class, white, and young. After a certain age the strictures softened for women, but appearances were retained. Married middle-class men were allowed affairs, but they were expected to keep up appearances, and there was a sharp distinction between screwing around with discretion and screwing around in a way that was embarrassing or insulting to the wife.

Ultimately, though, the trysts with Blanca didn't lead anywhere and that was the way it was supposed to be, at least in my mind. She was "fuckable" not "marriageable" in my family's classification of women and therefore not suitable as a *novia,* or formal girlfriend. And a *novia* was what I wanted at that point, so after a while I stopped seeing Blanca, although I could have continued having sex with her while I looked for a *novia,* or even after I had found one, so I guess I didn't want to see her any longer. She didn't seem upset at all when I told her of my decision, or, if she was, she was able to hide it completely.

The idea of a *novia* did not have a clear form in my mind, but it didn't interfere in any way with the satisfaction of the sexual instinct, or with anything else, and it had no special urgency attached to it; it simply formed part of an overall equation in which a man was to have a cause to fight for and a woman to cherish—and that was the extent of my concern with the matter.

CHAPTER NINE

As months went by, Batista's grip tightened, and the dark and tired political landscape gave way to new vibrant colors, fueled by youthful enthusiasm, idealism and candor. At the University a new set of student leaders was beginning to push aside the corrupt clique that had previously controlled the student federation. Union politics took a new direction, as challenges to the ruling officials were no longer based on specific grievances or demands but on rejection of their connivance with Batista and his government. The Triple A offered a way to rid the country of the dictator and to bring democracy and civilian rule back, and by so promising it helped to erase old antagonisms and forge new alliances, dividing the opposition into two clear camps: those denying the government legitimacy and prepared to fight and those willing to reach some sort of accommodation with Batista—*los duros,* the hard, and *los flojos,* the soft; the revolutionaries and the patsies.

In truth, however, neither I nor anyone I knew had any clear idea of what we meant by "revolution," although we had no qualms throwing the term around, referring to it frequently, emotionally captivated by it. At the University, the word "revolution" had almost mystical connotations, denoting no specific plan of action or objective but embodying a sense of epic idealism that united the anti-Batista students and gave them the impetus to brush discrepancies aside. The Batista military coup had magically transformed the previously languid campus into a spirited center of activity allowing, actually prodding, students to reconnect with their historical tradition of political militancy. The Federación Estudiantil Universitaria, the University Students' Federation, commonly referred to as the FEU, quickly became the country's most committed and vocal antigovernment force, with public meetings, marches and demonstrations succeeding one another with increasing regularity. I could hardly believe the pace and magnitude of the transformation, and felt uplifted and inspired by the campus's new atmosphere, and tried to spend as much time as I could there.

At the bank things could not have been going any better. Feliciano was taking care of the day-to-day duties of the steward and I found another employee, Reinol González, *el bizco*, the cross-eyed one, willing to work diligently on the preparation of an opposition slate for the forthcoming union elections. *El bizco* was a preternaturally intense individual highly committed to the Catholic Workers Youth Movement—the Catholic Church's answer to Communist labor unions—who combined the zeal of the missionary with a most un-Cuban gravity of character and deportment. Some people thought this was the product of his being an orphan, while others, in more convoluted thinking, thought that his disinclination to laugh and his dour Catholic militancy were the two connected outcomes of an ingrained idiosyncratic personality that had developed on its own instead of resulting from childhood circumstances. Whichever the case, Reinol was ideally suited for the job and we were on our way to challenging the union leadership, and although I still was the union head at the Banco Continental Cubano, I now had enough time to do my job, begin recruiting for the Triple A, keep in touch with the University and, once in a while, hit the books.

An old Spanish proverb runs *Quien mucho abarca poco aprieta*, he who tries to grab too much ends up with a weak hold on everything. I was aware of this but had a difficult time concentrating on just one thing. What I wanted most was to increase my involvement in University activities, to fight the government from that vantage point, to emulate the deeds of the 1920s and 1930s students who were in my mind cut from the same cloth as the Black Corsair and Ignacio Agramonte. I could see that I was well positioned as a union officer to have an impact, but I could not gather within myself enough zeal and commitment to that role to give it the required attention—it wasn't attractive enough, it did not strike the romantic and adventurous chord my young and wandering mind needed. The Triple A, on the other hand, offered an appealing field of action with its promise to deal a quick and deadly blow to the dictatorship, to rid the country of the military usurpers in one clean sweep, so I decided to concentrate my efforts there.

Recruiting for the Triple A was not as easy as I had first imagined. When I approached my friends from the Partido Ortodoxo, only a handful responded positively. Some were reticent about Aureliano and his role in the Prío administration, others, to my continuous surprise and dismay, wanted some accommodation with Batista through elections, and most, like Pepe Iglesias, seemed to have had the wind taken from their sails and had sunk into unshakable passivity. I found it very difficult to understand and accept that the same individuals who a few months earlier had been loudly clamoring for radical change, making speeches for the renovation of society, advocating an end to corruption and political shenanigans, would reject the Triple A's call. It was of no avail that I explained to them that our function would be one of supporting an armed action, not direct involvement, or that no commitment beyond this support was expected, or that after civilian rule and democracy were restored everyone would be free to follow his own political course. I thought these were reasonable and persuasive arguments, but they failed to impress most of my listeners. Even the handful willing to join me in supporting the Triple A seemed unmoved by, or uninterested in, the logic of my disquisition. Kiko Baeza, the pro-Franco Paquito, Macías and the few others who said yes had said so immediately, before I had a chance to explain exactly what was required of them.

With reluctance, and sadness, I saw that my romantic and idealized vision of the fight against the ogre Batista was not shared by those I had assumed would share it. So when Raúl Roa told me I should meet some of the Triple A operatives who were putting together a clandestine antigovernment newspaper, I looked upon this as an opportunity to work with people who, I hoped, felt as I did.

Roa referred to them as *monstruos,* monsters. In Cuban parlance this meant larger than life, superhuman in a positive sense. As I was, however, beginning to recognize the man's weakness for hyperbole and his proclivity to exaggeration, I wasn't sure what to expect, though I was still impressed by the fact that someone like Raúl Roa, proven revolutionary of the 1930s, close collaborator of Aureliano and pillar of the Triple A, thought so highly of them. Who were they? What type of subversive newspapers were they working on?

Roa had arranged for me to meet Jorge Tallet, one of the *monstruos,* that same afternoon right outside his office, and after a brief introduction he left us alone. I expected a *come-candela,* a fire-eater, a boastful and action-oriented type; instead I stood facing a mild-mannered and soft-spoken guy with a friendly smile on a round baby face who, although older than I, looked not a day over sixteen. We talked for a long time, but Tallet said little specific about what they were doing or who they actually were. He just mentioned that some people, himself obviously included, were putting together a newspaper attacking Batista and his rule, and that its publication should pave the way for the Triple A's armed insurrection. As we spoke, it seemed clear that neither of us knew much about this armed insurrection, who was planning it, when it was to take place or what it entailed. It was not even clear why Roa had brought us together since my task and his, even if both parts of one overall strategy, seemed unrelated. The only thing we knew, or assumed, was that we were engaged in the same effort to overthrow the government and bring back civilian rule. We talked for a while, and I parted without any new mission or objective but feeling I had found a kindred spirit.

There was something very peaceful, quiet and attractive about Havana University in the afternoon that lasted until late in the day when the sun began its retreat and before it took the quick plunge beyond the horizon with which it ends it daily sojourn in the tropics. In the morning, the Plaza Cadenas was a noisy epicenter of motion, as students, professors, uniformed *bedeles* and visitors mingled about, engaged in all sorts of animated discussions, and the place at that time exuded a sense of frantic activity and feverish diligence. What students didn't seem to do much of was going to class, since there was often little sense in doing this; in the Schools of Law and Social Science, classroom lectures were basically redundant, as the professors, if keeping to a dependable lecturing schedule, would just repeat what the textbook said. So why bother? It was more rewarding to be outside with friends or in the coffee shop in the school's basement sipping the Cuban brew and discussing politics or baseball or whatever young people talk about when their energy is abundant and their hormones reign supreme. So in the morning, when all but a few classes were held, the University was vibrant with sound and movement as if fueled by the rising power of the sun, but as the afternoon arrived and the soft Atlantic wind refreshed University Hill and the Plaza Cadenas, the buildings emptied and only occasional silent figures would be seen walking by and quickly disappearing, as if propelled by the invisible force of the breeze coming from the sea.

As I sat in the Plaza Cadenas after Jorge Tallet and I had parted company, I forced myself to accept another reality I found incomprehensible: the country was settling down under Batista. The high degree of uncertainty and nervousness of the first months was giving way to accommodation. With the exception of the Communist Party's newspaper, *Hoy*, which had no credibility beyond that party's ranks, the press had buckled under the new master and only sporadically would a forceful critical piece see the light of day. Surrendered, too, had the business community and the Catholic Church and every other civic group or organization that could have, and should have, opposed the arbitrary rule of the military, the suppression of elections and the discarding of the constitutional process. As I thought about it, I realized that there were factors at work I had never suspected before. After the coup I had visualized the country as neatly divided between Batista and his henchmen on the one side and the rest of us on the other. I had seen an unbridgeable chasm between a self-appointed master and his subjugated subjects, and had assumed that the latter would reject and forcefully oppose this arrangement. Now I could see I had been wrong. All kind of people with all kind of excuses were, if not openly flocking to Batista's camp, complacently adapting themselves to the new situation and, therefore, lending their support to his regime. Disgusting, I thought, but undeniably true, I had to admit.

It must have been late in 1952 when Fidel Castro asked Pepe Iglesias and me to go with him to his beach house and spend the night. He was politically courting Pepe, who remained head of the rapidly disintegrating but still substantial Havana youth section of the Partido Ortodoxo. I was asked along only because I happened to be with Pepe that evening in one of my last visits to the party's headquarters. Fidel still cut a rather ridiculous figure at the time as far as we were concerned, as he would come to the Prado Street building and shut himself behind closed doors with some young guys from the nearby countryside and harangue them mercilessly hour after hour. We would shake our heads in disbelief and smile to one another, and some of the more daring among us would go and knock at the door and run away, and inevitably Fidel would open the door and seeing no one there would swear and curse, and as many times as the intrepid pranksters repeated the deed, out would come Fidel, verbally fulminating and threatening and then slamming the door shut as he went back inside—and almost immediately we would hear his voice again, lecturing and exhorting and appealing and cajoling.

It was after one of those sessions, after all of Fidel's *guajiros* were gone, that he and Abel Santamaría,* one of his few Havana followers, came over to where Pepe and I were talking and invited us. At first we refused, pointing out that we didn't have bathing suits with us, but Fidel offered to drive to our respective homes to get them. In fact, he said, he could do this easily since he was taking Abel home and Pepe and I both

---

*Abel Santamaría accompanied Fidel in the attack on the Moncada barracks in July 1953. He was captured, tortured and murdered.

lived somewhere along the way. So Pepe agreed, although rather reluctantly, and I was happy to go along, partly because I had nothing better to do the next day, a Saturday, and liked the idea of going to the beach, and partly because I was curious as to what lure Fidel would try to use on Pepe, who, as far as I could tell, had no intention or inclination to get himself involved in any antigovernment activity.

In my mind Fidel was still an individual not to be trusted, given his in-laws' connections with the government, and I had not eliminated completely, although I thought it far-fetched, the possibility that he was actually an infiltrator, or agent provocateur working for one of the several secret police organizations run by the government—and by his brother-in-law.

I had seen Fidel many times before, but, except for the neighborhood meeting he attended while campaigning for Congress, I had never been with him for any length of time. Now, he talked and talked and talked. He was talking as we went by Pepe's house to pick up his swimming gear, he was talking as we dropped Abel in the Santos Suárez area, he was talking as he drove by my house, he was talking when I left the car to go inside to get my things, and he was talking when I came back. It was well past midnight, late by Havana standards, and I assumed we would go directly to the beach, but no, Fidel wanted to stop and eat. We stopped at a bar-restaurant sort of place that was on the way and which Fidel knew, and we ate there, but eating did not prevent Fidel from talking, and the meal took the form of a monologue on Cuba's problems, on the ineptness and corruption of its politicians and on the need for change. It was all couched in legal and constitutional terms with constant references to the 1940 Cuban constitution that Batista had trampled over and discarded, and I remember being excruciatingly bored by what sounded like a never-ending legal brief with every point repeated three, four, five times, as if to exhaust the listener into acquiescence.

Fidel was courting Pepe Iglesias because Pepe had been the charismatic leader of the largest group of young people in the Partido Ortodoxo, and since Fidel was beginning to advocate the creation of a new political force independent of the old politicians, Pepe would have made an ideal recruit. Fidel, of course, had no way of knowing what I knew then about Pepe, that he was going to sit this one out. Kiko Baeza, who had known Pepe since high school, had a psychological interpretation of Pepe's attitude. He thought Pepe had been affected by the death of an innocent bystander in a shootout in which he had been involved, and despite the earlier history of violence that had earned him the *el gatillo* moniker, he had developed a strong reluctance to engage in it again. It sounded good to me when Kiko expounded it, and it was consistent with what I could see of Pepe's character. If the man was not willing to oppose Batista with force, he was equally unwilling to help the government by supporting initiatives or compromises that would validate and legitimize the military coup, and this meant two things: he did have some integrity, and, as a result, he was condemning himself to political obliviousness. But Fidel didn't know any of this and was still talking when we arrived at his rented beach house at almost three o'clock in the morning, and I was shown a room in the back where there was a bed and fell asleep within seconds, still hearing Fidel's voice.

I wasn't sure exactly what it was about Fidel that I didn't like, but I knew first thing next morning what I did like about him—his wife, Mirta. She was not only pretty and friendly but radiated a kind of lightness, a gracefulness, that was in complete contrast to her overbearing husband. I got up around nine or ten o'clock in the morning, very late for me, and found my way into the dining room where Mirta offered a friendly smile and a breakfast of *café con leche y pan tostado,* which she went on to prepare and serve. She told me that Fidel had gone for a swim and that Pepe was still asleep, as was her son, Fidelito, and we spoke and I ate as slowly as I could. I have no recollection of any subject of conversation, definitely not politics, as her father was one of Batista's ministers and her brother the head of a pro-Batista youth organization in addition to his police activities, but remember only the sharp contrast between her personality and Fidel's, and how restful and comfortable it felt sitting at the dining room table of the beach house having breakfast and talking to her.

Pepe, a notorious late sleeper, would not wake up, so I went to the beach for a swim by myself. As I ventured out not too far from where I could touch bottom, I noticed Fidel in the distance, two or three hundred yards from shore, swimming long laps back and forth across the horizon. I enjoyed the warmth and the mild waves of the tropical sea, still uncertain about Fidel, and wondering what Pepe actually thought and how incongruous the Fidel-Mirta couple was, and thinking how Aureliano and the Triple A would soon make their move and turn things right side up. The evening before, Fidel had disparaged Aureliano and the Triple A, together with almost everyone else in Cuban politics, but since I wasn't sure where Fidel really stood, I didn't give his remarks much weight, and following Pepe's lead, didn't challenge his opinion or dispute any of his assertions. I wondered also whether Pepe's silence in the face of Fidel's unceasing barrage of views, assumptions, opinions and judgments was the result of the same reticence I felt to engage Fidel in discussion, or of Pepe's own increasing apathy, or just his acceptance of the obvious fact that Fidel could talk but couldn't listen.

Time went by without any news from the Triple A, and as the pre-Batista political scene continued to disintegrate, a new reality began to take its place. Those who had been the leading political figures and the electoral powerhouses of the two dominant parties up to March 10, 1952, were now, for all practical purposes, gone, as were their parties. All of a sudden, almost as if by magic, traditional electoral politicians had nothing to say and nothing to offer. Batista had forced them into a bind from which they couldn't extricate themselves. Either they accepted the rule of the military, hoping it would eventually bring some electoral opportunity in which they could reclaim their former influence and privileges, or they had to advocate and engage in armed resistance. The first alternative was unpromising since in any electoral deal Batista would hold all the trump cards and would arrange the terms of any contest to his convenience while, in addition, the anti-Batista militants would brand those members of the opposition participating in elections as traitors. The second alternative, fighting Batista, meant putting life and fortune at risk, and this was a highly unattractive option for the aging and corrupt individuals who had controlled Cuban politics before the coup. Caught between two unattractive choices, the rulers of the old order did nothing.

As the political ground shifted and the country restructured itself along new partisan lines, the void created by the vaporization of the previous order, following a basic law of political dynamics, began to be filled with new individuals and groups. The path was an uncharted one, since the emerging groups, other than the Triple A, were only embryonic formations, handfuls of young people getting together to discuss what should be done and to take some antigovernment action which, in most cases, consisted in distributing propaganda leaflets and delivering impromptu anti-Batista harangues in movie houses and other public places.

Well over three months after my meeting with Aureliano, I had been assigned to work with Manolito Cobo, and he raised my first doubts about the Triple A. Up to that point, all the Triple A members I had met were friends or colleagues of Aureliano, individuals who had been anti-Batista activists in the thirties and forties and who were involved in educational pursuits as university professors, schoolteachers, administrators or athletic coaches; they were to a man anticommunist leftists with a nationalist bent, and they all, something rare among Cubans, seemed genuinely modest. I liked them and realized that, like Aureliano, some had held government posts in the Auténtico administrations without enriching themselves, and I found that reassuring. But despite their similarities in background, in some ways my co-conspirators constituted an incongruous group. There was Roa, skinny, wiry, and constantly gesticulating while spewing tales, gossip, jokes, theories, conjectures and opinions on all possible subjects, and who was congenitally incapable, I was certain, of keeping a secret for long; and there was Salvador Vilaseca, tall, gaunt, parsimonious of movement and word and devoid of all social graces and who was, I was convinced, capable of keeping a secret forever. Somewhere between these two fell Willy Barrientos, tall, athletic, jovial and sports-oriented; and Mario Fortuny, the driver who had tried to disorient me on the way to the meeting with Aureliano and who had gone into hiding for some time with his wife, the woman I had met at the Víbora house, and who was now back aboveground, and who was expansive and friendly and sedate, with very pleasant and reassuring manners; and Ignacio Fiterre, who had been a high school math teacher reputed to be demanding and strict and known for the dread he provoked among students; and there was Reinaldo López Quintana, whom I barely knew, but who told me, in the only conversation we ever had one evening on the steps of the University Library, that he was going to be killed, and by whom, and who went on to describe exactly how it would happen and who a few days later was killed in precisely the manner and by the man he had foretold; and there was the inseparable pair Mario Escoto and Pepe Utrera, both teachers at Havana's Normal School, the former serious, reticent, and far from friendly, and the latter expansive, amicable, quite talkative and nicknamed *el cojo,* the lame one, thanks to a gunshot wound inflicted by the police during Batista's previous dictatorial incarnation. And the sobriquet outlived the limp, which was not very surprising given the propensity of the Spanish language to coin and use adjectives denoting physical handicaps—just as a *cojo* is a man with a mangled leg, a *manco* is someone missing the use of an arm, a *tuerto* one without an eye and a *chiclán* one with only one testicle.

I had never before been part of an underground organization and I didn't know what to expect from the Triple A, so I saw no contradiction between the subversive nature of the enterprise and the casualness that seemed to govern the members' interactions. It was closer to a club or a fraternity than to a clandestine organization, but I took this to be the natural adjunct of comradeship and was quite happy to join in and be accepted into such a group. But Manolito Cobo was the Triple A member I didn't like—and I didn't like him at all. Manolito possessed none of the positive attributes I found in the others. He was petulant, self-aggrandizing and blatantly concerned with potential future benefits rather than with ethics, ideals, dreams or even ideas; and I couldn't understand what he was doing in the Triple A, why I had been asked to work with him, or what that work could consist of. And he didn't have a clue either. He had been told to work with me. That was it.

So what do you do when you don't know what you are supposed to do but whatever you might do could affect the main undertaking you are involved in? When you don't know when that main undertaking is going to be undertaken, under what circumstances or by whom? Faced with this predicament, the two of us were left to nurse our mutual dislike into full-blown detestation. It was obvious that he disliked me as much as I disliked him, maybe even more, and that he was as mortified to be saddled with me as I was to being exposed to his crassness. We usually met at his place of business, a furniture factory cum warehouse where he put together sofas and couches and chairs out of flimsy wood from discarded boxes he collected from all kind of places including trash dumps. It seemed to me that his entire enterprise consisted of putting together a chair or a sofa or a couch that pretended to be something that it was not and could never be—a dependable piece of furniture. And after the ramshackle wooden skeleton had been hidden behind garish fabric, the item was ready to be sold on installments to some unsuspecting soul. What a way to make a living! The whole thing was repellent to me, and it must have been my reaction to the nature of his business that sealed the character of our relationship, since the more he talked and bragged about it, the more difficult I found it to hide my disdain.

The incipient disillusionment sparked by Manolito began to fester, as week followed week, month followed month, and we were ending 1952 with no sign of life, of any life, from the Triple A. Rumors would emerge periodically and word would spread that a confrontation was imminent, that arms were being gathered, that the military had gone on alert or that someone, somewhere, was about to do something—but nothing would ever happen. Batista's control was hardening, and the only visible opposition came from the University students who marched and demonstrated and shouted against the government through loudspeakers at the bottom of the steps leading to University Hill on San Lázaro Street.

But there was still the ongoing effort of Jorge Tallet and the *monstruos*. Jorge was the polar opposite of Manolito Cobo—it probably would have been impossible to find two more dissimilar individuals. Weeks, if not months, had passed since our first encounter outside Roa's office when he called me to a meeting to discuss the distribution of his newspaper, which was to be called *Liberación*. I was struck immediately by the fact that he was on time. Cubans had a very indifferent attitude towards punctuality, one that ranged from the irresponsible to the offensive and which, due to my lack of patience and compulsive personality, irritated me to no end. So when I arrived at the arranged place a couple of minutes early and found Jorge already there I was impressed.

Jorge Tallet was the son of a renowned Cuban poet, José Zacarías Tallet, and the nephew, through his mother, of one of the most romantic figures in Cuban contemporary history, Rubén Martínez Villena, also a poet as well as a hero of the fight against Machado. Jorge was completely unassuming in an environment where modesty was the exception and blowing one's horn, usually stridently and with little justification, the rule. The more we talked, first about the subject that had brought us together and then about a multitude of unrelated ones that went from politics to history to philosophy to movies to girls, my initial positive impression was not only confirmed, but surpassed.

Talking to Jorge Tallet was a new experience for me. He listened, and I began to realize what an extraordinary faculty that was, to listen; to actually hear what another person was saying. I didn't have to go far to understand its rarity; I was as prone to not listening as anyone else. I would hear the words, but as I did, I was already processing them through the machinery of my own views, experiences and preconceived notions. Rather than try to understand what someone was telling me, what he meant, what value there was to his words, I simply reacted to them as they left the other person's mouth, placing them immediately and mechanically within my own system of references and preferences; evaluating and judging, accepting and discarding what the person said, neither looking into nor trying to understand it. But Tallet was different. You could disagree with him and he would think about it, examine what you said, reexamine what he had said, compare the two, and the matter, whatever it was, would be truly open for discussion; and when he did that it was difficult not to feel compelled to oblige in return.

The five or six people putting together *Liberación* considered themselves an almost, if not totally, independent part of the Triple A. They had agreed to put out the newspaper for the organization, but to nothing else, and I began to know who these individuals were, what they were doing and what they thought. The group consisted of three Martínez—Julio César, Emilio and occasionally Emilio's father, Norberto—Carlos Franqui and his sidekick Rubén, and Tallet, and among the six of them they had almost all the skills necessary to design, write and print a newspaper. No one knew exactly how Emilio had secured all the heavy equipment required to print a full-size paper, all of which had been placed in a house in the residential Vedado neighborhood rented from an unsuspecting landlord. The group learned that the owner of one of the printing presses they were using was a policeman when the man dropped by unexpectedly to collect the lease money. The owner-policeman, when he realized what his press was being used for, turned right around and left without collecting. The members of the group held an impromptu emergency council to determine the best course of action—flee the house, find a new location for the equipment or silence the policeman before he had a chance to blow the whistle on the operation—and as they discussed these options, Rubén went out to search for the man. But the whole exercise became moot the following day when they learned the policeman, in an apparent precautionary move to avoid implication or explanation, had fled the country. Since nothing came of the incident, it seemed the man had panicked at the idea of having to disclose the use to which his property had been put.[†]

Printing a newspaper in those days was a noisy and complicated task with presses and linotypes and molten lead and bronze and huge rolls of paper, and Tallet and his gang were printing a subversive, hard-hitting antigovernment newspaper under the flimsiest of cover, in a private residence, across the street from a taxi stand and veiled only by a small sign leaning on the garden fence in front of the house that read, Escuela Nacional de Artes Gráficas, National School of Graphic Arts. But they kept at it against all odds, and the only significant obstacle they faced was near the end of the process, when they couldn't find a linotype operator willing to take the risk. They had approached several professed anti-Batista individuals who claimed they wanted to do something against the dictatorship and offered their services for free, but upon seeing the

[†]After Castro took over the country, Emilio Martínez became editor of the Havana newspaper *Diario Libre* and was eventually removed from this post and forced to flee the island when, trying to live up to the publication's title, he reproduced past pronouncements of Fidel Castro contradicting the new government policies and published a translation of Milovan Djilas's *The New Class*. Carlos Franqui joined Castro in the mountains and became the editor of the first official newspaper of the new government, *Revolución*. He eventually broke with the regime and went into exile in Europe. His sidekick, Rubén Hernández, became a loyal functionary of the new Cuban order. I lost track of the other members of the *Liberación* group.

actual material they were to print, refused. Eventually they found an operator who was politically disinterested and who simply wanted to know how much he would be paid. With the price for his labor agreed, he went to the house, never raised a question about the newspaper's content, did a first-rate job, got paid and left. *Liberación* was ready to hit the streets.

By the beginning of 1953, my frustration with the Triple A had begun to deepen. The new year arrived and nothing, absolutely nothing, had been done to topple, attack, weaken or challenge Batista's grip. My spirits had been lifted a bit when *Liberación* came out in December, as it was highly gratifying to see my feelings and ideas in print, in actual professional-looking print, and to read articles attacking Batista and calling for revolt and demanding a return to civilian rule. I especially relished the headline, large black letters reading "Navidades sin Batista," "Christmas without Batista," which was simultaneously instigation and longing, and encapsulated the best present I could imagine for the season. But that Christmas came and that Christmas went and Batista was still there, and still nothing from the Triple A; the organization was existing in a state of complete inertness, in some inescapable stupor in which nothing was attempted and nothing was accomplished.

Even though my romantic life continued to be plagued with frustrations, being a revolutionary more than made up for social disappointments and discomforts. The feeling of being involved in a transcendental task, in an effort to redress a collective wrong, and the idea of risking my freedom, if not my life, in the service of this purpose, did wonders for my ego. I was on top of the world and at that moment I wouldn't have traded places with anyone, hot little island, mosquitoes and all. In my head, I had finally joined the Black Corsair and Ignacio Agramonte in their unending quest for justice, and I no longer felt ashamed of the unheroic tenor of the time I was living in.

I still wasn't sure, however, what it meant to be a revolutionary, but I was pretty certain it included carrying a gun. My efforts to acquire one, although inconsistent, eventually paid off when Pepe Iglesias handed me a .32 caliber pistol. The only reason I knew it was .32 caliber was because he told me, and he also showed me how to work its automatic mechanism and he apologized for not having any bullets to go with it. It was unclear whether the gun was intended as a present or Pepe just wanted to get rid of it. He had placed it in my hands after one of the last meetings of the Ortodoxo youth section, which had been held at the Havana cemetery to honor some past revolutionary deed and ended up being taken over by Fidel Castro and his *guajiros*. It was painfully clear now that the youth component of the Ortodoxos had followed its parent organization on the path to oblivion, and Pepe's gesture was symptomatic of the group's surrender. I knew he was leaving politics for good and thought this was the reason for his getting rid of the gun, and I saw the gift as a sort of symbolic gesture—a way of formalizing his withdrawal.

I ran my fingers across the gun's black metallic surface, hard and perfectly smooth, lost in the contemplation of countless heroic deeds to come. Whatever element fuels the atavistic drives and fantasies of the young male mind had materialized within me, bringing a blithe trance to my senses. I knew I didn't need a gun for any of the antigovernment activities I was engaged in, or for anything else, and that it would increase my risk without providing any counterbalancing advantage, but still, feeling the pistol in my hand, looking at it, I wanted it—and took it.

My thrill was short-lived. Less than an hour later, as I stood up to get off a bus, the gun, which I had stuck under my belt, next to my right back pocket, slid down my buttocks, through the right leg of my baggy trousers—if only I hadn't been so damned skinny—and smacked loudly onto the wooden floor. I saw the four or five passengers near me look down at the gun, then at me and back at the gun, but I couldn't move, my mind went blank and I realized for the first time how cold one could feel in the heat of the tropics. The whole incident couldn't have lasted more than a few seconds, and all I remember is that no one said anything, or if they did I didn't hear it, and that my brain was stuck in neutral. My body must have been responding to some instinctual command as I bent down, picked up the gun from the floor, put it back under my belt and stepped off the bus.

"You're a stupid jerk," I told myself when my brain finally got back in gear, "a jerk many times over, a super-jerk." The seduction of the gun, the childish desire to stick it under my belt, movie-style, when I could have easily secured it in my pocket or carried it in a paper bag, had been unabated and inexcusable stupidity. Had a policeman been on the bus, I surely would have been arrested. For an antigovernment activist to be armed was no minor offense in the eyes of the Batista police, and the idea of being beaten or tortured terrified me, not just the physical pain but the helplessness that went with it; so my naïveté and idealism took a backseat to practical concerns, and I vowed to be more cautious even if it meant forsaking a bit of my revolutionary self-image.

The year 1953 began with blood, with the death of a student ironically named Batista, Rubén Batista, who was shot dead when the police opened fire on one of the student-led marches of protest; and with the first publicly spilled blood came the first substantial signs of a changing of the guard in the opposition's leadership. While the Triple A produced only rumors and frustration, new names and faces began to emerge and take leading roles in the fight against the dictator. Radical antigovernment leaders were elected to preside over the thirteen schools of Havana University, and the FEU became the fulcrum of opposition politics. Rafael García Bárcena, the high school teacher who passed review of his knife-wielding recruits from the window seat of a city bus, now rose to prominence by advocating a public and popular revolt against the government, challenging the Triple A's idea of a countercoup. His approach was not devoid of virtue, but his sense of the practical was so unconnected to reality as to be appalling, and he attracted the kind of dreamy followers who truly believed ideas and kitchen knives could carry the day against the weapons of an army. In April 1953 he marched his disciples into Batista's largest military garrison in an action that came to be derisively referred to as *la revolución de las navajitas,* the revolution of the razor blades, and which, as expected, failed miserably but not without securing its leader some renown; and meanwhile, Fidel and his *guajiros,* as reclusive and secretive as ever, kept on meeting and plotting.

Much has been said, written, imagined and invented about Fidel's attack on the Moncada military barracks. His July 26, 1953, operation on the eastern end of the island caught all other anti-Batista groups by surprise. We had assumed he was up to something, but no one ever imagined an action so bold—and so stupid. Jorge Tallet and I were by then in the habit of taking Sunday morning walks along the length of the Malecón, the boulevard by the sea that forms the northern edge of the city, stopping at some out of the way café to have breakfast and ending our walk somewhere in the colonial part of town. On July 26, 1953, a Sunday, we had been out a bit longer than usual, immersed in a typical discussion that began inevitably with politics and moved on to history, philosophy, women, police repression, books, movies, disappointment with the Triple A and whatever else came to mind. Not until we parted company and I boarded a public bus for home did I get the sense that something had happened, as I could discern the same apprehensive mood that had infused the morning air the day of Batista's coup, although now in a minor key.

None of us could explain why Fidel had attacked the Moncada military installation. From our point of view, his action never had the remotest chance of success and could serve only to produce an upturn of repression against all government opponents. We debated it for hours, days, dissecting the attack and its possible objectives, and its consequences and implications. Castro was captured and jailed, the casualties were buried, and reports, stories, rumors, anecdotes and concoctions started to filter in, and we were still unsure as to his motives, plans or objectives. But if we didn't understand Castro's action, one of the consequences of his move became crystal clear and reshaped the expectations and the dynamics of the opposition to the government: the time for talking was over. He had drawn a line between those temporizing with the dictator, whatever their excuses, and those ready to take up arms against him.

Some among us thought that Fidel had been trying to force the Triple A's hand. That knowing the organization to be well armed but engaged in a nebulous and slow campaign to gather military converts, Castro had planned to take over the Moncada Fort and then, as Batista forces regrouped and got ready to counterattack, to issue a public call for help. The call, directed specifically at the Triple A, would have been intended as appeal, and challenge, to the organization to come to his rescue and to join the effort to overthrow the tyrant. If this version was accurate, if Fidel's assault on the Moncada garrison had been an attempt to force the Triple A into action, it would have also meant that he had grossly overestimated the ability of that organization to do so.

All of Cuba knew the Triple A had a secret arsenal; an arms dealer working for the group had been arrested in the town of Mamaroneck in New York State and information about the arrest made public by the American authorities and widely reported by the Cuban press. Ex-President Prío, in exile in Miami, had provided the money, and the weapons seized were reported to be just one lot among several purchased; the rest were assumed to have found their way into Cuba. So the Triple A was well armed but doing nothing. The organization's continued explanation for its inactivity was the very reasoning I had been given by Aureliano: unwillingness to use untrained civilians as combatants and a commitment to recruit from the ranks of the military, which constituted a slow and laborious process. But there was a contradiction between relying on soldiers and stashing guns away; soldiers, for the most part, already have guns or are able to procure them from military arsenals. Thus it would only make sense to assume that the smuggled weapons were destined for people who did not have them, for civilians. If the organization's strategy rested on action on the part of disaffected military, why bother buying and smuggling weapons into the country? But whatever the answer to this question, the arms were there, Fidel knew it, and it was possible he may have been trying to force the Triple A's hand.

A news blackout had followed Fidel's attack, and, as always in these cases, rumors became rampant. Even as the blackout was lifted and information began to trickle in, very little was certain, not only about the accuracy of the reports but also as to whether this was an isolated act or the first stage of something larger that would take place not in remote Oriente province but in Havana itself. And we were still sure, hopeful really, that if something bigger was in the works, it would be the Triple A's doing. That was the logical conclusion to be reached given the fact that the Triple A was the only anti-Batista organization known to be armed. But not a sound, not a whisper, nothing from the Triple A, and as Fidel Castro himself was captured and put under army custody, and as his attempt at insurrection was clearly finished, nothing, and more nothing. The Triple A's silence had been deafening.

The immediate casualty of the failed July 26 attack turned out to be not the Batista government but the Triple A, which, by its lack of reaction, proved to be paralyzed, revealing that it had never developed the ability, and perhaps not even the will, to act, that it could not be counted on to come to the help of other anti-Batista forces in need. The organization had revealed its ineffectiveness; and in the eyes of those who thought it could have acted, but that it had chosen not to, it appeared mendacious and more interested in monopolizing the anti-Batista mantle for future political gain than in fighting the dictatorship. The perception of the Triple A as a genuine and reliable force, as an effectual instrument for ridding the country of military rule, collapsed overnight.

I lost my temper with Raúl Roa and had a sedate, but equally frustrating, discussion with Mario Fortuny, and neither of the two could come up with a satisfactory answer to the gun question, or to the Triple A's passivity, or to its total silence, or to its lack of response to the events of July 26. They couldn't explain the organization's failure to contact its members on that day or shortly afterwards, most of whom, like me, had had no idea what was going on and had spent the rest of that day, and the following ones, trying to reach someone in the organization, expecting to be instructed or, at the very least, informed. Frustration and anger led to skepticism, skepticism to disaffection.

The Moncada attack, by its drastic and dramatic nature, had laid bare the basic facts of the country's political reality and had made it impossible for the rest of us to ignore them. It was as if we—my generation, those my age—had been wearing rumpled shorts one day and found ourselves unexpectedly clad in pressed full-legged trousers the next. We had looked upon our elders, those who were there before us, as our natural leaders, as individuals who were wiser and understood what we didn't, and who were thus in position to show us the way. But on July 26 Castro *pateó el tablero*, kicked over the game table, and the old game could no longer be played, it had to be restarted, or replaced by something else, or forgotten about. The feeble efforts taken by the lingering ghosts of the traditional parties just a few weeks before—when they had signed a public document full of empty words and hollow promises of redemption, insisting that the only way to oppose Batista was by force—came as the swan song of the political generation that had come of age fighting tyranny and government abuse in the 1930s and 1940s, and was now exiting as a deplorable collection of venal politicians and corrupt former government officials.

Fidel Castro's action was an abysmal military failure and an extraordinary political success. Daring without luck leads to oblivion, but daring with luck is the stuff that makes legend. Logically, in accordance with the political tradition of the country and the expectations created by them, Fidel should have been killed by the military immediately upon his capture. Some accounts credit his survival to a scrupulous soldier and others to a pious clergyman, but more likely it was Fidel's in-laws who, close to Batista, were able to intercede for his life. Or perhaps Batista, who always yearned to be a popular politician and, consequently alternated periods of harsh repression with lenient permissiveness, acted on his own. Even if the providential intervention of a soldier, priest or family member had spared Fidel's life upon capture, it would have been very easy for the government to have disposed of him afterwards. But Fidel lived—and Cuba changed.

So there we were. No Triple A getting rid of Batista, no Aureliano rescuing the nation, no easy putsch to rub military faces in their own shit, no nothing, just us and Batista. The fog had cleared and we found ourselves in the front lines, with nothing between the repressive machinery of the dictatorship and us, and I was scared but felt taller, talked faster, and my stride had a new bounce.

At the bank those challenging the union leadership had gained so much support among unionized employees from banks throughout Havana that we began to take formal steps to field an opposition slate in the next elections for union officials, which in fact amounted to a fight for control of the whole union since whoever controlled the union in Havana controlled the union throughout the country. Because we were

young, inexperienced and idealistic—and thus not seen as a real threat—
the union bosses were not especially worried; if anything, they sounded
amused and treated us condescendingly, and their attitude was a blessing as it meant that they didn't feel any need to put Batista's police on
our tail, and we were left free to campaign and organize a small but
dependable cadre of committed activists.

After a couple of months' work we thought the time had come to mobilize whatever backing we had, to test our strength. We at the Banco
Continental decided to call a strike not only without the consent of the
pro-Batista union leadership, but against their wishes. It wasn't a full-
blown strike but a *huelga de brazos caídos,* a sitting-in slowdown, with
no specific labor demands, something that amounted to an open and public protest against the government, an act of political defiance, a statement that showed where we stood and which would, we hoped, set an
example for others to follow. The July 26 action of Fidel Castro and his
hicks had liberated us psychologically from our previous dependence on
established political figures and spurred us to action. It is amazing to realize how much a change of perspective can alter our view of something,
how what has a certain form and shape when seen from one angle become something totally different when observed from another. As if by
magic, the hold Aureliano and the Triple A had exerted on my imagination was gone. Fidel Castro, whatever his intentions might have been, was
the conjurer who broke the spell, destroying whatever illusions we had
left concerning our political elders—and setting us free.

It was the beginning of 1954. Castro was in jail. The Triple A seemed
to have evaporated and I was feeling good, very good, about being involved in a public action against the government. It was the strike's second day and I was having my shoes shined across the street from the
bank's main entrance when the police arrived. No blaring sirens, just dark
blue police car after dark blue police car and a couple of gray paddy
wagons that pulled up across the street from me, and then a line of uniformed men marching into the bank. I knew they would come. We all
knew they would come, we just didn't know exactly when; how long the
government would allow a political strike to last.

My first impulse was to run into the bank to join my fellow workers,
and I tried to get up from the shoe-shining chair, but the shoeshine boy
wouldn't let go of my foot. I tried to shake him off, but he held fast, insisting he still hadn't done my other shoe and that I couldn't leave with
one shoe shined and one not, and I told him I didn't give a damn about
having one shoe shined and the other not, but he said that wasn't right
and was still holding onto the foot with the unshined shoe when I saw

the first employees being marched out. The policemen were being selective; they were taking only the activists, the "troublemakers," probably pointed out to them by someone inside the bank, and that meant my second-in-command, Feliciano, and also Reinol, and Arturo Brizuela and about twenty others, most of them from the hole. So I sat back on the chair and told the shoeshine boy to go ahead and shine the other shoe while I tried to figure out what I should do, and now the boy got angry, telling me to make up my mind and stop fucking around, and so concerned was he with my strange behavior and so determined to complete his work that he didn't notice what was going on behind him, just across the street.

From the shoe-shining chair I tried to make eye contact with and signal those being walked to the paddy wagons, and it was Brizuela who first saw me and responded to my signals by moving his head from side to side and shaking his hand in a movement that meant that I should get away, and as he disappeared from view behind the wagon, Feliciano saw me also and, raising his hand waist high, let his index finger transmit a negative answer to my coded suggestion that I join them. By now the shoeshine boy was done with my second shoe and was almost forcibly removing my feet from the chair's footrests, convinced he was dealing with a nut case, a guy who not only had wanted only one shoe shined, but who was now gesturing, moving his hands and pointing his fingers in the air, and forming words in his lips without letting a sound out, so as I stood up he gave me a look that conveyed puzzlement and pity and none of his previous annoyance and exasperation. When I reached into my pocket for some money and he turned around to put his shoeshine tools away, he noticed for the first time the commotion across the street and asked in total surprise, "What's going on over there?"

The bank's employees carted away by the police while I was having my shoes shined were kept in jail for thirty days, but they didn't have it all that bad. They were not beaten and their families were allowed to supply them with whatever they needed; they had not been interrogated either, often a prelude to torture. Batista was beginning to mount an electoral circus to sanction his rule, so leniency was in. My friends had been locked away in the Castillo del Príncipe prison, in the center of Havana and not far from the University, and were kept together as a group, separate from the common criminals, and I went to visit them frequently.

The Latin American way of dealing with political prisoners has traditionally followed two quite divergent paths. Prisoners are tortured or killed, or they are handled with extreme consideration. In the first instance they are perceived as a menace and treated with peremptory harshness; in the second they are perceived as potential future holders of power and taken care of with preventive deference. It was the nature of Batista's rule to alternate between the two approaches, and this was fortunate for my coworkers who seemed in high spirits every time I went to see them; but it was even better for Fidel Castro, who ended up being the major beneficiary of the regime's fluctuations in its repressive mood.

After being captured and jailed, Fidel functioned more as symbol than active participant in anti-Batista revolutionary politics. Most of us, assuming a consistency in government action that was not there, thought that Fidel would be killed or kept in jail for a very long time, at least until Batista was gone. But he wasn't, and the resoluteness and the boldness of his assault on the military, and the publicity that went with it and with the trial that followed, made Fidel Castro the most talked-about person in the country. He was the hero of all the anti-Batista militants— but hero and leader are two different things.

A hero is an idealized representation of something we cherish and look up to, someone with whom we identify in our mind, a human figure we have shaped in iconic contours and then gone on to venerate. A leader is someone we follow by the force of his personality, deeds or ideas. The former influences our thoughts; the latter influences our actions. Removed from the center of political activities, expected by most to be disposed of by the government, having traveled from word to deed by taking up arms against the dictator—what most of us told ourselves we wanted to do even if uncertain as to whether we had the guts for it—Fidel in 1954 was hero but not leader. That would come later.

CHAPTER TEN

"He almost died! My God, he almost died! We thought he was leaving us!" Kiko's mother kept repeating hysterically over the telephone.

I had run into Kiko, completely by chance, the previous Saturday afternoon on my way to the University to pay the tuition for the year, forty-five dollars. He asked me what I was doing and when I told him he suggested I put the money to better use—to a good meal. There would always be time for paying the tuition and, in the overall scheme of things, he argued, having a good meal ranked far above paying—paying for anything—so we went to an Italian restaurant on Prado Boulevard, not far from where we had run into each other.

Kiko's approach to money had by now grown into a full-fledged philosophical theory, and as we ate he espoused it in detail, with references to European and Eastern philosophers, literary figures, famous poets, and to the lyrics of several popular songs. Buying, he explained, was a pleasurable experience, sometimes related to something you needed, but most of the time tied to nothing else than the satisfaction the buying action provided: the transaction, the acquisition. So you bought when you felt like buying. Paying was something else, a painful experience, usually but not always the byproduct of buying, and it occurred arbitrarily in time and space with all sorts of people trying to find ways of forcing you to pay for things you had never wanted, never needed, never thought of, never seen, never enjoyed and, sometimes, never bought. So paying was to be avoided whenever possible, and you should pay only under duress, when no other alternative existed.

While he spoke, he ate. He never ate in a rush but slowly, carefully, observing how each new serving of pasta reached his plate and each string of spaghetti found its proper place, and then he would pour the sauce, as methodically as a chemist mixing substances, over the pasta, and last he would turn his attention to the parmesan, which he would sprinkle with precision, almost punctiliousness, as if it were gold dust, and as uniformly as he had done with the sauce, and during this whole process he would be silent, totally immersed in what he was doing. Only when the preparation was complete would he then go back to the alternating, never simultaneous, sequence of eating and talking. Eating was for Kiko the epitome of pleasure, the most enjoyable of activities, and the more he elaborated on his buying-paying theory, the more he ate. We must have been at it for not less than three hours, until all other customers were gone and only our table was being served. The pasta kept coming, with both sauce and parmesan, and I ate more than I had ever eaten in my life, and Kiko ate easily three or four times as much. When we eventually left the restaurant I found it hard to walk, and it took my system a full two days to process the meal and all its after-effects.

It must have been then Thursday or Friday of the following week that I called Kiko and got the hysterical reply from his mother. The first thing that came to my mind was that the bout of tuberculosis that had made his overprotective family keep him from finishing high school had suddenly returned, especially after his mother said that he had vomited blood, that they thought he was going to die and had called the doctor. But the doctor, amidst the tears of the women and the lamentations of the father, told them that Kiko's lungs were perfectly fine. What was not fine was his stomach, and after much examination and a trip to the hospital he concluded that Kiko had perforated it—with spaghetti.

I began to doubt my interest in Neji, a girl I had been pursuing for some time with decidedly mixed results. Like it or not, whether I admitted it openly to myself or refused to let it surface, I was aware that there was something lacking in my interest in her. When I had first found myself infatuated with girls, Gloria and then Amarilis, nothing had mediated my feelings towards them. I couldn't have cared less about their families, or their social environment, or their political connections; nothing apart from the girls themselves was important, nothing beyond how I felt when I was with them, or when I thought of them, mattered. My feelings had been neither influenced nor mingled with or affected by any other consideration. But this wasn't the case now, and I was troubled by it.

I became slowly aware that my attraction to Neji was as much social as personal, social in a cultural, almost anthropological sense, not in the economic one the term commonly connotes. I was attracted by the political and intellectual environment in which she lived, as her father and uncle were well-known university professors and her sister Ada was married to Raúl Roa. I saw in her family the confluence of intellectual accomplishment and an enlightened political attitude, and formed an idealized version of both her and her surroundings. Courting her was an effort to get personally closer to a whole group, to rub shoulders with people whose interests matched mine, to break the isolation of my family's self-imposed aloofness and find a place of my own and to my liking.

These were still the days of the chaperone, the middle-class insurance policy for the preservation of female virginity until matrimony could be extracted as compensation, or until the goods showed signs of not moving and expectations were lowered. Josefina, Neji's mother, was our regular chaperone, which meant another admission ticket to the movies and another mouth to feed when we went to one of the café-restaurants that were open until late in the evening. I didn't mind that too much because it was part of the deal, but I did mind that as she ate she was consistently able to convey her dislike and disapproval of me. There were many reasons for a Cuban mother to dislike her daughter's suitor, most arbitrary and some quite sound, but I couldn't put my finger on what exactly about me bothered her. Maybe it was that she didn't know much about my life, or about my family, or about the part of town I came from, or maybe because I was involved in politics and with a labor union, or that I seemed to have been chronically underfed, or maybe it was the way I drove my sister Marta's car when I took them out. I didn't know, but as I realized that my own interest in her daughter was rather uncertain, Josefina's unspoken but forceful manifestations of her dislike for me shifted from nuisance to item of curiosity.

While visiting the house or having a bite after a movie, I began to ask Josefina innocent questions and make innocuous comments about all kind of subjects and people and incidents, wanting to see how she responded to them. I drew a blank. There was nothing she said, no expression on her face, no gesture, no body language that would clue me in to what was going on in her head. It was only after spending many an hour under her disapproving glare that I finally became aware of the subtle and indirect references to her husband, more insinuations than statements. Neji's father was the kind of person who should have been under psychiatric care but who in an underdeveloped environment can usually pass, at least in the eyes of some, for an eccentric genius. As a cardiologist, he was totally committed to the therapeutic benefits of the excretory function, to which he ascribed salutary benefits that reached the miraculous and went well beyond his immediate cardiac concerns. His medical mantra was: ¡Cagar, cagar, y cagar! To shit, shit, and shit! He went on to endow the human dislodging of its inner solid waste with powerful salutary properties—and to bring about these beneficial properties a sporadic and indifferent defecation would not do, oh no! To unleash all the potential beneficial and curative power of defecation, taking a shit had to be a happy and joyful occasion, the kind that is looked forward to, enjoyed during and relished afterwards, and it had to be indulged in as often as possible, not less than three or four times a day.

At the University, Professor Juan B. Kourí was famous for his crudeness and habit of referring to human sexual organs not in medical terms but in coarse street terms, so penis was dick, and vagina cunt, and sexual intercourse fucking, and so on, and those who didn't think he was a genius thought he was a foul-mouthed creep, and those who thought neither saw him as a raving lunatic. And his antics in the consulting room and in the classroom had their home counterpart as he often went about the house stark naked, without a stitch of clothes on, regardless of whether there were only family members in the house or also visitors, asking everybody present how many times they had shit that day, and stating frequently, whether related to any ongoing conversation or not, that his brother Pedro, another doctor, was the best parasitic expert in the world and that he, Juan, was not only the best cardiologist in the world, but the best doctor, period. It must have been hard for Josefina, or for any half-sane woman, to put up with such a man, especially when one considers the middle-class standards of Cuban society at the time and their accompanying inhibitions and restraining mores.

The family adhered to the genius interpretation of the man's quirks in order to bridge the gap between their middle-class standing and his behavior. For some reason I couldn't explain, I thought him a crook, a con man, a phony; I simply couldn't swallow all his theatrics as being anything else, it just didn't make sense for a crazy person to appear so blatantly crazy, to trumpet his insanity in such a manner. As a result, I failed to show the right attitude towards his talent and brilliance when displayed in my presence, and was unable to hide completely my lack of appreciation for the show, and this, I concluded, was the reason Josefina didn't like me. Maybe I was right or, most probably, not, but in either case I was perfectly happy with my interpretation and it didn't take too long for my interest in the family and all its members to come to an end.

The Havana University professors were an odd bunch. As unusual a character as Dr. Kourí was, he had nothing on Rafael Portela and Elías

Entralgo, two among the small minority of professors who were dedicated to their academic careers, who held classes dependably and who were frequently on campus. Portela taught political economy, a mandatory subject in both the Law and the Social Sciences Schools, and had built a nationwide reputation for flunking students. The stories about him were legendary, and at examination time students from all over the island who needed to pass his course to qualify for their degree would flock to Havana and anxiously wait for their turn to be subjected to his implacable questioning. Professor Portela gave only oral examinations, and they would always follow the same, well-known, pattern. He would ask question after question until he could identify the student's area of weakness, and would proceed to prod in that area until the student revealed the total depth of his ignorance. Professor Portela would then take great pleasure in pronouncing the student *¡suspendido!* failed! loudly enough for all those outside the examination room waiting their turn to hear.

Portela failed about 70 or 80 percent of those who took his examination. Most who persisted eventually obtained a passing grade, and a degree, but it took a large number of them years—ten was not unheard of. This was especially hard on those who did not live in Havana, and who were thus forced to trek to the city—by no means an easy trip for the poor ones or for the ones who lived in remote places—once or even twice a year just to return home, in most cases, frustrated and humiliated anew. There was no doubt in anyone's mind that Rafael Portela was the most hated man at Havana University.

Professor Elías Entralgo, on the other hand, was a widely admired individual, although he had some of the intransigence of Portela. He channeled his idiosyncrasies in a less openly spiteful manner, and as a result most of his bizarre actions were laughed off, especially by those who had not been directly exposed to them. Students couldn't miss more than two of Entralgo's classes, it was absolutely forbidden to miss more: a third miss and you were out. No appeals heard and no excuses accepted. To preempt any request for reprieve, he scheduled all his classes at seven in the morning, thus eliminating all potential conflicting commitments. And by seven he meant no later than five minutes to seven, since it was at precisely five before seven o'clock that he would have the door to his classroom closed and locked. Those arriving even a second later would be turned away, their knocks at the door and their pleas unanswered as Professor Entralgo would not budge and would not allow anyone to let them in. As he had affirmed on the first day, in one or two weeks at the most everybody would arrive on time and no one would be knocking at the door—and he was exactly right.

The strangest part of Entralgo's classes, however, was the nonacademic component he integrated into his course requirements. He was appalled, he explained at the beginning of the year, by the very low number of Havana University students engaged in sports, and he considered this lack of interest in physical activity both unhealthy and unethical. So he took it upon himself to remedy the situation and made playing softball a mandatory requisite for his course, and once a week the entire class had to show up at the University's athletic field. No excuses were accepted here either, and only in the case of a blatantly crippling physical handicap would he permit a student to forgo softball—and play chess instead. And the manner in which he ran the softball game was in unison with the manner in which he ran his classroom—concerned and absolute control. He wanted the students to learn but to learn his way. He had no tolerance for divergent views and used rules and regulations to advance and protect his authority. He suffered no opposition, intellectual or otherwise.

He formed two teams out of class members, and kept records of performance on the field, as meticulous as those he kept for class attendance and participation, and he announced that there would be prizes at the end of the year for the winning team, for the best pitcher, and for the leading batter and fielder. This was somewhat odd for two makeshift teams made up of both men and women, and whose age and physical ability ranged widely. But what was totally unexpected was that the professor appeared at the first game in full softball regalia, and appointed himself captain and starting pitcher of one of the teams.

What followed was the logical consequence of what had preceded it, and an unequivocal admonition that the Cuba we lived in was not Batista's doing, but that the doings of Batista were the result of the Cuba we lived in. By chance, because no one knew the quality of the players as the two teams were formed, Entralgo's side, with Entralgo on the mound, was trounced and the pitcher-captain-professor was personally humiliated when he hit a one-hopper line drive to left field and was put out at first by a combination of the outfielder's strong arm and the professor's aging legs. Those of us on the winning team relished our victory and saw the whole thing as a tragicomedy resulting from the aberrations of a well-meaning but very peculiar professor.

Little did we know. Next game, a week later, Entralgo appeared again in full softball regalia but this time accompanied by two big and strongly built black men who were, according to him, University *bedeles*—one of whom, we learned later, had been a professional baseball player— and both of them were to be on his team. Our protest went unaccepted.

The professor limited himself to stating that being University employees the two men had the right to play and said nothing about why they were both to play for his side. He never lost a game again.

Entralgo was the totalitarian, wanting control over thought and action, and it came to no surprise when I learned he was a member of the Cuban Communist Party. Portela was the authoritarian, the sadist despot. He needed no rationalization to impose his arbitrary will and to dispense pain as he saw it fit. He didn't want you to perform in any prescribed way; he just wanted you to buckle under the weight of his power and he made no attempt to explain it, to justify it or to embellish it. And the year before I was supposed to take his course Portela was set upon by a group of students as he emerged from one of his orgies of failures, and they broke his arm, and the news spread like wildfire. The following day scores of students expecting a replacement to be conducting examinations in his stead descended upon Havana University and were cheerily milling around the Law School when the dreaded and hated figure appeared on the portico of the school's building with his broken right arm in a sling, and looking down on them with a set face and a firm voice said, "I still have my left arm to flunk you with." *

These odd souls, Kourí, Entralgo and Portela, were, irrespective of anything else, among the few professors committed to their work, and who were interspersed into a large majority that showed little or no dedication to their professorial duties. Most professors were around only when they had to be, which was, at least in the case of the Law and the Social Sciences Schools, almost never. It was not altogether unusual for students in these schools to have no idea what some professors who had occupied chairs for years looked like, or even if they actually existed. The University was, in fact, as corrupt as the country's government agencies and political practices had ever been. This realization came to me in stages, but when it was all in, it hit me hard. I had idealized the institution, and had assumed that its role as the political conscience of the nation required it to be above the sins and practices its officials, faculty and students claimed to oppose in Cuban public life.

My disappointment was deepened, in part, by none other than Raúl Roa. Already frustrated with him over the Triple A's inactivity, I began to see the man as duplicitous, strong on pose but weak on deed, critical in theory of the same things he accepted in practice; allowing, and thus

*Fearing for the man's life, the University sent him out of the country and appointed a temporary, and benevolent, substitute to his chair. Professor Portela did not return to the University during my stay there.

condoning, professorial misconduct and irresponsibility—misconduct
and irresponsibility he had the power to stop.

By the end of 1953 the anti-Batista camp had turned into a free-for-all,
with many a militant an isolated individual floating in a vacuum and
searching for kindred spirits with whom to cooperate, create a common
strategy, form a plan of action, open up a front. Havana University, despite my growing misgivings, still offered the opportunity to vent anger
and frustration—to march, demonstrate, shout and fight the police, to
let emotion hang all out, and feel good about your antigovernment
activism. It was a psychological recharge station, a morale booster, especially after a public meeting, or when one attended the student federation's sessions where the roster of students who had died fighting oppression and dictatorial rule was read aloud before going into the day's
agenda, and as their names were called, " . . . Anacleto Bermúdez . . .
Angel Laborde . . . Julio Antonio Mella . . . Rafael Trejo . . . ," those in
attendance would respond, ¡Presente! and you would feel a chill through
your spine, at least the first couple of times. And all those interested in
fighting the government, whether students or not, would go by the University, and it was there that I got to know those who, with Tallet, had
put out the anti-Batista newspaper and who had by now also cut all ties
with the Triple A, and it was with these people that I decided to make
common political cause.

The bank strike was a political victory. We showed that the pro-
government and corrupt union leadership could be challenged, and the
publicity accompanying the arrest and month-long incarceration of my
coworkers had helped to get our message across and create, in combination with the increasing frustration of middle-class Cuba, some momentum in our favor. All of us in the "hole" now decided to join up with
opposition members in banks throughout the city, and give final form to
our own slate of candidates for the upcoming election of union officials. I
was offered one of the three leading spots but declined partly out of deference to Reinol González, who had done most of the liaison work with
the other banks and who was more deserving of the spot than I was, and
partly out of my general lack of interest in union politics. But under the
pressure of those who wanted me on the slate, as the only union steward of a large bank who had been openly opposed to the bosses and their
pro-government stance, I accepted a spot on it.

It quickly became clear that those running the union had underestimated us, as well as the dislike and disapproval among the membership of their identification with the Batista regime. As election day approached we seemed to be getting stronger and they weaker, and when the votes were counted, the results were quite close, much closer than anyone had expected them to be; and we then knew we would win the next time around, in a year. We had openly politicized the quest for control of the union, we had made it very clear that we wanted to turn the union into an anti-Batista force and on such basis our slate had received an impressive amount of support.

I had no doubt that union activism was a political sideshow, a complement, an auxiliary, not the main provider of the thrust needed against the government; but I could not identify any potential provider of that main thrust. The disappearance of the traditional parties first, and then of the Triple A, had left the opposition without institutional anchors, and I felt adrift.

The Partido Socialista Revolucionario was mostly Tallet's idea. The old and traditional political parties had ceased to exist, so we had to create our own, one modeled after our ideas and aspirations for a different country and for a different society. We didn't know what kind of country we wanted — different, yes, but how? — or what kind of society; and it was lucky we didn't know because if we had, each of us would have had a different version of the future, and we would have poured all our time and energy into disagreeing and arguing over abstractions whose only bases would have been dreams and ignorance. So when Jorge Tallet called a meeting, five of us came, Carlos Franqui, Norberto Martínez, Paquito Almoína, Tallet and I. We all agreed on the need to form a party, one truly different from what had existed before, and we didn't discuss any other issue but spent the rest of the time debating the pros and cons of adopting *noms de guerre*. Did we need them, or did we not? How would we use them? It was amazing how long we went on discussing this while postponing all other questions. After an entire evening we had decided, aside from the adoption of revolutionary names, only one thing — to meet again.

It was hard to keep track of the music, but there was now something disturbing, almost maniacal, about it, as if different instruments were all playing different tunes and superimposing each on the other, blended in an arrangement that had no pattern, no order, no sequence that could be made sense of, or that I could follow or identify. Life has a sound track, people have sound tracks, moods have sound tracks, and everything goes with its music. Now in Cuba the maracas and the clavichord, the timbales and the violins, the organ and the bongo drums became enmeshed in a giant muddle of unsynchronized sounds in which each instrument took up its own rhythm just to abandon it immediately for another one, popular and classical, Cuban and Spanish, Mexican, Argentine and American, and it sounded like tangos by Mozart, or Benny Moré singing a Bach cantata, or Schubert playing *cha cha cha*. We could see, feel and hear the confusion and dislocation engulfing the country, but we didn't know what to do. Fidel Castro did.

Fidel seemed to be guided by an instinct the rest of us lacked, and he cleverly let others become the immediate beneficiaries of his attack on the Moncada garrison. There were those among us who thought they could use Fidel, build a movement upon his deed but under their own control, and they all, unwittingly and to the eventual chagrin of most of them, became Fidel's foot soldiers. Some founded and organized cells of the 26 of July Movement while Castro sat in his prison, well aware of their actions and happy to let them use his name, delude themselves. Those who had been lured to the spectral ranks of the Triple A, or who had followed García Bárcena's demented revolutionary dream, or who had wanted to overthrow Batista but didn't know how, or who could no longer contain their desire to strike at the dictatorship—they all became potential recruits for Castro's ranks.

Other than the general aim of overthrowing Batista, and bringing back civilian rule and electoral democracy, there was no explicit ideological connection uniting the various opposition factions. Ideology— with the exception of the shared contempt for Marxism, engendered by the local Communists' history of revolutionary betrayal and connivance with dictators—was not a question. There was, of course, an ideological bent to our ideas and values, but being almost exclusively a white middle-class assemblage, our beliefs were assumed and generally uniform, with no glaring divergence forcing them to the surface. Only when dealing with the *ñángaras,* as we disparagingly referred to the Communists, did ideology become manifest, and then only to reaffirm that we were all pro-democracy, anticommunist and anti-Soviet. The recruiting appeal of the Castro-inspired emerging movement was thus based on the promise of action, not on words; on presenting itself as a combative alternative to the passivity of the Triple A; on offering the promise of a structure where no structure had been left standing; on providing a refuge for those out in the revolutionary cold.

Many fled to the new movement; mostly students who needed some organizational prop to complement their emotionally satisfying but erratic discharge of anger and frustration in meetings, marches and confrontations with the police. But we, the cast of the almost imaginary Partido Socialista Revolucionario, knew better, or so we thought. We certainly didn't need Fidel: I, because I still disliked him and didn't trust him despite acknowledging his bravery and daring, and the others probably for different but equally personal or irrational motives. And it was more rewarding this way, having our own party, at least for a while. There was no one to direct us, so we had to think hard about what we really wanted and how we could best achieve it. To be on our own was humbling and thrilling and intriguing and perplexing, like setting our minds astir, cranking them up and finding that they actually worked. We were like toddlers stumbling while finding their legs, when the act of walking is more important than getting anywhere.

In truth, we were neither socialist nor revolutionary, not in any real sense. In the haze of our environment and the muddle of our political vocabulary, "socialist" meant that we had some social concerns, and "revolutionary"—well, I am not sure what "revolutionary" meant, we just knew that no anti-Batista group worth its political salt could be anything but "revolutionary." It was never clear, or that important, whether the term referred to substance, form or both; whether it defined goals envisioned, methods used or some symbiotic relationship between them. We, however, didn't have to concern ourselves with disentangling such convoluted cerebral knots; we just cut through their Gordian complexity and called revolutionary whatever we wanted, and it was the act of labeling that imprinted the revolutionary seal on what we sought and on what we did.

In our microscopic and phantasmagoric party we came to realize that beyond getting rid of Batista, almost no one among all his enemies seemed to know what they wanted—or if they did, they weren't saying. The Communists did, and said so with dependable and predictable tediousness—they wanted whatever Moscow told them to want. We also knew that whatever the Communists were after, we were not. We wanted some things for the country, and some things for ourselves. For the country we wanted a vaguely defined regeneration of its public life, although we had to accept that regeneration meant going back to a previous state of health and we couldn't find a previous state of good political health anywhere in Cuban history. So it would have to be an inauguration, the introduction of something different, bright and, above everything else, honest. Honesty was the key ingredient, the magic component that would bring everything else in tow: fair elections, reliable politicians, efficient administrations and the enlightened discussion of problems followed by their constructive solutions.

What did we want for us, personally? That was different. It was fine, in fact thrilling, to feel like we were paving the way for the political changes to come, helping to save the country and bringing about a new era, and we especially enjoyed the idea of getting rid of Batista and his gang of thieves and murderers. And then what? I didn't see my future as a politician or a government bureaucrat, as just one more cog in the slow process of creating and nurturing the new state of affairs, the new Cuba. I discussed these concerns with Jorge Tallet and with Kiko Baeza, and the three of us saw such a path as boring and unappealing, as ordinary and unadventurous, and who would want to lead that kind of life?

Tallet, who was in the last stages of getting a doctorate in philosophy, would much rather write recondite treatises on weighty and impenetrable topics; and Kiko wanted to write witty and amusing short stories sitting at the tables of good restaurants, and I was not sure what I wanted other than to travel, to see what the world had to offer beyond the inescapably oppressive heat of my tropical surroundings. We were beginning to come to grips with the notion that we were incorrigible dreamers willing to charge the ramparts of oppression but that our motivation would lapse when confronted with the tedium and mendacity of ordinary political life. We discussed politics and our activities, but as time passed we broadened our horizons, and it was those two, Tallet and Baeza, with their very different styles and ambitions and with quite dissimilar approaches to life, who led me to new books and new ideas, who brought some sanity into the political mental asylum Cuba had become.

It was for real now. We won the elections. We were the Union. We thought we had power and were elated. A year had passed and we had tried again, basically the same slate and exactly the same ideas, but when the votes were counted this time we had more votes than the official one. The union bosses were unhappy, but they appeared willing to let us take over, or so they said right after the elections results were known. But the government didn't give a damn about election results or votes counted, and the next day it declared the election null. We had received more votes than the other guys, but that wasn't the Batista way. He and his people were not about to let one of the country's largest and most influential labor unions be taken over by the opposition, so the result of the vote was cast aside, the election abrogated, put in the trash can in tyrannical fashion, and that was that. And no one on our side knew exactly how to react. It was Monday morning, the day after the election, and we in the hole were in high spirits and joking around and planning how we were to run the union, and the telephone rang and we were dumbstruck. We shouldn't have been surprised, since the official ukase overturning the election result fitted in with what we had been saying about the government, but we were.

Right away we called the people who had headed our slate, and they proposed calling a meeting to discuss the situation and suggested initiating some legal action, although it was not clear what any legal action would accomplish under a system that had no regard for legality. It was obvious they had also been taken by surprise and had no concrete or useful notion as to what to do next, so we in the hole, without consulting anyone and without wasting another minute, took matters into our own hands—we decided to call for a citywide bank strike.

Striking is a kind of warfare, and like any war, it requires preparation, planning and the right mental attitude. We, however, had decided to strike on the spur of the moment and had certainly not done the necessary homework, and that became evident very soon. But even if we had properly prepared, we still wouldn't have been able to achieve much beyond the symbolic value of a gesture, taking a public stand against a dictatorial regime in protest of an arbitrary and unfair action. We were not thinking in rational terms, though, we just wanted to hit back, so we stopped working. We called for other bank employees throughout the city to join us, and based our right to be calling a strike on the fact that Reinol and I, both in the hole, had been on the robbed slate. The government had shown its true colors and those running the union had been unmasked, notwithstanding their assurances to us of the night before, as Batista's pawns. We had the right, the obligation, to retaliate, and so convinced, we dispatched messengers to the headquarters of every bank in Havana. The strike was on.

I went down to the banks' exchange center, where employees from all banks went early in the morning to deliver and pick up checks and documents which they would bring back to their offices for processing. I entered the room and loudly shouted, "¡Estamos en huelga!" "We are on strike!" I then saw activity in the room come to a complete halt with all eyes turned to me. It was a satisfying, brief, but totally exhilarating moment when at the sound of my voice those in the place ceased doing what they were doing, and when all union members present, the vast majority there, began marching out in response to my summons.

I had made the call, thrown the gauntlet down, and those working in the place had responded. I felt so good in fact that I treated myself, not to one, but to two *pastelitos de guayaba*, the flaky pastry-like guava treats, before returning to the hole, anxious to tell my co-strikers that the banks' central exchange had closed. This meant that no bank could conduct business normally or properly and that all operations in Havana had been paralyzed or seriously disrupted. Given the financial dominance of the city over the rest of the country, disrupting banking and financial transactions in Havana affected the whole island.

The main office of the Banco Continental Cubano was like a beehive gone berserk, and as employees came in we immediately told them a strike was on, and they turned around and walked away. The nonunion managerial staff was huddled in a corner, not sure what to say or do, probably awaiting orders from above, and every so often one of them would venture into the hole, which now was functioning as the strike's headquarters, to find out what we were up to, and to whisper expressions of support. Frustrated clients gathered on the street, in front of the bank's glass doors, struggling to find out if any transactions were going to be conducted; and no one among us had any idea what would happen next. Arturo Brizuela appeared to have become the self-appointed director of operations; he was glued to a telephone and was giving instructions to those around him in a composed and efficient manner, as if carrying on a regular business task. I looked around and found Reinol on another phone, his lazy eye paralyzed in place as if it had joined the strike, discussing some meaningless and interminable theoretical point about the strike with a journalist at the other end of the line. I realized that the Communist Party must had issued some instructions concerning our strike and that Brizuela, whom we suspected of being a card-carrying party member, was their man in place, and that Reinol and the Catholic Youth Movement he belonged to didn't have the foggiest idea what to do.

Feliciano walked in, back from breakfast across the street, satisfied and content as ever, and sat next to me as I stared at Brizuela and then at Reinol. "The Communists are trying to take over and the Catholics are lighting candles," I said to Feliciano in a tone that must have carried surprise and annoyance. He smiled, and in his usual slow and placid tone said, "Take over what? The strike? There is nothing to take over. We certainly have tipped over the chamber pot, but no one controls the shit. Man, you better go up and talk to Martínez." José Martínez was the executive vice president, the man who actually ran the bank, the person with whom I had to deal on any issue of consequence and whose sister I had been dating of late.

Martínez wasn't an easy man to read, so I had no idea whether my friendship with his sister had endeared me to him or had had the opposite effect. He had made clear to me in previous conversations his personal dislike for Batista and his regime, and his desire, within the confines of his position, to help. I went to his office, which was on the second floor of the building and told him we were striking, which he already knew, and why, which he already knew. I went on then to tell him that my concern was protecting the strikers from reprisals: the few individuals now in the hole from police violence and the employees heeding our call from the loss of their jobs. To my surprise, his answer was straightforward and positive. He couldn't prevent the police from marching into the bank, he said, but he would both alert those in the hole of any police activity he learned of and under no circumstances, and he repeated this, under no circumstances, would the bank take punitive action against the striking employees. It was more, much more, than I had expected and it made me wonder whether Batista's grip on the country was as a firm as I had assumed.

The strike was a resounding success—for a day. On the second day, the police burst into various banks' offices and arrested all the union employees they could find on the premises. Although they were not working, many employees had gone in, trying to find out whatever information or instructions they could. A few, whom the police incorrectly assumed were leading the strike, were arrested at home, but we, who had started the whole thing, were left alone. Perhaps it was just a question of time, and had the strike lasted longer we might have been taken in, but by the end of the second day our grand scheme was on its last leg, and the next day it gave up the ghost. We had issued no instructions to follow, had no plan to implement and had provided no guidelines or advice. We had set the strike in motion but had done nothing to keep it going, to establish lines of communication, to coordinate our actions, to gather resources and seek support. And without instructions, guidelines, information or support people just started to go back to work.

From the beginning the strike had been plagued by confusion, disorganization and fear. We introduced much of the confusion and disorganization ourselves, through our lack of experience, while the fear was the apprehension inherent in any risky action. Some strikers were scared of the police, of being arrested and beaten, others were afraid of losing their jobs, and adding to the confusion was the desire of some not to appear weak or irresolute in the eyes of co-strikers while in fact opposing the strike.

I had passed the word around to the Banco Continental's employees that our management had assured me no reprisals would be taken, but there was always the possibility of the government forcing the bank to take some action. The fear of the strikers was real, and assuaging it the key to prolonging their willingness to stay away from work; so for the strike to have lasted longer, we would have had to counterbalance that fear with assurances about the righteousness of our cause combined with an effective playing down of potential negative consequences. We were sure about the former but uncertain, and then most probably unconvincing, about the latter.

The Communists, for all of Brizuela's telephone calls and cool demeanor, didn't help much, and it was probably their intention never to help much since they didn't cherish the idea of anyone else establishing claims over any part of the labor movement. The Catholics helped even less, they contributed nothing of practical value, just prayers and candles, at best. Martínez had provided a degree of comfort and encouragement by showing that those with interests to protect were inclined to hedge their bets. For me it was the end of my interest in labor leadership. Calling the strike, openly challenging the government, had been daring and exciting. Learning that the effective mobilization of workers required catering to their worries, dealing with their apprehensions, comforting them, holding their hands and reassuring them about real and imaginary perils convinced me that this was something I was not cut out for. It was not that I didn't understand my coworkers' concerns for security, or that I thought myself above them, or immune to similar preoccupations. It was the simple realization that this was something I didn't want to have to deal with—like acknowledging the need for bridges and roads but having no inclination towards engineering. It just wasn't for me.

The Partido Socialista Revolucionario began to fizzle also, as Tallet, who had zero tolerance for institutional dependence, lost interest in the party. He was still willing to collaborate in specific undertakings, but almost as soon as the party took on some organizational substance, he went back to abstract philosophical disquisition—and to the admiring observation of women. I had been left in a state of disoriented frustration by the changing political situation and was less willing than Tallet to let it go, but I was forced to admit that having a party, an organization, before you knew what you wanted it for, was putting the cart before the horse—that to determine the "how," it was necessary to know the "what."

CHAPTER ELEVEN

Their guns were drawn, pointing at us, and there were four or five or maybe six of them, it was hard to tell, and as their guns came out, they yelled at us to get up and keep our hands where they could be seen, and to stand against the wall. Everyone else in the restaurant sat frozen in their seats, their faces betraying the same confusion and fear I felt, and they stared at us with a commiseration that was more disturbing than the policemen's guns.

Earlier in the evening I had run into Juanito and Ramón Papiol, acquaintances from the Partido Ortodoxo, who were with Carlos Olivares whom I knew from the University, and with a couple of other people I knew vaguely from Ortodoxo gatherings, and they invited me to join in a little celebration of Ramón's release, two days earlier, from the army intelligence detention center. So we went to eat and have something to drink, and as we ate and drank, and as Ramón recounted his experience with the repressive military unit, the undercover plainclothes cops burst into the restaurant.

They handcuffed and dragged us from the restaurant into the cars waiting outside, and after a short drive we found ourselves being marched through a back entrance into the dreaded Buró de Investigaciones, the headquarters of the secret police, the same building where the unlucky owner of the Víbora house had been thrown out the window. Once inside, we were led straight down into a dank and dimly lit basement, our handcuffs removed as we were ordered into a large, dark cell with only the faint white outline of a toilet visible in contrast to the blackness of the back wall—and the door slammed shut behind us with the clattering resonance of metal.

With the cold concrete floor against my back and the sound of the closing door reverberating in my ears, a chill swept over me. It was fear, but a fear very different from the clear and focused dread of the pistols pointed at our heads when I thought we might be shot, deliberately or by accident, and killed right then and there. The cell unleashed a whole array of nightmarish scenarios that battled for possession of my mind, as if my psyche were trying to determine what constituted the gravest or most imminent danger, where it lurked, and I needed to identify, arrange and prioritize the various undefined worries knocking at the door.

We were lucky not to be alone. Being with others helped us, most definitely me, to stay calm, at least in appearance, and subdue the anxiety inspired by knowing yourself to be at the mercy of those you knew to have none of it. We talked for a little while about what was going on and why we had been arrested, but we didn't talk for long, as each one of us prepared to deal in his own way with our common predicament, and I followed Ramón Papiol's lead as he took off his jacket, folded it neatly into a square pillow, laid it on the cement floor and lay his head on it.

The cell was absolutely dark and the building quiet and I must have been asleep for a while when I heard the cries. They were faint, muffled by my own sleep-induced stupor, but unmistakable. They seemed to float down the hallways on the thick and musty air, passing through cell wall after cell wall until they reached my ears. I knew what I was hearing and I didn't want to hear it, but I couldn't dismiss it or ignore it, so I lay down, uncertain, unable to sleep, yet unwilling to focus on the wailing and the image of what must have been producing it. It turned eerier when, after a little while, I realized I knew the crying voice. It was Lucas, someone I knew only as a friend of the Papiol brothers, and though I was not especially familiar with his voice, I had no doubt that it was his.

"Acuérdense, somos rateros, rateros, no presos políticos." It was a plea, not a reminder, "Remember, we are thieves, thieves, not political prisoners," and it came from the cell next to ours, startling me out of whatever sleep I had been able to get. We all stirred, looked at one another, and felt like laughing but we couldn't. I asked the Papiol brothers if that had been Lucas in the middle of the night, and they both said it had sounded like him, and none of us had any idea what to say or do as the faint light of early morning filtered in. So we wondered aloud about breakfast, unwilling to talk about anything else, and we couldn't have been awake for more than a few minutes when a heavy-set uniformed policeman with a thick black mustache appeared in front of the cell and called my name.

Fear comes in many forms—the adrenaline-induced nervous energy right before a fistfight, the stomach-churning apprehension of coming to bat with the bases loaded, the paralyzing shock of finding your illegal pistol on the floor of a public bus, the dread of a police gun pointed at you—and after one night in that cell, I was pretty sure I had experienced them all. But when the policeman called my name that morning, when he opened the cell door and motioned for me, and only me, to come out and follow him, I felt a kind of fear I had never felt before, a zombie-like sensation that disconnected my mind from my body, and as I followed his instructions I could see myself from outside my body, and although my movements were not impaired, my entire being felt unbearably heavy, as if instead of walking, I was dragging it behind me.

My mind was talking to me from someplace out of my head, telling me that I was being taken to some interrogation room, maybe the same one where the owner of the Víbora house had been brought before he was pushed out the window, trying to sort out what kind of information they could have on me, what they would ask, what I should say. Would they know about my union activities, or about my participation in students' demonstrations and marches, or, most troubling of all, about my links to the Triple A? I didn't have any idea, and as I followed the fat policeman down a long corridor and up some stairs, I realized the depth of my ignorance and unpreparedness, how I didn't even know why they had taken us in the night before. The mind struggles to give comfort and support, and since mine couldn't provide specific direction or a clear strategy, it simply enveloped me in a dense soporific fog as a protective shield against panic.

As we reached the first landing and made a right turn to continue climbing up, I could see the building's main entrance and receiving hall, and there, sitting on a bench with a very pale face and her hair undone, was Lucas's wife. I swallowed hard and felt my knees buckle. I had seen her before only a couple of times, but there was no doubt it was she. It was only then that the full impact of the night screams hit me, that I fully remembered the sound of police cars in and out of the building all night long. Whatever doubt I might have had about where I was being taken vanished. All of a sudden the stupor left and my mind was clear as my protective mental shield shattered into a thousand pieces.

We climbed another flight of steps and went into a long corridor with doors on both sides. "There, to your right," the policeman said from behind me. I stopped walking and faced the dark wooden door. "Push it," he commanded. It was just a moment, a split second, before I did what I was told, but in that brief span of time I felt the impact of contradictory desires freezing my will: the reluctance to face what was behind the door and the need to know what was there. I pushed the door open because I knew I had no choice.

I couldn't believe it. I thought my mind was playing a trick on me. I rubbed my eyes to clear my vision and take me back to reality, but things were exactly the same when I reopened them. "En frente de la máquina." "In front of the machine," commanded a voice from inside the room. The burly policeman stayed by the door as I placed myself as instructed and as the voice emerged into view with a rectangular piece of metal in his right hand. "Here, hold it in front of you, by your chest," he said.

They were taking my picture. That was it! This was no interrogation room. No desk, no table, no chairs, nothing other than the big camera and the wooden platform to stand on while they took your mug shot. I felt giddy. I felt like laughing and have always wondered what that picture of me looked like. Disheveled, unwashed, hair uncombed, in the crumpled shirt and jacket in which I had slept on the cement floor, holding the rectangular metal bar with the numbers in front of me, and trying not to let my relief show on my dirty face.

The apprehension was palpable among my companions in the cell as I was brought back. They could see I hadn't been hurt, but they still had no idea what was in store for them, and their eyes gaping wide with curiosity and anxiety gave away their concern. "They're taking our picture, that's all," I said as the policeman called one of the Papiol brothers out and signaled me back in.

Our immediate concern pushed onto the back burner, our minds now returned to food. We had not eaten since our interrupted meal the night before, and we were starved. The *rateros,* the burglars, in the next cell were having breakfast brought to them and they sent the delivery man over to us with the shouted admonition: "Si quieren comer, este es el hombre, el único, no hay otro." "If you want to eat, this is it, this is your guy." And he came to our cell, and even before we could see him, he asked us how many we wanted. "How many what?" one of us replied. "Café con leche y pan con mantequilla, no hay más nada." "Buttered bread and coffee, that's all there is." I guess we really couldn't have expected anything more. "Six," we replied.

We weren't familiar with the routine of the place, but by the way the policemen were moving, by the excitement in their voices, by the nervous tension that permeated the air, it was clear that something was afoot. In the meantime, the *rateros,* who had not communicated with us beyond the information about breakfast, had been taken out of their cell and we saw there were three of them, and they were very young, about our age, and as they went by they didn't even glance in our direction, as if avoiding contamination.

The worst part of being held prisoner is the absolute severance of any link to the outside world. We had no way of finding out what was going on out there, not even why we had been locked up. As the hours passed with no one providing us with any information, our anxiety, frustration and anger grew steadily. There was no lunch and we didn't know how to get hold of the delivery man who had brought us breakfast, and in contrast to the relative stillness of the previous night inside the prison, only broken by the arrivals and departures of patrol cars and the cries of Lucas, noise was now permanent and everywhere, people were shouting, cars were pulling in and going out with blaring sirens, and the metal doors could be heard squeaking open and slamming shut. We waited, the six of us cooped up in the same cold cell, with no food, until late in the afternoon, almost evening, when another uniformed policeman, not the morning one, came and marched us to the front desk. Rafael Salas Cañizares, Batista's chief of police, was talking to a couple of officers at the desk. I had seen his picture in the papers many times, but I now realized no photographic image could do the man justice; his physical presence seemed to actually exude the stench of killings and beatings and abuses and torture. As we were formally booked he looked at us contemptuously and asked who we were.

One of the officers behind the desk answered his question, "These ones were caught last night, before the bombs went off. They had nothing to do with that," and he added, "and we don't have a cell for them now, *estamos abarrotados,* we are filled to the brim."

Salas Cañizares looked us over once more, and now his expression showed less contempt than loathing. "¿Seguro que no hay lugar?" "Are you sure you don't have room?" He asked no one in particular. "Seguro." "Sure," responded the same officer who had spoken before. "¡Mándalos entonces al carajo!" said Salas Cañizares, the rough equivalent of "then send them to go fuck themselves."

So, just like that, we were free. It took a moment for the idea to fully penetrate; the alacrity and arbitrariness with which our release had been decided left some lingering doubt, but once we realized we could really go, we went. We were quick to get out of the building, and quicker to hit the street, and we all took off in different directions, except the Papiol brothers who went together. I looked for a public phone and called home. My parents were quite worried assuming I had been arrested but not knowing why or by whom or where I was being kept. Had they known I was being held in the Buró de Investigaciones, they would have been even more concerned. They sounded relieved.

I sat down on a bench to wait for a bus as the porcine features of Rafael Salas Cañizares danced around my head, and I thought about how whimsically our fate had been determined. He knew we had done nothing but wanted to keep us in jail nonetheless, and was willing to let us go only because there wasn't room to keep us in. Had there been another empty cell, we would still be there—for as long as he, or whoever else was in charge, would have wanted.

All along I had assumed, without giving it much conscious attention, that the political events I had gotten involved in would be governed by a degree of logic, by some form of rational cause-and-effect mechanism, by a predictable sequence that would let me see and gauge the dangers coming my way, and thus I had felt that through my actions I could control the risks I was taking. But as I sat on the bench early that evening waiting for the bus, I realized the extent of my miscalculation. A breeze was blowing in from the sea, refreshing, after the stagnant air of the cell, and I understood that I could never control the implications of my actions; I lived in a reality I could neither manage nor predict. And only then did I first fully realize that what I did and what I knew were only part of a much larger equation, that the actions of others in the fight against Batista, as well as my ignorance of these actions, affected me as much as what I knew or did myself. It was an unsettling realization, a realization that brought with it yet another kind of fear. Not the earlier fear of being beaten, tortured or even murdered—those were concrete. This was a new fear, perhaps more apprehension than actual fear, the sensation of losing control, an until then unfamiliar feeling that events were spinning out of my grasp, that I didn't have a say in my own fate, and this feeling hovered above me like a menacing dark cloud.

The explosions the night of our arrest must have been the work of either renegade Triple A operatives, or of freelance militants inspired by Fidel. Those who touted their efforts in the name of Fidel and the Moncada attack had begun to move towards the still amorphous 26 of July Movement because the movement, at this stage, encouraged a symbolic identification with its commitment to violent action without affording, or requiring, organizational linkage. But whoever had been responsible for the bombs, their act was indicative of the emerging strategic shift of much of the opposition. The national political landscape was now, more than ever, firmly divided into two opposing camps. On one side was Batista, his government, his open allies, and anyone who while claiming to oppose him was willing to legitimize his rule by partaking in some electoral charade. On the other side all those who truly wanted to bring the government down: Castro, the University students, and a multiplicity of small, newly formed and independent organizations. The Communists, who had come down hard on Castro's Moncada attack, still carried the flag of popular mobilization, but the majority of the government's opponents were gradually turning towards violent confrontation as the only effective way to fight the regime.

From his prison cell, Fidel Castro was the poster child of those favoring armed violence and, as such, acted as a magnet for small groups of independent activists and for freelance revolutionists. Through his Moncada deed he had become a national figure, a hero to the opposition throughout the whole country, a potential redeemer of Cuba's political woes, the only individual providing for a glimmer of freedom and for a sign of hope. Fidel Castro was starting to fill the existing vacuum in the nation's political psyche; beginning to get closer to the heart and imagination of the country in a manner Aureliano had never been able even to approximate; becoming a symbol, the human incarnation of the fight against evil, whose actions were bound to be projected into the field of legend. And people began to flock to him or, more accurately, to align themselves behind his flag. Fidel was emerging as the figurehead of the anti-Batista struggle; Cuba was giving birth to a new *caudillo.*[*]

My personal dislike for Fidel immunized me to his appeal as I couldn't separate the private from the political, but my antipathy towards him didn't blind me to the long shadow he was casting over the land. It was disturbing but also somewhat compelling—in a car wreck sort of way—to watch the opposition buckle under the idea of Fidel-the-hero, to see everything now measured in reference to his daring but failed attack, to observe Fidel steadily gaining control over the course and agenda of anti-Batista activism. Although in prison, Fidel was able to communi-

---

[*] *Caudillo* is one of those terms whose precise meaning intellectuals love to debate. Ultimately, however, a *caudillo* is a leader who is identified in the eyes of his supporters with a cause. The common rendition of *caudillo* as simply a military dictator misses two important points: (1) that the *caudillo* does not have to be a military man; and (2) that force alone does not qualify him for the role.

cate with the outside world, claim moral authority over the rest of the
opposition and leave all potential rivals behind. This process was unfolding before my eyes and I was disturbed and puzzled by it, although
I never dreamed it would reach the magnitude it eventually did.

My preoccupation at the moment was limited to the glorification of
a fiasco, to the drawing of mistaken conclusions from a direct attack on
the Cuban army carried out without an adequate plan, without the resources for success and without a fallback strategy. Fidel deserved a certain amount of praise, for sure—he was, after all, still the only one to
have taken any armed action against the government—but his deed was
not the proper gauge by which to measure anti-Batista activity, or the
best model to follow. There was no reason—no sound reason, that is—
to believe his approach was the only or most effective one. If anything,
the evidence pointed in the opposite direction. His leadership credentials, although impressive since his attack on the Moncada barracks, were
not superior to those of other committed anti-Batista activists like the
University students who were proving their mettle in repeated bloody
confrontations with the police. But reason was no longer relevant—if it
had ever been. I was perplexed by how Fidel was bringing anti-Batista
forces under his spell, and the more I thought about it, and the more
pronounced the rise in Fidel's standing, the less I grasped the reason why.

I sought understanding with Kiko Baeza who took my bewilderment
with compassionate amusement and who tried to reassure me with historical, psychological and sociological explanations. But, being Kiko
Baeza, he went on to point out the weaknesses, lack of insight and su-
perficiality often inherent in the same answers he was giving me. He was
not one to concern himself with understanding; he saw such an effort as
futile and meaningless. He preferred to simply observe, taking pleasure
in noticing the folly and capriciousness of what went on around him,
more interested in its human aspects and humorous implications than in
sorting out causes or formulating interpretations. "That's how heroes
become heroes and saints become saints," he would say, and he made
me relax and often laugh, but he didn't help me to understand.

Jorge Tallet helped—some. He didn't have the answers I was seeking
either, but he would entertain my questions, so we discussed the incomprehensible willingness—psychologically, rhetorically and politically—
of the opposition to subordinate itself to Castro. Granted that some of
those praising him in public, especially the new student leaders at Havana University, reserved plenty of criticism and snide comments for private conversation, but this attitude in no way hampered the growing
exaltation of Fidel. It was as if finding fault with Fidel, or expressing any

criticism of his Moncada action, was no longer permissible, as if doing so constituted a sin, a taboo. Why?

I never found a satisfying explanation, but I couldn't fail to see the mechanics and some of the phenomenon's implications. Neither the student leaders nor anyone else would dare criticize Castro publicly until they had pulled themselves to his level, that is, until they had confronted the government, arms-in-hand. In the convoluted game of revolutionary political competition, Fidel Castro had raised the ante, he had led a frontal armed attack against the dictator, and since he was the only one to have done so, he had come to monopolize the mantle of true opposition to Batista. Anyone wanting to remain competitive had now to ante up in the same coin. The fact that the attack had failed, that Castro was alive thanks to his in-laws' influence, or to Batista's whim, didn't matter. I couldn't help but feel that the situation made little sense, but at the same time couldn't ignore that, sense or no sense, this was the logic ruling our reality.

Every revolutionary wannabe was now scrambling to organize and find a place in some armed effort, to partake in a deed of violence that would validate his standing and serve as imprimatur to his political credentials. And now, for the first time, I began to doubt such brazen tactics. Fidel's armed blunder and the virtual vaporization of the Triple A had led me to question the efficacy, wisdom and even desirability of armed action that was not part of a wider plan; a plan that included propaganda and mobilization and political education, and above all, clarity of goals. The Communists had a point, I reluctantly acknowledged, when they argued that taking up arms in rebellion without engaging in any other form of political activism was either ineffective or led to undesired consequences. I began to see sole concern with armed action as detrimental to sound and effective political reform, as an impediment to the acknowledgment that what was necessary to eradicate was not just the ongoing dictatorship but the rottenness of the basis upon which it rested. I started to look upon this commitment to violence as detracting from the need to attack the root of the problem, what made our dictator and his ilk possible, and as taking attention away from the importance of constructing a reliable constitutional and democratic order. The point, I now thought, was not to overthrow Batista the man but to do away with what he and his system and his cronies stood for: illegitimacy, arbitrariness, military rule and official banditry. I was either maturing or looking for an excuse not to fight.

The music was changing again, although I couldn't put my fingers on precisely how. All the old rhythms were still there and the cacophony had not gotten any less discordant or any less loud, but it was as if the sounds were now coming from a farther distance, as if I were hearing them from another room or from far away.

For the first three years of the Batista dictatorship I had been completely immersed in the politics of the new situation, nothing else had mattered, even my desire to travel and see the world had been put on hold as all my energy and determination went into doing something about the country's condition, into striking back. The frustration with the Triple A first, and the growing adulation of Fidel Castro now, started to give me pause, to generate a subtle but undeniable sense of detachment, as my emotional commitment began to make room for a critical appraisal of what was happening around me. My desire to see the country free of Batista and his henchmen had not flagged, but the question of how to go about it, what means to use, started to rise, to give me concern. Up to then I had uncritically accepted all anti-Batista actions without distinguishing between them. I no longer felt that way.

Havana University was a microcosm of Cuba, and much of what was wrong with the country at large could be found at the institution I had idealized and still saw as a bastion of political idealism, and as the spiritual center of the fight against the dictatorship. I became increasingly aware that the University was ailing—educationally, administratively, even politically—and could no longer retain, at least in my eyes, the moral authority to lead others in the fight against oppression and corruption. I knew I was shifting my focus, taking a detour from my ultimate goal, but I was certain that an essential step towards eliminating Batista's regime was to clean our own house. Reorganizing my thoughts and reappraising my objectives allowed me to be active in the fight against tyranny without shutting my eyes to reality, without partaking in the surging glorification of Castro and without being seduced by the facile promises of another Triple A.

I had seen my union work as a way of making people face the harsh fact of military rule and of aligning them against it, but I had come to fully accept that union work wasn't my thing, that it didn't motivate me. So I began to drastically curtail my involvement in these activities, trading places with Feliciano, who became the head steward at the bank. I theoretically remained his second in command but in fact did little or no union work, and let Reinol be our liaison with other antigovernment labor groups, and I gave my full attention to the University.

I began my new crusade by voicing my growing anger and disappointment with Raúl Roa—the dean of my school, my ex-superior in the Triple A, and Neji's brother-in-law—in a loud and public confrontation. I spoke up at a meeting he was holding in his office with students, and accused him of allowing erratic professorial behavior and of mismanaging the Social Sciences School. And while everything I said was undeniably true, what I was doing was just not done—it was not only unconventional, it was taboo; it went against the accepted political correctness of the time to call attention to the frivolous manner in which the University schools were run, to the absenteeism of the faculty, to the inadequacies of the curriculum, to the lack of concern for the needs of students, to the administrative disorder in which the institution operated, and, very especially, it was unheard of for a student to attack a faculty member who was a known opponent of the government.

The other students in the room sat aghast during my verbal assault; they couldn't believe I was actually saying what I was, that I was holding Roa personally responsible for the ills of the school and challenging him further by questioning his sincerity, insisting that he ignored the kind of problem in the school that he claimed to oppose in the government. Roa was livid and could barely contain his anger; anger fueled, I was sure, by the knowledge that my accusations were justified and that everyone in the room, although unwilling to join me, knew it. He offered some lame excuses, promised to look into some of the things I had mentioned and cut the meeting short. I had managed to secure two things: Roa's everlasting enmity and the reputation among my fellow students of being boneheaded or crazy.[†]

Taking advantage of accumulated vacation time, of the flexibility of my work schedule and of the relinquishing of union responsibilities, I immersed myself in the University, trying to escape from the political dislocation Fidel Castro and the disintegration of the Triple A had brought to my life. Occasionally I returned to the Moon and tried to view things from there, searching for some clarity to help me find new bearings. I wanted to engage in political activity that would allow me to keep fighting Batista in a way I thought proper and logical, in a way I could find acceptable, and I was having a difficult time discovering such a way. The Partido Ortodoxo youth section and the Triple A had vanished from under my

---

[†]After Castro took over in 1959, Raúl Roa became Cuban ambassador to the Organization of American States and, before the year was over, minister of foreign affairs, a position he kept until 1973. He remained loyal to the Castro regime until his death in 1982.

feet, swallowed by dynamic forces I could see but not control and which ran counter to logic or, at least, counter to my understanding and expectation. As I involved myself more in Havana University life and became active in its politics, I started to feel an increasing sense of discomfort, of frustration, caused first by the hypocrisy in Roa's management of the Social Sciences School, and then by the manner in which the student leadership of the University had been overhauled.

It was in accordance with Cuban political tradition for the University's student federation, the FEU, to take the leading role against dictatorship and oppression. No other institution was up to the task, and this was perfectly in line with the University's history, with the predisposition of the student body and with the island's political tradition. So there was no question in what direction student politics were headed, and the election of a new executive body for the FEU was only a matter a selecting among individuals who stood for the same course of action—openly confronting the government, demanding the ouster of Batista, and the return to electoral democracy and the rule of law. Each school's student body elected a president by direct vote and then the elected school presidents, thirteen in number, elected a president of the FEU from within their ranks, and whoever was elected to this position was expected, at this juncture in Cuban history, to be a leading figure in the struggle against the dictator.

The two different approaches to the fight against the Batista government, direct armed confrontation and popular mobilization, had competed for adoption by the opposition from the very day Batista staged his coup. Without giving much consideration to their pros and cons, I had been drawn by the former, hence my membership in the Triple A, and had thought disparagingly of the latter. The attraction of the first was part gut reaction and part a naively idealized notion of its execution. Popular mobilization, which I took to mean the creation of widespread awareness of the Batista regime's ills, and of the need to institute new policies and create a new attitude, appeared as a dreary endeavor devoid of dash and adventure. My experience as a union leader had confirmed in my mind the dullness of such a task, and the Communists' advocacy of this approach had made it smell of rhetorical bunk. But now, although I still couldn't get my heart behind it, I had to admit that there was merit to the popular involvement approach, so when the newly elected president of the FEU, a proponent of civic involvement and popular mobilization from the School of Education, was quickly and peremptorily forced out of office by militant advocates of armed confrontation, I was appalled. Removal from office through intimidation seemed quite out of place in the very institution and among the very people who opposed Batista for his tyrannical rule and lack of regard for the law.

There seemed to be a growing discontinuity, a contradiction, between the stated objectives of the anti-Batista forces and their own behavior. Roa blithely accepted corruption in his own school while he called for the heads of those who abided by the same immoral practices in governmental and political functions. Anti-Batista students had no qualms about using strong-arm tactics to scare someone out of office, in fact staging a coup, because they didn't agree with him; as if claiming to be fighting for freedom and democracy at one level granted them license to transgress that same freedom and democracy at another. It was painful to realize that the sins of Batista were not limited to him and his band of murderers and thieves, but the evidence couldn't be ignored, and I began to think that the manner in which the dictatorship was fought and the means used to get rid of it were as important as having the dictator gone.

As I reluctantly began to accept the value of popular participation in the fight against the government, I had to figure out what I could do about it, how I could contribute to it. I had turned away from union work, unable to overcome my aversion to the tedious details required to perform well the duties of a steward and had warmed up to the idea of becoming part of the University's student government, which, given the preeminence of Havana University in anti-Batista politics, would have put me in a position to reach large segments of the population. This, however, was somewhere in the future; first I would have to climb the ladder of student leadership. I was familiar with the path and knew it would take some time. So what could I do in the meantime?

Fermín Flores came up with an idea. He was an old acquaintance from the Ortodoxo youth section, a man who fused elocution with incantation to produce a mesmerizing concoction of voodoo and political speech, a unique oratorical style that was guaranteed to transfix any audience. I ran into him one evening and, as we discussed the political situation, I told him about my change of heart concerning anti-Batista tactics. He, who had always preferred popular mobilization to armed confrontation, suggested that we stage our own public antigovernment rally, in our own neighborhood, Luyanó.

It took quite a bit of effort and finagling to organize the rally. We had to choose a location, find speakers, secure seating—park benches were not suited for the occasion since generally there were too few of them and usually improperly placed—and get the word out, advertise the meeting. We purposely ignored anything regarding official permission; permits were required for such gatherings, but we figured that since we didn't recognize the government as legitimate, we couldn't very well ask its permission to hold our rally.

We eventually chose a small park, one square block, with an elevated platform in the center that could serve as dais for the speakers. Finding people to address the meeting was not difficult—Flores and I would both speak and we invited the Trigger, our former leader Pepe Gatillo, to join us. Even though he had been politically inactive since the collapse of the Ortodoxos, he quickly, and surprisingly, accepted our offer. Our roster was completed by another former comrade from our Ortodoxo days, Mario Rivadulla, a good orator. The hard part was letting people know about the rally, making sure they knew when and where it would take place. Newspaper and radio were out of the question given the threat of government reprisals against the media, and because their citywide readership and audience didn't lend themselves to our makeshift local operation. We also knew that only a few days, three or four at the most, should pass between the public announcement of this type of antigovernment convocation and the act itself. If more time elapsed, especially given the fact that we could make only one serious effort at getting the information out, people would either forget or the police would discourage potential attendees by letting it be known that trouble was expected.

So our only real option for publicizing the meeting was distributing leaflets. Our tactic was to surprise people into attending before they found anything better to do that evening or were scared away. We decided that the leaflets should be distributed only in the neighborhood two or three days before the rally. But we had no leaflets, and without leaflets we would have no meeting. Flores had approached several printers he knew, but they all refused to have anything to do with printing a flyer that called people to attend a protest gathering in strong antigovernment language. Flores was out of printers and I didn't know any, the only thing that occurred to me was to go and see my uncle Miguel, the Communist honcho.

In the traditional Latin fashion that protects family links by not letting extraneous disagreements intrude, Miguel and I never discussed politics. I knew what he thought and he knew what I thought. There was then no unnecessary preamble, just the normal family niceties, after which I told him we were trying to organize an antigovernment public action but couldn't find a printer for the leaflets announcing it. He listened to me and without asking any questions gave me the name and address of a print shop, also in Luyanó, and told me to take the work there. That same day I went to the address Miguel had given me. A man came out and I told him what I wanted. He most probably had been alerted to my visit since he made no comment, just took a look at the proposed text I had brought along, asked me how many copies were needed and told me to come back the following day to pick them up. And the next day they were ready, and two days after that we were distributing them.

That was our last organizational hurdle. Flores, in a burst of creativity, had turned the absence of adequate seating accommodations in the park into a propaganda asset. It was indeed customary for public political gatherings to provide chairs for those attending; it was not only a question of custom but of common sense. Revolutionary circumstances, however, called for revolutionary solutions. We were not going to provide chairs because conditions called for the people to be alert and "on their feet." So in our leaflets we called the people of Luyanó to a *mitin sin sillas,* to a meeting without chairs.

Surprisingly, and almost disappointingly, the rally took place in total peace. No interruptions, no police invasion, and an audience we thought good in numbers, well over one hundred, but that didn't seem to share completely the intensity of our enthusiasm for anti-Batista rhetoric. They applauded what we said, but not wildly, and appeared somewhat curious about us, especially when Flores turned his back on them in the middle of his peroration and conducted some audible but cryptic exchange with an unseen alternate audience. Rivadulla spoke first, Flores second, I third, and Pepe, the best orator among us, last. Our listeners reacted similarly to each of us, except for the wider eyes for Flores' incantations, and showed more interest in references to specific practical issues—the need to improve public transportation, to create jobs, to tackle our economic overdependence on sugar, to build more and better schools—than to the fate of democracy and freedom in our land.

I hadn't thought much about what I was going to say at the meeting, assuming that words would come when the time came. I had spoken before at Ortodoxo youth gatherings, at union rallies and at Havana University public convocations, and had come to think there wasn't a whole lot to speech making. If you had your ideas and you said what you wanted to say as clearly as possible, that was that. But as I watched our audience take in Rivadulla's words and then Flores's mystically coated political harangue, I sensed the presence of a form of energy in the crowd I had never felt before. Their attention seemed to directly affect the speakers, as if what I had always considered a straightforward one-way process had metamorphosed into a two-way give-and-take. I could see the deliveries of both my predecessors on the improvised podium affected in a subtle, but noticeable, manner by the reactions and attitudes of the crowd. When my turn came, I found myself carefully scrutinizing the audience as I spoke, trying to see how they reacted to my words. Most of them were clearly far from affluent and a good number of them black; they were not my middle-class bank coworkers, or the politically motivated Ortodoxo activists, or the middle-class and politically active university students, but just a group of regular Cubans. And as I touched on practical issues and problems with which they were concerned, their heads moved forward, towards me, and their faces showed increased attention, and as I discoursed on principle and abstraction, their heads fell back and their faces reflected flagging interest. I didn't know at first if my eyes were playing tricks on me, so I began to experiment, trying to control with my choice of subject and words how my listeners swayed back and forth. It was surprisingly easy to do and I began to indulge in the game; and as I directed their reaction, their reaction started to influence what I was saying.

As instructive as the communication between speaker and audience was, the Luyanó park meeting taught me something more important by bringing me face-to-face with an aspect of political reality that my romantic naïveté had tended to neglect and belittle—the preoccupation of most people with those issues and problems that affect their daily life, and their limited interest in abstract ideas and general principles. It was not that I was unaware that "bread-and-butter" issues were important political subjects. By then I had read enough to know where the French Revolution ended and the Russian one began, and of more relevance to our situation, I knew also about the Mexican Revolution and what it had meant, how what began as an electoral dispute ended up transforming a society. Still, this was all abstract knowledge, intellectual disquisition. That night, in the small park in Luyanó, the human side of politics, the substance of what most people were interested in and cared for, became real, and it was obvious it couldn't be ignored.

I was forced to think about politics in general and about my role in particular. I had no trouble recognizing that, in a country like Cuba, advocating changes in government that didn't imply changes in how people lived was a meaningless proposition. My political friends and I had seen the return to democratic rule as a first step in the regeneration of the country without giving much attention to what the subsequent steps would be, obsessed as we were with the overthrow of the military dictatorship, personally affronted by Batista and by his actions. The more I thought about it, however, the more convinced I became that there was something hollow in our approach. Yes, we had paid lip service all along to the need for social reform, but the truth was that we didn't have an inkling of what that meant, other than being "fair" and "equitable" and "socially responsible"—a concern for social issues which, if left unexplained, was nothing but yet another abstraction.

And as I wrestled with the question and tried to make sense of it, and as I was also trying to decide whether or not to run for president of my school's student body, Kiko called and invited me to dinner. It was an expensive restaurant and Kiko was in an expansive mood, a mood that indicated he had money to burn. He had gotten a job, he informed me as soon as we met, the first real job he had ever had, and given his attitude towards money and his ideas about it, he had managed to secure the most improbable of all possible employment: that of *cobrador*.

Cuba was still largely in the cash era with the use of checks limited almost exclusively to business transactions, and paying with cash meant that someone had to collect it, and this was the *cobrador*, bill collector. Insurance companies, public utilities and a multiplicity of other institutions sent their *cobradores* all over the land and these men, with their old briefcases, tired expressions and worn ties over old short-sleeved shirts, were visible in all urban areas, especially in Havana. Large institutions would have their own collectors, smaller ones would use collecting services, and it was one of these services that had employed Kiko.

How Kiko came to be hired for this job, no one ever knew. He wouldn't say and we didn't ask since asking would have been an unacceptable intrusion into his privacy and this, for whatever reason, we didn't do. Most of us were sure, however, that Kiko had not actually sought the job, that it had been foisted on him by his father or by an oversolicitous family friend or by one of his sisters, and that he had agreed to undertake it so as not to appear unappreciative. There was no other possible explanation—and there was no other possible outcome than Kiko losing the job as fast as he had gotten it.

It was a truly exceptional month; a tour of Havana's best restaurants as two or three times a week Kiko would call with an invitation to dine, and his words would always be pretty much the same: "I collected so much today. Let's find a good place to eat." And there would never be more than four of us at dinner, and Kiko never overate in the manner he had done when he almost killed himself with pasta, and he would talk about his experience as a *cobrador*, and about the people he had met and how they reacted to a bill collector descending upon them, especially one who didn't look like a *cobrador* at all. He would imitate their expressions as they realized what he was, which went from surprised embarrassment to undisguised annoyance to blatant antagonism and, in some instances, to true desperation. And Kiko would delight in reproducing their arguments and in the long list of excuses they offered for not paying, for asking for extensions, for requesting that he come back some other time when someone else who happened not to be there that day would definitely be there with the money.

Kiko's recitals on his saga as *cobrador* although extremely funny were totally devoid of malice or cruelty. In fact, he felt sorry for those he was to collect from and who often could ill afford whatever it was they were now supposed to be paying for. And as there were those who put all their creativity into explaining their tardiness, there were those who took paying on time as a sacred duty and who, in some cases, were able to do so only at the expense of something of higher necessity, and in such instances Kiko would exercise all his persuasive talent to convince them that they didn't have to pay, that the world wouldn't end if they used the money for food or for their children or for something else they needed. This was the reason we couldn't dine out everyday, he would explain, he wouldn't accept payment from those he thought couldn't afford it. And he would state this as the most natural of all things without ever a trace of self-righteousness or sanctimony. For him it was not an ethical issue but a practical proposition, you paid only if you had no choice, and you definitely didn't pay if there were more important things to do with your money, and it all tallied with his philosophical decoupling of the buying and paying acts.

The month came to an end, as we knew it would, and as we also knew it would, so did Kiko's job. Not only was Kiko fired, but his employers demanded the money he had blown in dinners, and threatened to call in the police and have him arrested. They gave him forty-eight hours to produce the money, so we met that night at Julio's house after scavenging around for every peso we could get our hands on, and the money owed was a large sum for us, over three hundred pesos, and after putting together all we had been able to dig out during the day, we were still short around fifty, and since I was the only one with a steady job and had been the primary beneficiary of Kiko's largess, I called my sister Marta and convinced her to lend me the money.

Two days later I saw Kiko, who looked his absolutely normal self and was telling the story of how flustered his employers had been when time came to turn in the money he had collected and he simply told them he didn't have it, that he had spent it; and how at first they thought he was joking and how, when they realized he wasn't, they became outraged and began shouting and threatening him; and how he just sat there until they were done with the shouting and the threatening, and had given him the forty-eight hours to produce the money after mentioning police and jail time; and how he then told them he had one request to make, and how they were puzzled and asked him what it was; and how he then gave them a list of about ten people whom he thought were in such bad economic straits that they deserved special consideration; and how then, according to Kiko, those questioning him really lost it.‡

The police cars pulled up to the house, lights flashing and sirens blaring—three or four of them, according to the neighbors across the street. Two policemen with submachine guns forced their way inside through the front door, and two others, equally armed, ran to cover the back entrance. The rest stayed outside, covering both sides on Villanueva and Rodríguez Streets. They shouted and threw stuff around and demanded to know where I was. I wasn't home, my mother told them, so they asked a few more questions and left leaving instruction that I should report to the local police station as soon as I returned.

My mother told me when I called that evening. It had already been a couple of hours, but she was still upset. I asked if they had given any indication why they were looking for me, and she said she had asked the officer in charge several times but he had never given her an answer. Although my father and my brother, as well as my two sisters, had been home at the time, the policemen showed no interest in anyone else. I immediately thought back to the bombs that had been set off the night I was taken in with the Papiol brothers. Part of the problem with my new position as revolutionary freelancer was that I never knew what anyone else was up to, and this police visit was a forceful reminder of that. I had to find out what was going on.

‡Kiko Baeza, true to his theory that buying and paying were two disconnected operations with no relation to one another, was on the brink of financial disaster when Fidel Castro came to power and, as one of the first measures of his government, canceled all personal debts. Kiko went to work for the Cuban diplomatic service and, either out of gratitude to Fidel or inertia, but definitely not out of ideological commitment, remained loyal to the regime until his death in 2001, having served for some years as director of the Cuban Cultural Center in Prague and, upon his return to the island, as head of the country's cultural radio and television stations.

I called Jorge. He suggested we go consult with his father who was, in addition to one of the country's best poets, a prominent journalist with friends and influence at several Havana newspapers. It was almost midnight by the time we arrived at *el viejo* Tallet's home, a modest apartment on San Lázaro Street that looked more like a book repository than living quarters. I had never met anyone, poet or not, who looked more truly bohemian than José Zacarias Tallet, with an unkempt mane of red hair covering his head and part of his face while his person and demeanor conveyed no affectation. He must have been in his late fifties or early sixties but seemed younger, and held to a facial expression that let you know that, as he sat there facing you, his mind, or at least part of it, was somewhere else.

The elder Tallet, who had been in his newspaper's office until a few hours earlier, had not heard of any imminent anti-Batista activity that could explain the sudden police interest in me. We discussed the matter for a little while and he advised me to turn myself in and that if I had not been released by morning, he would mobilize his friends in the press to look into the matter. To understand the basis for this advice one must take into account that during his years in power Batista fluctuated between the repressive dictator he was and the popular politician he wanted to be, and that since his return to power in 1952 he had tried to legitimize his rule by allowing periods of relative permissiveness, usually in conjunction with some electoral machination. This meant that, sometimes, to a certain degree and under the right circumstances, the press wielded some influence.

It was almost two in the morning when I walked into the police station on the Calzada del 10 de Octubre, about six blocks away from my home, and turned myself in. The desk sergeant looked my name up, found it somewhere among his papers, eyed me intently but expressionlessly and asked a policeman to take me to an outside patio. The patio was a cemented rectangular passage that had a tall wall to its left and a series of doors to its right, five or six of them. Attached to the wall was a long bench, also cement. I was told to sit on it, which I did facing the almost deserted patio with only an occasional policeman walking by.

The longer I sat there, the surer I was that I should not have come, that old man Tallet's advice, although well intentioned, had been mistaken; it might have been common sense or, perhaps, the effect of sitting outside on the cement bench as the night got cooler and the hours began to pass with burdensome monotony. I was not in a cell, but I felt totally isolated, and maybe it was this sense of isolation more than the drop in temperature that began to make me shiver. By the time I could feel the morning approaching I was absolutely convinced that I should never have turned myself in, and as I pondered the consequences of my mistake I saw the police captain in charge of the station walk in.

He came into the building, stopped at the front desk, spoke to the sergeant for a brief moment, came out into the rectangular patio, passed me without a glance in my direction and went through one of the doors facing my bench. It was a while before he came back again, maybe twenty minutes, maybe longer, I couldn't tell, but when he came back he came directly at me, and I saw that he was now hatless and in shirtsleeves, and I had a clear view of his face, a face I had seen before.

"Are you Marcial's nephew?" he asked, and without giving me a chance to reply added, "Paquito's son?" "Yes," I said. He moved closer, rested one foot on the bench, shoved his face up to just a few inches from mine, and without raising his voice asked, "¿Quién carajo te mandó a venir?" "Who the fuck told you to come here?" I began to answer, but he cut me short, and still without raising his voice looked straight into my eyes, "Listen carefully, under no circumstances, none! are you to turn yourself in again." He paused, but it was clear he was not waiting for me to say anything, so I simply nodded, acknowledging that I understood, that I'd gotten his message. He kept his glare on my face, as if to make sure his words had actually made their way through my thick skull, and then in a slightly louder voice told me to get the hell out of there.

The next evening my uncle Marcial came by the house and took my father and me to a room where the three of us could be alone. The police captain was passing word down to us through his brother, one of Marcial's oldest friends, that my name was on a list of anti-Batista activists who were to be rounded up and "disposed of" in retaliation for any future acts of violence against the government. Apparently the police had gotten wind of a plot earlier in the week and had come to get me in case anything happened. Luckily for me, nothing happened and I had been let go. The captain didn't know why my name was on this list and had no power to remove it, but he wanted us to be aware of it. Turning myself in had been, Marcial was told, a very stupid move, since the ominous request to dispose of the people on the list couldn't be misunderstood or ignored. Marcial, usually a happy-go-lucky character in permanent high spirits, conveyed this information with gloom and concern, and my father's face grew ashen as he kept looking at me. When the state of my actual circumstances sank fully in, I felt threatened, afraid of what the police might do to me if I fell into their hands, and disgusted by my previous evening's lack of caution; but with the inflated self-perception and absence of sense characteristic of most twenty-year-old males, I also felt proud.

My father and I had had one, only one, conversation about my political activism. He had tried to dissuade me from any potentially dangerous undertaking with reasons ranging from the inherent corruption of Cuban politics to the unscrupulous tendency of older people to use younger ones to do their fighting for them. He was, at the same time, careful to let me know he respected my convictions—he just wanted me to be "realistic" about them, not to let others take advantage of me. I, in turn, told him that I understood and appreciated his fatherly concern and that I would try to act intelligently and responsibly but that as he was committed to his religious beliefs, I was equally committed to my political ones. I am sure my answer did not satisfy him, but although he and my mother frequently expressed concern about my safety, on no other occasion did he question my antigovernment militancy.

My mother, on the other hand, questioned my political activities loudly and frequently. Partly to placate her, and partly out of my own increased concern with safety, I began avoiding my own home as much as possible. Without any concrete plan or schedule, I would sleep over at relatives or friends as often as I could. When I was home, I would make sure to have a clear plan and path of escape should the police descend on the house again. It is questionable whether this forced foresight would have been of much actual help, but it made me feel better, and I needed to feel better about my safety because it was becoming evident that an increasing number of those opposed to Batista shared none of my newfound doubts about the effectiveness of violence. Antigovernment activists, sometimes on their own and sometimes in small groups, were, with mounting frequency, placing bombs and shooting policemen and soldiers and, needless to say, the dictator's thugs were retaliating in kind.

CHAPTER TWELVE

There was no way I could defeat Juan Nuiry for the presidency of the Social Sciences student body, since he had the election sewn up. Not that it was going to be rigged, just that he held all the cards. He had been around for a while as a full-time student and as a candidate whereas I was a newcomer in both respects; he was already vice president, I had no official position in student government; he had the support of the outgoing president and of all those active in the school's electoral politics, I had the support only of a small group of ordinary students; and to top it all off, he had a knockout of a sister actively campaigning for him among the male students while I had no weapon to match that in my meager arsenal. I knew I had no chance of winning, but I decided to run anyway. There was something about being invited to address student meetings, about everyone knowing who you were, about seeing your name in big printed characters on the posters hanging on the walls of the cafeteria and the classrooms that brought a certain satisfaction—a juvenile, attention-seeking kind of satisfaction for sure, but satisfaction nevertheless.

It was as I campaigned one morning, engaged in a futile attempt to make the race competitive, that I met Joan Campana. I came across one of my few enthusiastic supporters, Rubén, sitting on a bench with an attractive girl who was wiping tears from her cheeks. I was about to turn around, not wanting to intrude, when Rubén called me over, introduced me and went on to explain the reason for her distress.

She was an American student from Yonkers, New York. After majoring in Spanish at home, she had arrived in Havana, her first time out of the United States, eager to take courses at the University and to put her long years of language work to the test. Now she was ready to quit, to go back home. She couldn't understand what Cubans said to her. Nothing in her education had prepared her for the speed with which Cubans spoke, for the way they chained one word to the next without pause, jamming complete phrases and sentences into one, to her incomprehensible, sound; for their total lack of regard for word endings, treating them as unnecessary nuisances to be discarded at all cost. She had not been warned about Havana's vast slang, rich in Hispanicized African terms and with sprinkles of Caló, Spanish Gypsy language. Rubén, who spoke English, was trying to console her and tried to enlist my help. Since I didn't speak any English, he thought she would feel better if she was able to converse with me in Spanish.

He was trying to hammer the point in that she just had to give herself some time to get used to the way we Cubans went about grinding, almost pulverizing, the Spanish language. The three of us had lunch together and Joan and I spent most of the afternoon walking around the University and chatting, mostly about Cuba, New York and academic life in Cuba and in the United States. Her understanding of the language was actually quite good. She could talk about almost any subject with fluency, and had no difficulty understanding me as I slowed my speech and toned down my Cuban diction enunciating more the way my mother had instructed me to speak as a child. It was clear that nothing was amiss with her knowledge of Spanish and that Rubén's diagnosis had been accurate. Practice and patience—lots of patience, that's all she needed. I told her what I thought and proposed that we get together again. She agreed.

To suggest that Joan Campana became my girlfriend would be inaccurate. We were friends and spent a lot of time together; she was interested in getting her Spanish up to Cuban speed, literally so, and I enjoyed the company of an attractive girl who could tell me about a foreign land I only knew through the movies. If those who saw us frequently together wanted to believe that romance was also present, I was not going to go out of my way to enlighten them; if nothing else, it pleased my vanity.

Joan Campana was a window to the outside world, a way of escaping my increasing frustration and ambivalence. As we sat down on a city bench, or took walks along the seashore or rode to the countryside for a glance at rural Cuba, I forgot about my mounting doubts fueled by the surge in violent confrontation and the narrowing of the political alternatives from which to choose. On at least two separate occasions, bombs went off within our hearing when we were strolling down the street or having coffee at some outside café. Joan couldn't understand how blasé the general reaction was, as everyone carried on with what they were doing as if they hadn't heard a thing. Cubans were in some ways quite fatalistic, and by now the frequency of the explosions had increased to such an extent that they were beginning to be taken as a part of daily life, as an unavoidable risk. But I tried to convey to her, I'm not sure how successfully, that underneath the lack of visible reaction lay true concern for the increasing unpredictability and danger. Or maybe I was just telling her how I felt.

My mental escapades with Joan were supplemented by long discussions with Jorge Tallet, mutual attempts to discover a path that would allow us to keep fighting the government without betraying other principles — or making fools of ourselves. He was basically in the same predicament I was. Writing a column for one of the largest daily Havana newspapers, *El Mundo,* which dealt usually with nonpolitical subjects, he had gone out of his way to include denunciations of government abuses, and his name was bound to be on the same nefarious list as mine or on a similar one. We agreed on the need for widespread popular participation in the opposition to the government, and on the pitfalls inherent in any violent action that wasn't an integral part of a well-thought-out political strategy. We discussed the works of Gustave Le Bon, Curzio Malaparte and Ortega y Gasset on the psychology of the masses and on the techniques for a violent takeover of the government, and we knew that violent action could easily transmute from means to end, and this wasn't empty theoretical speculation — it was happening in front of our eyes. Tallet and I didn't conclude anything in our discussions because there was nothing for us to conclude, events were doing it for us.

As my sense of political isolation grew, I increased my contacts with Baeza and Tallet. In their very different idiosyncratic ways they were islands of sanity in a world that was going berserk. Kiko had gone back to writing doctoral dissertations and under no circumstances would he contemplate getting a degree himself, something he could have easily managed in at least a couple of fields. Tallet, a brilliant student, had been offered a greatly sought-after job for a graduating philosophy student, an assistantship to the most distinguished philosophy professor at the University. He turned it down.* Both of them saw academic life as lacking, intellectually and ethically. So at a time when many of my dreams

---

*After the fall of the Batista government, Jorge Tallet became the third-highest-ranking officer in the Cuban Ministry of Foreign Affairs and, in disagreement with the regime's policies, left the island in 1962.

had vanished and some of my convictions were flagging, Jorge Tallet and Kiko Baeza showed me that honesty and integrity did indeed exist.

My ability to study, read texts and pass examinations increased all of a sudden when I found an antidote to my hyperactivity or to whatever prevented me from long stretches of memorizing efforts. I met Mario Condi during Professor Entralgo's softball games when we both played on the same losing team, and at one point he told me he was having trouble with a subject and suggested we study together. I had never studied with anyone and wasn't inclined to do so, but he put it as a request, as a favor, and I acceded.

It turned out to be the best studying move I ever made. The textbook we tackled was written in dry and syntax-deficient semilegalese and it took me sometimes a couple of tries before I could figure out the meaning of some of its sentences or paragraphs. But Mario wouldn't get it. He wouldn't get it the first, the second or the third time—just rereading the words wasn't any help. I would have to decipher them for him, to explain their content in as simple and plain a language as possible. This forced me to concentrate on understanding rather than memorizing—and it was like magic. Once I was able to explain something to Mario I remembered it quite well, at least for the next few days—all that was needed to pass the test. So I began to study with Mario whenever possible, even registering for courses just to have him as a studying partner. It was a useful arrangement for the two of us. He got passing grades and I could accelerate the rate at which I took the required subjects since there was no limit to the number of them a free student could take.

One afternoon I arrived at the University and was told Mario had been in a fistfight. Fistfights were rare occurrences at Havana University. Shootouts were part of the institution's accepted canons of behavior, but fistfights were not, so I was puzzled and sought Mario out and eventually found him. He told me it was true, he had had an argument with another student and they had gotten into a scuffle and a few punches had been thrown. He explained that the argument started when he and this student were debating which of the two was better versed in administrative law. The other student based his claim on the high grade he had obtained on the subject while Mario thought such a claim weaker than his own. The student, Mario explained, had gotten a good grade in the examination, that was true, but had studied the subject only once. He, on the other hand, had studied the subject five times, true he had flunked it the first four times, but that was not relevant—he had studied it five, mind you, five times! As we spoke he was still so outraged at the falsity of the other student's claim and so convinced of the superiority of his own that it became clear why the fight had ensued.[†]

In March 1955 Batista let Castro out of jail in one of the many inexplicable twists of a mind caught between a dictator's need to rely on force to stay in power and a wannabe politician's longing for popularity. Under different circumstances, and in a different latitude, Batista's psyche could easily have been material for a classical tragedy, but in our tropical island burnt by the relentless sun it was destined simply to set the stage for the bloody rendition of a farcical play.

By July Castro was on his way out of Cuba, but promising to return. This was a threat against Batista as well as a challenge to anyone aspiring to lead, and reap the eventual fruits, of an antigovernment revolt. The student leaders understood the challenge perfectly well and responded by ratcheting up the violence of their demonstrations and by planning the assassination of government figures, and the remnants of the traditional political organizations went into erratic rigor mortis spasms of violence, efforts of their political corpses to pretend they were still breathing by killing a policeman here and setting off a bomb there. It seemed that whoever had a gun wanted to fire it and whoever could arm a bomb wanted to detonate it, as everyone hoping for a place in post-Batista politics sought a violent deed through which to register his claim.

Castro's 26 of July Movement was still a loose amalgam of small groups and revolutionary freelancers fighting the government in whichever way they could. As Castro was let out of jail and went into exile in Mexico, more and more of the anti-Batista fighters began to identify themselves with his movement; but this was still more the result of a generic desire for institutional affiliation than the product of effective proselytizing or organizing by Castro. Just as the man, after the Moncada attack, had begun to fill a leadership vacuum, his movement was now starting to fill an institutional one.

Violence reigned supreme with no apparent scarcity of people ready to kill and be killed. I still participated in the students' antigovernment demonstrations, which, although less frequent, were bloodier than ever.

[†]I last heard of Mario Condi when I was back in Havana in January 1959, right after Batista's downfall. I didn't see him but learned through a mutual friend that he was the presiding judge in one of the newly formed revolutionary tribunals.

I was attracted to these marches even though much of their original political punch had been superseded by more spectacular, and more violent,
antigovernment actions. But before long even these student-police confrontations, almost always on San Lázaro Street, at the base of the mon-
umental steps leading into the University campus, were escalating from
traditional fists-against-billy-clubs melees to shootouts.

Usually student demonstrations began with a rally in the main campus square in which one or two speakers would harangue anywhere
from one hundred to three hundred individuals. The rally would be followed by a march down the long, broad steps, the *escalinata,* that constituted the formal entrance to the University. By the time the students
moved from the square to the top of the *escalinata,* not more than fifty
yards, their number had been reduced by half. From there it could easily
be seen if the police were already on the scene, in formation, a few blocks
away on Infanta Street. If the dark blue line was not there, two-thirds to
three-fourths of the students left would march down the steps chanting
antigovernment slogans. But if the police force was already in place,
only half or less of them would descend the steps and head for the street.
As the police, once they were in place, began to move in the students'
direction, a few more of the marchers would defect, scared into retreat
by the advancing row of swinging billy clubs. Those remaining, always
led by the school presidents, would lock arms, chant louder and march
faster.

The result was always the same: the clash of bodies, the swinging of
the clubs, some students on the ground, a few of the most aggressive
demonstrators punching or wrestling with a policeman, shouts, curses
and finally students fleeing back to the University, some of them bleeding, and the medical students, easily identifiable by their white tunics
and a seemingly lesser proneness to desertion, always among the last to
abandon the fray.

In the last couple of marches in which I participated, however, the
script changed. As we fled up the *escalinata,* and the policemen were left
on the street milling around and waiting for instructions, shots rang out
and the policemen ran for cover. Armed students positioned at the top
of the steps, or inside one of the buildings facing San Lázaro Street, had
opened fire on the police who, after their initial flight, would turn
around and return the fire. The traditional hand-to-hand combat that
had characterized student demonstrations was fast being supplanted by
gunfire—and as Havana University went, so did the country.

Cuba was now a free-for-all, and despite the increasing identification
with the 26 of July Movement, no opposition group or organization

held sway over more than a handful of militant oppositionists. The Batista police, despite their superior resources, found it impossible to keep in check what had become a veritable guerrilla force of individual and small groups of fighters and disrupters; a stalemate ensued in which Batista couldn't control his enemies and Batista's enemies couldn't overthrow him. And as acts of violence against the government and its repressive forces multiplied, the brutality and arbitrariness of the repression grew in tandem.

As expected, I lost my electoral bid for the presidency of the Social Sciences student body. I felt like a political orphan, but, at the same time, my unwillingness to make common cause with individuals and groups whose ultimate political objectives I didn't know, or couldn't agree with, became stronger. It was not that I was prescient about Cuba becoming communist. I, like almost everyone else at the time, would have dismissed such a notion as absurd. My objections were rooted in the contemporary history of the country and in my growing skepticism that those now fighting Batista, and loudly protesting their commitment to honest and responsible government, would live up to their rhetoric. The more I observed the dynamic of opposition politics, and how it shared many of the vices of the government, the deeper my doubts.

I was glad to have Tallet and Baeza to share my preoccupation with, even when their individual reactions were far apart. Kiko was convinced that Batista's ouster would bring about only minor substantive improvements but thought that getting rid of the military was worth the effort. Life would not change much, he concluded, but it would be more enjoyable. Tallet, more cerebral and perhaps more naive, thought more as I did: those fighting Batista had an opportunity to make a real difference but seemed intent on blowing it. Discussions of what was to be done after Batista were gone, other than mandatory and hollow references to freedom and legality that interested no one now. I accepted that the emphasis had to be on getting rid of the dictator, that this was still a necessary step, but thought that without a clear vision of what was to replace him and his system, without a commitment to a feasible and positive political project, the exercise was skewed, twisted in the wrong direction.

I don't remember exactly when or how we began to talk about leaving Cuba. In the convoluted processes of my mind, I am certain that concern for personal safety played a larger role than I was willing to admit to myself at the time. I was moving towards my degree as fast as I could, taking as many examinations as I was able to manage. It was obvious that Havana University would not remain open for long, now that it had become arsenal and firing ground for antipolice action. The commonly held notion that the University's charter as an autonomous institution protected it from police invasion and takeover couldn't survive the increase in tension and violence. My fixation with getting the degree before that happened had more to do with my compulsive nature, I am sure, than with any practical value the degree had for me at the time.

Tallet and I had been discussing for some time the reasons for getting out of the country: gaining a new perspective, and taking a respite from a situation that had become uncontrollable and in which we didn't seem to have a proper place. I was spending very little time at home now, avoiding both the police, which had come twice more looking for me, although without the theatrics of the first visit, and trying to accommodate the increasingly stern, and often also lachrymose, admonitions of my mother. Without knowing exactly what use we would have for them, Tallet and I secured merchant marine permits for working on ships. We thought it could be a handy option to have, but for the most part our talk about leaving Cuba was in the realm of the theoretical. That is, until Tallet ran into Paquito Almoína. Paquito, who had gone to high school in the States and who was in a political limbo of his own, member of a renegade Triple A faction that had fallen prey to internal discord, told Tallet that he was going to New York for a while, and told him how easy it had been to obtain a green card from the American embassy.

When I had previously considered leaving Cuba, I had thought Europe, not the United States. But if I truly had a chance to get a permanent immigrant visa to America, that would certainly be a worthy detour. I could get to know New York, raise some money and continue on my way to Europe—France, Italy, Germany, England, Spain. I had some more talks with Joan Campana, wanting to find out all I could about New York, and she provided as much information as a young Catholic woman born and raised in Yonkers could.

I was skeptical about Paquito's story and so was Tallet. Although we knew nothing about U.S. immigration policy, there was no way it could be that easy. Just go to the American embassy and get a permanent residence permit? But we had Paquito's assurance, so Tallet, who had been to the States and who spoke English, went to the embassy to find out. Sure enough, Paquito's information seemed accurate. Jorge was given an application for a green card and told what else was required: a physical examination by an embassy-approved physician, five hundred dollars in a bank in the States, a personal interview with an American official and an affidavit of good conduct issued by the local police. I saw the last two as the kickers, the mechanism by which the embassy rejected applicants—probably most of them. My doubts then remained and I was unwilling to let my hopes fly too high, but I was also determined to go through the exercise. The idea—to travel out of Cuba, to know New York, to go from there to Europe—was too good to let it pass without a try.

Meanwhile the music had stopped. Now there was just noise—unadorned, unrhythmic and completely unmusical. It was as if the sound track were no longer something separate from the action, something that molded our reaction to the action, that colored its perception. Action and noise had been symbiotically fused—forged into one and the same thing. The bangs of the explosions, the piercing cries of the police sirens, the reverberation of gunfire, the arguments, the threats—that was all one could hear. There was no other sound.

I took my last exams in September and the University was closed down in November. There were no classes and no student activity, but the bureaucratic mill kept on grinding, so I was able to retrieve my degree from the Records Office before the year ended. I was not so lucky with the police certificate of good conduct the American embassy required. The friendly captain was gone from the local police station and no one there would issue the affidavit. I didn't dare to go in person to request it, but one of my father's employees took in my written request. They didn't tell him anything, just took the paper. The man went back twice and never got an answer. Eventually my uncle Marcial, my connection to the old captain, who had never been involved in politics and who was well known in the neighborhood, gave it a shot, but still no answer, no information.

I had filed the formal application for a green card and visited the embassy-approved doctor. All I had left was to deposit the five hundred dollars in a bank in the States and secure the good conduct affidavit. I was doubtful of the wisdom of doing the former without having secured the latter, since obtaining the money involved resigning from the bank. I could have borrowed the amount from my sister Marta or from another relative but would rather not take that route, and I was inclined to believe the bank would provide the funds if I resigned. They didn't have to, especially if they assumed I was leaving anyhow, but they could well be willing to ease my departure since they would be getting rid of a union troublemaker and, more important, I was still occasionally seeing Carmen Martínez, the sister of the head of the bank, and her brother might be happy to see me go.

By the end of 1955, violence was the only acceptable political coin of the realm. I was not disturbed by the violence itself as much as by its lack of direction, by its use as a means unconnected to clear and specific ends. I no longer wanted any part of it. The current free-for-all convinced me that the fight against Batista should have taken the path of civic confrontation and mobilization, providing the opportunity to sort out what best to do after Batista. Short of that, the pattern of Cuban history was bound to remain unchanged: from corruption to dictatorship, from dictatorship to revolution, from revolution back to corruption.

Paquito Almoína got his green card and left for New York. Tallet had complied with all the American embassy requirements, including the police affidavit, and was sailing through the process. I didn't know what to do, but I had to do something. I decided to ask for the interview with the embassy official without the paper from the Cuban police. I wasn't sure the request would be granted, but I went ahead, and to my surprise it was granted without any question.

My appointment was late in the morning of a beautiful and, by Havana standards, cool and crisp December day. But I couldn't enjoy the weather—I felt like I was walking into a blind alley. I tried to prepare myself for the interview but quickly realized I had no idea what to expect. I saw the interview as the embassy's tool to reject applicants, but Tallet had been in a few days earlier and reported no difficulty. His circumstances, however, were different—all his papers were in order, he had never been arrested, he spoke English and he had been to the States before.

My interviewer was so young that I mistook him for a clerk or secretary, thinking he was leading me to the actual embassy official; but he was it. He pleasantly asked me to have a seat in fluent and only slightly accented Spanish while he examined the file on his desk. Oh, shit! I thought, here we go. He looked from the file to my face a couple of times without changing his expression. Eventually he put the folder down and said, "You don't like the government much, do you?" He was not really asking but just letting me know what he knew. As he spoke some more it was clear he did know about my various political activities— Partido Ortodoxo, bank employees' union, Havana University—and he was making general comments, not passing judgment or requesting explanations. I kept waiting for the barrage of questions I was sure would come my way, but none came. He didn't make a single direct reference to Cuban politics, but his expression and demeanor appeared to convey sympathy for my activism, or at least tolerance.

He eventually asked me where in the States I intended to go, to which I replied New York, and whether I was going to work or planned to go to school. I don't remember what I said, but I took the opportunity to mention my inability to get the police affidavit. "Don't worry," he said.

"You don't need it," and as he spoke he jotted something down on my folder and then he stood up to shake my hand. "¡Buena suerte!" he said, and I turned around and left his office.

There is a certain perversity in human nature, at least in mine, that refuses to accept some unexpected good, so I had difficulty coming to terms with the fact that all my worries and my apprehension concerning the visa were fading without trace. I went to a café, ordered some coffee and went over the interview in my mind from beginning to end, several times, to see if I could have misinterpreted it, but I couldn't find any room for doubt. The embassy official couldn't have been more positive, or friendlier, or clearer. My residence application was going forward and only the money was left now to be taken care of. Then, as I sat in the café, it hit like a bombshell and I felt my legs shake. I was going to leave Cuba! It was as if up to then I had been speculating, playing mental games, telling myself tales, but not quite believing that I was undertaking a major, drastic, change in my life. And now, here it was!

The meeting with Martínez at the bank went smoothly. I still couldn't read the man, but by now it didn't matter. What did matter was that he told me he understood my desire to get away from Cuba and said the bank would help. In fact, he offered a thousand dollars, not to pay for my resignation, of course, but to help me reorient my life. In light of his understanding and generosity, I went one step further and asked him to hire my brother, at the time out of school and unemployed, to fill my vacancy. This was going to be my fallback position if the money had been refused, something to ease the impact of my departure on my family, none of whom knew yet about my plans. But I was genuinely surprised when Martínez immediately assented. He either was a hell of a nice guy or he really wanted to see me go.

With the money matter solved all I had left was to tell my family and pick a departure date. My parents were also glad to see me go, if for different reasons. They had become truly worried about my safety, and my mother shed some happy tears when I gave her the news. My father, never a verbally expressive man, gave me a long hug that needed no words. The hiring of my brother by the bank was an extra bonus. They appreciated both the fact and the gesture. My brother, a happy-go-lucky character like our uncle Marcial—they even looked alike—took the whole thing in stride. He was thankful, but the idea of going to work failed to excite him.

At my mother's request I decided to wait until after my birthday, at the end of January, to leave. My plan was simple: look around New York for a few days, get a job in the city and learn some English. Tallet had suggested enrollment at Columbia University's English-language program so I wrote to them and secured admission to the session running from April to June. There my plans stopped.

I quit the bank on December 31, 1955, and my brother began work on January 2, 1956. Avoiding unnecessary risks, I kept away from home as much as I could and had ample time to wander through the streets of Havana, go to bookstores to check maps and fly to the Moon. I could still see the Earth clearly from there, especially the places I had been recently locating on maps. I could see New York, the New York of the movies, in uncanny detail, but I no longer could see Cuba. Every time I tried to fix my gaze on the island all I saw was haze, a gray cloud hovering over where the island should have been.

I had to dispose of the gun Pepe Iglesias had given me a couple of years back and which I had kept concealed in the backyard, carefully wrapped, behind some loose bricks. I didn't want it to be found by the police or to fall into the wrong hands, so I took my last risk. I put the gun in a paper bag and took it to one of my cousins, a psychiatrist, who had told me some time before he was looking for one. I wasn't completely sure giving it to him was a good idea since he clearly showed the touch of insanity inherent in his profession, but I didn't want to leave it behind in my house.

The day finally arrived, a Sunday morning early in February, and a number of relatives came to see me off. We arrived early and I checked my luggage before we went to have breakfast in the airport restaurant. After breakfast most of my relatives left except my father and my uncle Marcial who stayed to see me actually take off. It was a National Airlines direct flight from Havana to New York. Paquito Almoína was to pick me up at the other end, Idlewild Airport, and Jorge, who also had a birthday coming that he wanted to spend in Havana, was to follow in a few days. I was in high spirits, excited about finally being on my way and looking forward to my first trip out of Cuba.

The airline employee was very polite, but he kept processing other passengers as he asked me to wait. Eventually another airline official came and they both huddled behind the counter, and the newly arrived one led me to the side and informed me I couldn't board the plane. He was very apologetic, full of assurances that this had nothing to do with the airline. My name was on a list of people who were not to be allowed out of the country so they couldn't let get on the plane—the goddamned list again!

It was as if an abyss had opened under my feet and I was in a free fall. I explained that all my papers were in order, to which he assented. I pleaded. I begged him to double check the list, which he did and told me again my name was on it and he couldn't let me go, and that it was not up to him. My father and my uncle were by now next to me. They also asked and also pleaded. But the airline representative was not to be moved. Nearly all the passengers had now boarded the plane. Events were telling me that the smoothness of the process until that moment had just been a trick of fate, a cruel joke, to compound the pain of the ultimate blow. My spirits sunk as I reluctantly accepted the inevitable.

"Then just give me my luggage back," I said to the bearer of the bad news. The man's eyes opened wide and his face moved towards mine. "What did you say?" he asked. "My luggage, I want my luggage back," I replied. "Who took it?" He now inquired in a voice that had lost all its early politeness. "You people did," I replied on the verge of losing my temper.

It was as if the airline official had been hit on the head with a brick. He turned around, not once, but twice. Looked at me, looked in the direction of the agent who had dealt with me originally, and with his eyes fixed on him, a few feet away taking care of a laggard passenger, he called the man over in a loud and irritated tone. Both airline employees now huddled again near the area where luggage went through on its way to the airplane. The agent I had been talking to, who was older and obviously the senior one, kept gesticulating and pointing to the plane. I didn't know what was going on, but it was clear the older man was in a nasty mood when he got back to me. He was obviously torn inside because he could barely get his words out of his mouth. I was certain he was going to tell me they couldn't retrieve my luggage and I was readying myself, preparing for the violent explosion of all my disappointment and frustration.

"Just get on the plane." He must have hissed, because I heard the words but didn't see his lips move, and as if to make sure there no was misunderstanding of what he meant, after all his assertions that there was nothing he could do about it, he extended his arm, stiff as a statue, with his index finger pointing to the boarding gate. I gave my father the quickest hug I ever gave anyone and ran through the gate and onto the tarmac and onto the ladder at the front entrance of the Super-Constellation.

Despite the delay, there were several window seats available. I took one that was not over a wing, sat down and realized that I was covered in sweat. It took a long time, I thought, for the plane to rev its four engines and take off. Relief overwhelmed me as we took to the air. I couldn't believe how lucky it was that I had checked my luggage earlier, on my way to having breakfast with my relatives just out of mindless convenience.

As we left the Cuba shoreline behind and began our slow climb, as the green waters turned blue and the Cuban coast faded from sight, I looked down and saw a beautiful brigantine with all its white sails unfurled moving at full speed. Although a few thousand feet in the air, I had no trouble recognizing the ship, it was the Black Corsair's and it was moving in the same direction as the plane.

EPILOGUE

The Cuban political situation continued to deteriorate. Cities became battlegrounds between the government's repressive forces and urban guerrillas that surged in all forms and shapes. By December 1956 Fidel Castro was back in Cuba, in the Sierra Maestra. In March of the following year, in a move to counterbalance Fidel's increasing political prominence, a number of Havana University students, in cooperation with other opposition groups, almost succeeded in killing Batista in an assault on the presidential palace. In the reprisals that followed the best-known student leaders were murdered. Whatever competition Fidel might have had for the top opposition spot was now gone.

Batista fled the country on New Year's Day 1959 after having lost the active support of the military and the confidence of the American embassy. I arrived in Havana five or six days after Fidel descended from the Sierra Maestra and began his triumphal trek to the city. The consolidation of Fidel's control over all the opposition groups that had fought Batista was not yet complete and armed civilians were all over, all kind of militias, some occupying police stations, others directing traffic, others guarding buildings and others just being there.

The ambience was one of great jubilation, of exhilaration and festivity, of open and widespread glee. Those who regretted Batista's departure, and there must have been some who did, were nowhere to be seen. It was as if Havana was throwing a big party and the whole city had been invited.

Many of my old friends and acquaintances were now army and police officers, ministers, undersecretaries and ambassadors, and some of my former union colleagues were running the national labor confederation. In the excitement of the situation, I felt that perhaps my misgivings had been unwarranted, that maybe I had been too hasty in my judgment, or too afraid to take more chances. As I had received offers to join one government office or the other, or to be commissioned in the new military, I decided to return. I needed some time to make the necessary arrangements so it was not until late in the summer of that year that I was back in Havana.

Tension and animosity had replaced euphoria and camaraderie. What in January had been one camp united in celebration had now become two antagonistic bands separated by rancor and mistrust. I found some of my former anti-Batista friends cloaked in the mantle of freedom and others raising the banner of social reform. I had assumed all along the two goals were compatible and still felt that way. As I spoke to friends on one side and the other, I could not separate personal ambition from social commitment, petty interests from national concern.

I stayed for ten days.